FRANK AIKEN'S WAR

FRANK AIKEN'S WAR

THE IRISH REVOLUTION

1916–23

MATTHEW LEWIS

UNIVERSITY COLLEGE DUBLIN PRESS

PREAS CHOLÁISTE OLLSCOILE BHAILE ÁTHA CLIATH

2014

First published 2014
by University College Dublin Press
UCD Humanities Institute, Room H103,
Belfield, Dublin 4
Ireland
www.ucdpress.ie

ISBN 978-1-906359-82-9

CIP data available from the British Library

The right of Matthew Lewis to be identified as the
author of this work has been asserted by him

Typeset in Scotland in Adobe Caslon and
Bodoni Oldstyle by Ryan Shiels
Printed in England on acid-free paper by
CPI Antony Rowe, Chippenham, Wilts.

Contents

—

Acknowledgements

—

I have incurred many debts while researching and writing this book. I owe a particular debt of gratitude to Marie Coleman for first suggesting the topic, and for supervising the resulting doctoral thesis at Queen's University Belfast. I would also like to extend my very special thanks to Fearghal McGarry, my secondary supervisor, and to Keith Jeffery and Joost Augusteijn, the thesis examiners. Their comments, suggestions and advice have been invaluable. Likewise to Eoin Magennis, Rory O'Hanlon, and Mark Feighery for sharing their knowledge of the subject in interviews and/or correspondence, and for providing many useful leads.

The research for this book was made possible by an award from the Arts and Humanities Research Council, which I hereby gratefully acknowledge. I had the pleasure of drafting and redrafting the manuscript during postdoctoral fellowships at the Centre for War Studies at University College Dublin and the Centre for the History of Violence at the University of Newcastle, Australia. For the former opportunity, I thank Robert Gerwarth and the European Research Council; for the latter, I thank Philip Dwyer and the Faculty of Education and Arts. The production of the book has also been assisted by funds from a New Staff Grant at the University of Newcastle. I thank the School for Humanities and Social Science for making this possible.

I have discussed aspects of this project with many people over the past number of years, and have benefitted greatly from their thoughts and insights. These include (in no order): Robert Lynch, Brian Hanley, Sean O'Connell, Liam Kennedy, and Michael Hopkinson. Special thanks go to Shaun McDaid and William Mulligan, for their thoughts on various pieces of draft work. Likewise to Noelle Moran and Conor Graham at UCD Press, and the anonymous reviewers, for their guidance in the process of transforming the thesis into a monograph. I am also grateful to an array of colleagues who have suggested readings and sources, or otherwise offered ideas and advice. In particular I wish to acknowledge Erica Doherty, Stuart Aveyard, Mary Clarke, Caomihe Nic Dhaibheid, Brian P. Murphy, Chris Magill, Gajendra Singh, Tomas Balkelis, Mark Jones, James Matthews and James Kitchen.

In addition I would like to thank the staff at the following libraries and archives: Queen's University Library Special Collections, the National Library of Ireland, the National Archives of Ireland, Trinity College Library, the Archives Department at University College Dublin, the Cardinal Tomás Ó Fiaich Memorial Library, the Irish Military Archives, Kilmainham Gaol Museum, the National Archives Kew, the Public Records Office of Northern Ireland, Louth County Archives and Belfast Central Newspaper Library. Very special thanks go to Mary McVeigh and the staff at Armagh Local and Irish Studies Library, who have always provided such a pleasant and welcoming atmosphere in which to research, and also to Dhruba Banerjee at Mint Productions for providing a DVD copy of their documentary, 'Aiken: Gunman and Statesman'.

Lastly, I want to thank my fiancée Kim for her love, patience, and unwavering support throughout the research and writing of this book. The finished product is dedicated to her.

Abbreviations

—

A/G	Adjutant General
AOH	Ancient Order of Hibernians, Board of Erin
AOHIAA	Ancient Order of Hibernians, Irish American Alliance
ASU	Active Service Unit
BMH CD	Bureau of Military History Contemporary Documents
BMH WS	Bureau of Military History Witness Statement
CBS	Christian Brothers School(s)
CI	County Inspector (RIC)
CO	Colonial Office
COFLA	Cardinal Ó Fiaich Library, Armagh
C/S	Chief-of-Staff (IRA)
DÉD	*Dáil Éireann Debates*
DELG	Dáil Éireann Local Government Department
DIB	*Dictionary of Irish Biography*
D/O	Director of Organisation (IRA)
FJ	*Freeman's Journal*
GAA	Gaelic Athletic Association
GHQ	General Headquarters (IRA)
GPO	General Post Office (Dublin)
ICA	Irish Citizen Army
IG	Inspector General (RIC)
IMA	Irish Military Archives, Dublin
INF	Irish National Foresters
INAAVDF	Irish National Aid Association and Volunteers Dependants' Fund
IRA	Irish Republican Army
IRB	Irish Republican Brotherhood
JP	Justice of the Peace
KGM	Kilmainham Gaol Museum
LCA	Louth County Archives
MP	Member of Parliament
MSPC	Military Service Pensions Collection
NAI	National Archives of Ireland

NEBB	North Eastern Boundary Bureau
NLI	National Library of Ireland
O/C	Officer Commanding (IRA)
ODNB	*Oxford Dictionary of National Biography*
PRONI	Public Records Office, Northern Ireland
RDC	Rural District Council
RIC	Royal Irish Constabulary
TCD	Trinity College Dublin
TD	Teachta Dála
TNA	The National Archives, Kew
TSCH	Department of Taoiseach
UCDAD	University College Dublin, Archives Department
UDC	Urban District Council
UIL	United Irish League
USC	Ulster Special Constabulary
UVF	Ulster Volunteer Force
WO	War Office

ONE

INTRODUCTION

—

Frank Aiken was one of independent Ireland's most prominent politicians and international statesmen. A founding member of Fianna Fáil, and a close confidant of Eamon de Valera, he served in numerous high profile ministerial roles in a career spanning 50 years. As Minister for External Affairs in the 1950s and 1960s, he also gained considerable international recognition as Ireland's representative to the United Nations where, in his determined attempts to carve out a distinctive Irish identity in the assembly, he became known for his pursuit of a non-aligned stance on issues such as the representation of the People's Republic of China and nuclear non-proliferation.[1] Retiring in 1973, he was widely respected throughout southern Irish political circles for his service to the nation in both its domestic and international affairs, a sentiment that was expressed repeatedly in the many tributes offered upon his death on 18 May 1983.[2]

Like many of his political generation, Aiken was a product of the politics and violence of the Irish revolution, the tumultuous seven-year period in which Ireland experienced a war for independence, partition, and a bitter civil war. Between 1916 and 1923, Aiken's involvement in the conflict facilitated his transformation from a teenage farmer to a provincial activist and guerrilla leader, and eventually to chief-of-staff of the Irish Republican Army (IRA). As a republican organiser, a Sinn Féin local government representative, and the commandant of the IRA's Fourth Northern Division, he became the central figure of the revolutionary movement in his native Armagh and its hinterlands of south Down and north Louth. Despite his later prominence in Irish politics, however, this aspect of Aiken's past is remarkably obscure. For decades it received little notice from historians or commentators alike, beyond occasional discussions of his role in the civil war; specifically, his futile attempts to secure unity between rival republican factions in the wake of the Anglo-Irish Treaty, his early neutrality in the conflict, and his issuing of the ceasefire and dump arms orders that eventually brought it to an end in May 1923.[3] It was only in the late 1990s that other aspects of his role in the revolution began to attract greater attention, with sensationalised revelations of his complicity in sectarian atrocities, and of his involvement in the joint-IRA offensive, an abortive plan for a republican invasion of Northern Ireland in May 1922.[4]

Even amid this growing interest, however, Aiken's role in the Irish revolution has remained largely unexplored. There are various reasons for this lack of scholarly enquiry. In many respects, it is symptomatic of both the scarcity of source material for his earlier years (an issue discussed in more detail later) and the more general dearth of research into his life and political career. Yet it is also a reflection of the fact that up until the mid-1990s Irish historians rarely engaged with the subject of republican politics and violence in the six counties that became Northern Ireland in this period. With the advent of the more recent 'troubles' in 1969, it was perhaps thought unwise to explore such a topic lest it should inadvertently serve to glorify or legitimise physical force republicanism, or for fear that it might further fuel sectarian bitterness by drawing attention to past atrocities. Consequently, throughout the 1970s and 1980s, scholarly discussions of events in north-east Ulster were dominated by the high politics of partition, or the histories of unionism and constitutional nationalism.[5] The violence experienced in the region was typically character-ised in terms of sectarian rioting, exemplified by intense bouts of inter-communal conflict in Belfast, Derry and various towns throughout east Ulster between 1920 and 1922. Sinn Féin and the IRA received little attention, and a consensus emerged that republicanism was too weak, too disorganised and too unpopular across the six counties to have been of any particular relevance there.[6]

It is only since the mid-1990s that historians have shown a greater interest in Ulster's experience of the revolutionary period, and with it the fortunes of the republican movement in what became Northern Ireland. Eamon Phoenix's 1994 study of northern nationalism revealed a wealth of new information con-cerning Sinn Féin's activities in the province between 1918 and 1922. This was followed in 1997 with the publication of Joost Augusteijn's comparative local analysis of the IRA, which included Derry amongst its six case studies. Looking beyond published work, moreover, in 1998 Charles Stephen Day completed an excellent doctoral thesis on the subject of political violence in the Newry and south Armagh area between 1912 and 1925.[7] It is only really in the past decade, however, with the release of new source collections, and, perhaps, the prevailing political stability in Northern Ireland, that this handful of studies has expanded to form a distinctive branch of the historiography. Amongst the most important additions since 2000 have been Robert Lynch's *The Northern IRA and the Early Years of Partition*, Jim McDermott's *Northern Divisions: The Old IRA and the Belfast Pogroms*, Tim Wilson's *Frontiers of Violence: Conflict and Identity in Ulster and Upper Silesia*, and most recently Fergal McCluskey's *Fenians and Ribbonmen: The Development of Republican Politics in East Tyrone*.[8]

A number of scholarly biographies of republican figures from Ulster have also been published by historians such as Fearghal McGarry, Tom Feeney and Marnie Hay.[9]

The greater awareness of Aiken's revolutionary past that has emerged in recent years owes much to this body of research. It was Lynch's history of the northern IRA, for instance, that highlighted his central role within the organisation in the six counties during this period, particularly in 1922, and the considerable violence that he oversaw in his 'unique fiefdom' in the borderlands of Armagh, south Down and north Louth. Lynch's study was also the first to add substance to allegations of Aiken's complicity in sectarian atrocities during the conflict, rumours of which had first surfaced in republican propaganda in 1986, and were subsequently publicised in Toby Harden's *Bandit Country: The IRA and South Armagh* in 1999.[10] Indeed, the confirmation of these revelations – which concern Aiken's responsibility for republican reprisals that claimed the lives of six Protestant civilians near Newry in June 1922 – has drawn the most attention to his role in the Irish revolution. Its inclusion as a point of focus in an RTÉ documentary on his life and career in 2006 captured the notice of both commentators and historically minded members of the Irish public.[11] Yet in the absence of a biography or a published study of the conflict in the borderlands of Armagh, south Down and north Louth, Aiken's place in the conflict, its significance, and the broader context of republican politics and violence in which it occurred, remain obscure.

Therein lies the premise of this book. It is not a traditional work of biographical history; the limitations of the sources alone rule out any such straightforward approach. Nor does it claim to be a comprehensive local study of the revolutionary period. Rather, it seeks to combine elements of both of these approaches to shed new light on Aiken's role in the conflict, and to elucidate the provincial experience of republican activism in which he played such a crucial part. This approach is desirable for two reasons. First, Aiken's experience of the conflict was so closely bound with that of the wider republican movement in Armagh, south Down and north Louth that it would be difficult to gain a sufficient understanding of either in isolation. Secondly, it will allow the study to address a range of themes and historical debates concerning the Irish revolution, and revolutionary republicanism in particular, that have rarely been addressed within the unique social and political context of six-county Ulster. These include, but are not limited to, the factors motivating individuals to engage in armed struggle, the dynamics of sectarian and intra-nationalist violence during the conflict, the social structure of the republican movement, and the nature of revolutionary republican ideology.

The approaches adopted by the study inevitably raise certain questions. First and foremost, given that biographical analysis requires a degree of empathy with the subject, how does one write objectively about an individual who was involved in morally abhorrent acts such as the killing of civilians? In this respect, the book's biographical aspect aspires to an approach that Robert Gerwarth describes as 'cold empathy', an attempt to reconstruct the life of the subject 'with critical distance, but without reading history backwards or confusing the role of the historian with that of a state prosecutor'.[12] So far as is possible, therefore, the facts will be allowed to speak for themselves, and the analysis offered will seek to explain – not to judge, justify or excuse – Aiken's actions.

The local study aspect of the book also presents certain issues. In particular, how should the geographic parameters be selected? Unlike most local histories of the revolutionary period, which tend to focus on an individual county, this study takes a somewhat unconventional approach.[13] It transcends both provincial and county boundaries in recognition of the fact that, for Aiken and his comrades, the conflict did not conform neatly to local administrative units.[14] The Fourth Northern Division, for instance, had its origins in a handful of Irish Volunteer companies in the districts of Newry and south Armagh, but by 1921 had expanded to encompass Armagh, south Down and north Louth. This was an acknowledgement of the structure of local republican networks, and longer-standing social, economic and cultural ties in the region. Accordingly, the study takes Armagh, south Down and (to a lesser extent) north Louth as its broad geographic focus, though out of necessity it will often focus more intently on one or other component area within this larger borderland region.

There is also the question of how one ensures that the experiences of an individual locality are contextualised in an effective way. In this respect, the study adopts the guiding principle of previous local histories of the revolutionary period. The Armagh, south Down and north Louth region will provide the focus for an in-depth analysis of the various themes and issues encompassed within the subject, but so far as is possible an engagement with other regional histories and relevant secondary texts will be used to place these local findings within a broader national (or indeed international) context.[15]

Some readers might question the periodisation adopted for the study. The period from 1916 to 1923 is only one of a number of possible chronological frameworks within which the Irish revolution can be considered.[16] It is employed here for the simple reason that it proves the best fit for the subject at hand. Although Aiken showed some signs of political activity prior to 1916, it was only after the Easter rising that his revolutionary journey truly began. Furthermore, while it could be argued that his revolution stretched beyond the collapse of the IRA's civil war campaign, and perhaps only ended when he entered the Dáil as a Fianna Fáil Teachta Dála (TD) in 1927, it is clear that 1923 marked a watershed in both the republican struggle and Aiken's own role in it, and he himself recognised this.[17] The years 1916–23 also provide a logical timeframe within which to explore the provincial experience of the revolutionary republicanism in Armagh, south Down and north Louth. Prior to 1916, separatism was a marginal political viewpoint in these areas, and it was only after the Easter rising that the movement became a significant political force locally. The year 1923 also provides an appropriate end date, marking the collapse of any significant republican resistance to the newly constituted order both north and south of the border.

The research for this study has presented considerable challenges in terms of source material. Although Aiken left a sizeable collection of personal papers, the majority relate to his later political career. A large quantity of the Fourth Northern Division's records appear to have been destroyed at the close of the civil war, and few contemporary documents relating to the Sinn Féin organisation across Armagh, south Down and north Louth appear to have survived the period.[18] Furthermore, Aiken was notoriously reticent about his role in the conflict. He rarely discussed this aspect of his life with family members and declined to submit a statement to the Bureau of Military History. This may have been an indication of trauma resulting from the conflict. Certainly, there is anecdotal evidence to suggest that speaking of the civil war could make him agitated and emotional.[19] It is just as likely, however, that his aversion to recording his experiences was simply a reflection of the contentious nature of the events in which he was involved. In his later years, for instance, when an acquaintance hinted that he should write a memoir, he is said to have replied 'I am not doing any writing [. . .] because anything I could say would be challenged by someone else'.[20]

Notwithstanding these considerable limitations, there are a greater variety of sources for the subject than one might expect. Despite his reluctance to discuss the conflict, Aiken did record some of his experiences in a handwritten statement and a personal chronology of the conflict. The former appears to have been composed in 1925, when he was IRA chief-of-staff. The latter was compiled around 1933, possibly in preparation for his Military Service Pension application.[21] In the 1950s, he also granted interviews to both Ernie O'Malley and Florence O'Donoghue.[22] Generally speaking, these reflections focused on his attempts to intervene with southern leaders to avert the civil war in 1922 and hint at a determination to prove his own absolution (as an opponent of the Treaty) from any sense of collective culpability for that conflict. It is also entirely possible, however, that he chose to emphasise this aspect of his past for political reasons, or in a conscious effort to shape his own legacy. Alongside Aiken's own testimony, moreover, 25 of his comrades from Armagh, south Down and north Louth provided witness statements to the Bureau of Military History. Among these is a richly detailed account written by his former adjutant, and life-long friend, John McCoy, which Aiken read and endorsed

as an accurate portrayal of their activities during the period.[23] McCoy and two
other former divisional officers also provided remarkably candid interviews to
Ernie O'Malley in the 1950s.[24]

In addition, there is a wealth of material with which to research the history
of the republican movement in Armagh, south Down and north Louth during
this period. The Kilmainham Gaol Museum in Dublin, for instance, holds a
substantial collection of papers relating to the Fourth Northern Division,
among them a revealing memoir of events in Dundalk in 1922 by former
quartermaster Padraig Quinn.[25] The Louis O'Kane collection at the Cardinal
Ó Fiaich Memorial Library in Armagh contains a wealth of material relating
to the local republican movement in this period; though unfortunately for
conservation reasons an aged collection of tape recorded interviews with IRA
veterans has been inaccessible during the research for this book. In addition to
these collections, some contemporary correspondence and reports regarding
the local IRA, and occasionally Sinn Féin, survive amongst the personal
papers of figures such as Richard Mulcahy, Michael Collins and Maurice
Twomey. Combined with information from local and national newspapers,
police reports, and other official records held at the Public Record Office of
Northern Ireland, the National Archives, Kew, the National Archives of
Ireland, and the Irish Military Archives, there is no shortage of material with
which to study the politics and violence of the conflict in the region.

Drawing on these collections, this book aims to construct a portrait of the
personal and provincial experience that was Frank Aiken's Irish revolution.
What emerges is a multifaceted narrative of an individual's pathway to and
from revolutionary activism, a political movement's futile struggle to gain
ground amid a largely hostile population, and the violent excesses of militant
nationalist ideology. If this restores some complexity to the way in which
Aiken's formative years are understood and remembered, beyond the prevailing caricatures of the reformed gunman or the sectarian thug, it will have
achieved its first goal.[26] If it provides readers with a more nuanced view of the
nature and the dynamics of the conflict at a grassroots level in Ulster during
this period, beyond the simplistic discourse of tribalism and sectarian hatreds,
it will have achieved the other.

NOTES

1.   Dáil Éireann Members Database, http://www.oireachtas.ie/members–hist/default.asp?
housetype=0&HouseNum=19&MemberID=1 (accessed 18 Feb. 2013); Aiken served as Minister
for External Affairs from 1951 to 1954, and again from 1957 to 1969; for more on this phase of his
career see A. Bhreatnach, 'Frank Aiken and the Formulation of Foreign Policy: 1951–1954, 1957–
1969' (MA thesis, University College Cork, 1999).

2.   *Irish Times*, 19, 20, 21 May 1983.

3.   See, for example, D. Macardle, *The Irish Republic* (London, 1937), pp 759, 761–3, 846; L. Skinner, *Politicians by Accident* (Dublin, 1946), pp 151–69; M. Hopkinson, *Green Against Green: The Irish Civil War* (Dublin, 1988), pp 169–71.

4.   T. Harnden, *Bandit Country: The IRA and South Armagh* (London, 1999) pp 135–7; *Irish Times*, 17 Nov. 1999; 'Aiken: Gunman and Statesman' (Mint Productions, 2006); R. Lynch, 'Explaining the Altnaveigh massacre' in *Eire/Ireland*, 45: 3 & 4 (fall/winter, 2010).

5.   See, for example, E. Phoenix, *Northern Nationalism: Nationalistic Politics, Partition and the Catholic Minority in Northern Ireland 1890–1940* (Belfast, 1994); A. C. Hepburn, *A Past Apart: Studies in the History of Catholic Belfast* (Belfast, 1996); J. F. Harbinson, *The Ulster Unionist Party, 1882–1973: Its Development and Organisation* (London, 1973); P. Buckland, *Ulster Unionism and the Origins of Northern Ireland* (Dublin, 1973); M. Laffan, *The Partition of Ireland, 1911–1925* (Dublin, 1983).

6.   See, for example, Laffan, *The Partition of Ireland*, pp 73–6; C. Townshend, *Political Violence in Ireland: Government and Resistance since 1848* (Oxford, 1983), pp 340–4; J. Bowman, *De Valera and the Ulster Question, 1917–1973* (Oxford, 1982), pp 72–3.

7.   Phoenix, *Northern Nationalism*; J. Augusteijn, *From Public Defiance to Guerrilla Warfare: The Experience of Ordinary Volunteers in the Irish War of Independence, 1916–1921* (Dublin, 1996); C. S. Day, 'Political Violence in the Newry/Armagh Area, 1912–1925' (PhD, Queen's University, Belfast, 1998).

8.   R. Lynch, *The Northern IRA and the Early Years of Partition, 1920–1922* (Dublin, 2006); J. McDermott, *Northern Divisions: The Old IRA and the Belfast Pogroms* (Belfast, 2001); T. W. Wilson, *Frontiers of Violence: Conflict and Identity in Ulster and Upper Silesia 1918–1922* (Oxford, 2010); F. McCluskey, *Fenians and Ribbonmen: The Development of Republican Politics in East Tyrone* (Manchester, 2011).

9.   F. McGarry, *Eoin O'Duffy: A Self-Made Hero* (Oxford, 2007); T. Feeney, *Seán MacEntee: A Political Life* (Dublin, 2009); M. Hay, *Bulmer Hobson and the Nationalist Movement in Twentieth-Century Ireland* (Manchester, 2009).

10.   Lynch, *The Northern IRA and the Early Years of Partition*, pp 48, 145–9; Harnden, *Bandit Country*, pp 134–8; the first publication to reference Aiken's complicity in sectarian reprisals was R. P. Watson's *Cath Saoirse an Iúir: Newry's Struggle* (Newry, 1986), a local history pamphlet that appears to have been produced by members (or sympathisers) of the provisional republican movement, and which carries a clear political message. A passing reference to its production appears in the memoir of IRA 'supergrass' Eamon Collins, though he mistakenly refers to it as a memoir; see Eamon Collins, *Killing Rage* (London, 1997), p. 317.

11.   'Aiken: Gunman and Statesman'; for commentary see *Sunday Independent*, 17 Dec. 2006.

12.   R. Gerwarth, *Hitler's Hangman: The Life of Heydrich* (New Haven, 2011), p. x.

13.   See, for example, D. Fitzpatrick, *Politics and Irish Life, 1913–1921: Provincial Experience of War and Revolution* (Dublin, 1977); P. Hart, *The IRA and its Enemies: Violence and Community in Cork, 1916–1923* (Oxford, 1998); M. Coleman, *County Longford and the Irish Revolution, 1910–1923* (Dublin, 2001); J. O'Callaghan, *Revolutionary Limerick: The Republican Campaign for Independence in Limerick 1913–1921* (Dublin, 2010); M. Farry, *The Irish Revolution, 1912–23: Sligo* (Dublin, 2012).

14.   The validity of the county as a geographical unit for local studies of the Irish revolution has been questioned, see J. Augusteijn, 'The emergence of violent activism among Irish revolutionaries, 1916–1921', in *Irish Historical Studies*, 35: 139 (May 2007), pp 329–32.

15. Fitzpatrick, *Politics and Irish Life*, p. x.

16. P. Hart, *The IRA at War* (Oxford, 2003), pp 11–12.

17. See, for example, Aiken to de Valera, 1 June 1923, University College Dublin Archives Department (hereafter, UCDAD), de Valera papers, P150/1752.

18. O'Hanlon to Aiken, 9 May 1923, UCDAD, Twomey papers, P69/35.

19. *Irish Times*, 13 Nov. 2008.

20. 'Aiken: Gunman and Statesman'; *Irish Times*, 13 Nov. 2008; U. MacEoin, *The IRA in The Twilight Years, 1923–1948* (Dublin, 1998), p. 913.

21. Untitled statement by Frank Aiken, *c.*1925, IMA, Bureau of Military History Contemporary Documents (hereafter, BMH CD) 6/36/22; 'Chronology', *c.*1933, IMA, BMH CD 6/36/22; copies of these documents are also held in the Aiken papers, UCDAD, P104/1308. Aiken's Military Service Pension was released by the Irish Military Archives in Jan. 2014; Frank Aiken, Irish Military Archives (hereafter, IMA), Military Service Pensions Collection (hereafter, MSPC), MSP34REF59339.

22. 'Notes of interview with Frank Aiken at Leinster House 18/6/52', National Library of Ireland (hereafter, NLI), O'Donoghue papers, Ms 31,421; Frank Aiken, UCDAD, O'Malley notebooks, P17b/90.

23. John McCoy, IMA, Bureau of Military History Witness Statement (hereafter, BMH WS) 492; I am very thankful to Dr Eve Morrison for this revelation.

24. Johnnie McKay [McCoy], UCDAD, O'Malley Notebooks, P17b/90; Mick Donnelly, UCDAD, O'Malley notebooks, P17b/116; Mick O'Hanlon, UCDAD, O'Malley notebooks, P17b/106.

25. Padraig Quinn memoir, Kilmainham Gaol Museum (hereafter, KGM), McCann Cell Collection, 20/M5/IP41/08.

26. See, for example, 'Aiken: Gunman and Statesman'; *Sunday Independent*, 26 June, 14 Aug. 2011; 'Frank Aiken: A man of war, a man of peace', www.politics.ie/forum/history/157924–frank–aiken–man–war–man–peace–6.html (accessed 6 Dec. 2013).

TWO

A PRELUDE TO REVOLUTION

—

Francis Thomas Aiken was born on 13 February 1898 in Carrickbracken, Co. Armagh, a rural townland situated within a mile of the village of Camlough on the main road to Newry.[1] At the turn of the century, Carrickbracken had a population of 284. Its inhabitants were a mixture of farmers, agricultural labourers, and textile workers employed at the nearby linen mill in Bessbrook.[2] The youngest child of James and Mary Aiken, Frank was born into a prosperous farming family which held considerable influence in the wider Camlough area by virtue of its relative wealth, property holdings and nationalist political connections.

The Aiken family are believed to have had their roots in the Ederney area of Co. Fermanagh. Frank's grandfather, Thomas Aiken, was of a Presbyterian background, but was said to have married a Catholic and subsequently left the district to settle in Truagh, Co. Monaghan. An alternative version, recorded in local folklore, suggests that his departure was due to his alleged links to the United Irishmen. Either way, it is evident that his choices in life, whether personal or political, resulted in his estrangement from his wider family circle.[3]

Frank's father, James Aiken, came to Newry in the 1870s. He established a construction business in the town, with premises in Monaghan Street, and it is believed that he was responsible for a number of the churches built in the south Armagh area during these years.[4] In 1881, he settled at Carrickbracken, and acquired substantial holdings in the decades that followed, including land and rental properties in Carrickbracken, Derrymore and Newry.[5] By 1911, the family was farming around 56 acres and letting as many as 38 houses, the latter including a cluster of properties in the High Street area of Derrymore known as 'Aiken's Row'. The farm and lands at Carrickbracken alone held a rateable valuation of £43.[6] The total holdings, however, were valued closer to £177.[7] To put this into context, 52.9 per cent of those living on agricultural holdings in Co. Armagh at this time resided on properties with a rateable valuation of £15 or under.[8]

Although a relative newcomer to the area, James Aiken quickly integrated into the local community. This was facilitated by his marriages into two well-known families; the Cardwells and the McGeeneys. His first marriage, to Catherine Cardwell, ended tragically when she died in March 1885, most likely as a result of complications arising from childbirth. This was followed by the death of their daughter, Mary, less than three years later in January 1888.[9] His second marriage, to Mary McGeeney, took place in 1887, and the couple went on to have seven children; James, Mary (May), Magdalene (Madge), Annie (who died in infancy), Gertrude, Nano and, finally, Frank.[10]

James also became active in local politics during these years, at a time when the nationalist home rule movement was only just beginning to make headway in the region. Positioned on the provincial boundary between Ulster and Leinster, the Aiken's hinterland of Newry and south Armagh marked a political frontier which various southern Irish nationalist movements through-out the nineteenth century had consistently had difficulty penetrating.[11] This became particularly pronounced from the 1870s onwards, when longer-standing nationalist demands for the repeal of the 1801 Act of Union were re-articulated in the cause of home rule, and a clear gulf emerged on the issue between the Catholic-nationalist south and the Protestant-unionist north-east. Conse-quently, it took a decade of concerted efforts before this latest nationalist movement – represented by the Irish Parliamentary Party (hereafter the Irish Party) from 1882 – became a significant political force locally. This was confirmed with the election of Alexander Blaine as the South Armagh con-stituency's first nationalist MP in 1885, an event which marked the beginning of three decades of constitutional nationalist dominance in the region.[12]

James Aiken's first steps into local nationalist politics came in 1881, when he was appointed as vice-president of the Camlough branch of the Land League. Later that same year, he was also elected as a poor law guardian for the Camlough division.[13] There is little evidence of his activities in the former role, or his specific views on the land issue. It is likely, however, that they reflected those of other local nationalists, who were primarily concerned with ensuring that the informal rights afforded to tenants under the 'Ulster custom' were appropriately defined and observed. This much was indicated in testimony provided to the Bessborough Commission in 1880 by Canon Charles Quin, the Camlough based parish priest for Lower Killeavy, and an ardent and influential south Armagh nationalist.[14] Nevertheless, the only firm evidence of James Aiken's stance on the land issue, or indeed his role in agitating for reform, came in 1884 when during a meeting of the Newry Board of Guardians he successfully proposed a resolution calling on the government to 'introduce a measure during the present session to extend the benefits of the Land Law Act to leaseholders, and reducing the percentage on loans.'[15]

More is known of James's activities as a poor law guardian, a role in which he served until the end of his life. He routinely attended the meetings of the

Newry Board of Guardians, and regularly contributed to discussions on the day-to-day business with which the body was typically concerned, such as the collection of rates and the maintenance of the Newry workhouse. As might be expected of a shrewd businessman, his interjections usually concerned financial matters, on which he consistently advocated retrenchment.[16] It was perhaps fitting, therefore, that in 1889 he was named as one of three special defendants in legal proceedings brought against the guardians by the Local Government Board (LGB). This concerned a decision to refer four suspected rabies patients to a Cavan folk healer named Philip McGovern, instead of following the usual, more costly, practice of sending them to Paris for treatment at the Pasteur Institute. The LGB refused to pay for the 'McGovern cure' and instead sought to make James and his fellow defendants liable for the expense. The dispute was eventually settled with the Newry guardians opting to cover the costs for the treatment from their own coffers.[17]

James Aiken became a prominent nationalist figure in Newry and south Armagh through his service in these roles. Throughout the 1880s and 1890s his attendance was regularly noted at local nationalist conventions and events.[18] Following the Parnell split in 1890, he took an anti-Parnellite position, as did the vast majority of south Armagh nationalists. This united stance in the region was due, in part, to the considerable influence of the clergy. At various points in 1891, Cardinal Logue, Primate of All Ireland and Archbishop of Armagh, used the scandal arising from revelations of Parnell's affair with Kitty O'Shea to denounce the disgraced leader. Driven as much by political motives as by moral outrage, Logue sought to use the situation to reassert the church's influence within nationalist politics, and successfully marshalled the clergy in a concerted campaign against Parnell and his supporters.[19] Locally, this agenda was vigorously pursued by the aforementioned Canon Charles Quin. In his zeal he forced the dissolution of the William O'Brien's Gaelic Club in Camlough, an act prompted by the Gaelic Athletic Association's (GAA) support for Parnell. He also proved pivotal in securing the selection of the anti-Parnellite Edward McHugh as the preferred nationalist candidate in the 1892 election, a nomination seconded by James Aiken. McHugh subsequently went on to defeat the sitting Parnellite MP Alexander Blaine.[20] This unified anti-Parnellite stance in South Armagh was not entirely attributable to the influence of the church, however. It also reflected a more general tendency against factionalism in the area throughout the 1885–1918 period. Though distinct divisions were often noticeable during the selection of election candidates, fears that a split vote might benefit unionism ensured that intra-nationalist electoral battles were relatively rare.[21]

The 1890s saw James attain further status and influence locally. In 1893, he was appointed as a justice of the peace (JP). Following the reforms of the

Local Government Act in 1898, he was co-opted as a member of the new
Newry No.2 Rural District Council (RDC) and was subsequently elected as
its chairman, though his attempt to secure election to the new Armagh
County Council for the district of Richhill failed miserably when he received
only 12 votes. He was also appointed as chairman of the Newry Board of
Guardians at this time in recognition of his past service, a move facilitated by
the fact that the nationalists had now secured a majority on the body.[22] It was
in this latter role that he revealed his more radical inclinations, adjourning a
resolution welcoming Queen Victoria on her visit to Ireland in 1900 'until
Ireland became free.'[23]

Within a year of his new local government appointments, however, James
was forced to relinquish his duties due to ill health. He died four months later,
on 12 August 1900, aged 59. Frank was two years old at the time, and his
father's death was the first of three close family bereavements that occurred in
his childhood years. In 1908, his older sister Gertrude died shortly after
turning 15. This was followed in 1913 with the death of his mother Mary, at the
age of 48. It is difficult to know how these bereavements affected Frank,
though the death of his mother had a particularly important impact on him
and his sister Nano, who were aged 15 and 16 respectively. As the youngest,
their mother's passing hastened their transition into adulthood. Although
they were looked after by their older sisters May and Madge, and to a lesser
extent by their extended family, in reality the pair had little in the way of
authority at home. It was perhaps as a result of this shared experience, and
their close ages, that they became particularly close, and together went on to
develop shared interests in both the Irish language and revolutionary republican politics.

Frank's early years provide a number of possible clues as to the origins of
his nationalism, beyond the obvious influence of his family background. Like
many of his peers from the Newry and south Armagh area, he later attributed
his youthful politicisation to the influence of folk tales of the area's turbulent
past. There was certainly a rich history from which to draw such stories.
Though south Armagh was largely untouched by the seventeenth-century
Ulster plantation, determined attempts to settle the area in the late 1700s
generated considerable conflict between newly arrived Protestant settlers and
dispossessed native Irish Catholics. The subsequent emergence of the Peep
O'Day Boys (the forerunner of the Orange Order) and its Catholic equivalent,
the Defenders, prompted considerable violence in the region. Indeed, the most
notable local incident, an attack by the Defenders on a Protestant schoolmaster
and his wife in Forkhill, in which the victims had their tongues cut out and
fingers hacked off, remained deeply embedded within the northern unionist

psyche. Though originally little more than a rural protest group, the Defenders organisation became politicised through its involvement with the United Irishmen during the 1798 rebellion. In the decades that followed, however, it retained much of its original character as an expression of 'social banditry', using intimidation and underground courts to maintain social norms, and carrying out sporadic attacks on local authority figures. Outbreaks of violence and unrest involving the group, and successor organisations such as the Ribbonmen, continued well into the nineteenth century, with agrarian outrages and attacks on officials, such as tithe collectors, proving particularly virulent in the 1810s, 1830s and 1850s.[24]

Combined with local narratives of the penal laws, the United Irish rebellion and the famine, this legacy of violence and banditry provided the basis for a folk memory of local resistance to English intrusion, invasion and misrule; a theme which was in keeping with a particular view of Irish history that formed a central tenet of revolutionary republican ideology.[25] Aiken later claimed that it was the 'horror stories from the old about life during the famine' that had the greatest impact on him, a rare insight which he offered to an academic researcher in 1972 while explaining his initial involvement in the revolutionary movement.[26] He was not alone in expressing such sentiments, however. His future friend and IRA comrade John McCoy, for example, later recalled his grandfather's tales of 'Redmond Count O'Hanlon, Johnson of the Fews, a famous Priest hunter, [and] his own recollections of the 1848 rising and the local activities of the Fenian days.' To McCoy's mind, these stories had 'unpredictable results and helped to mould my later actions.'[27] The legend of the seventeenth-century bandit Redmond O'Hanlon, in particular, held a special resonance for McCoy, and for other future revolutionaries in the region. An impressive mythology had formed around the outlaw, who operated in the area around Slieve Gullion throughout the 1660s and 1670s.[28] Tales of his exploits were well known locally, and were often retold in an overtly politicised manner. In March and April 1913, for example, the *Frontier Sentinel*, the area's main nationalist newspaper, published a serialised biography of O'Hanlon in which he was romanticised as the original 'Irish guerrilla patriot'.[29] The real allure of the legend, however, lay in the fact that O'Hanlon was a remarkably common surname in south Armagh. This ensured that many youths (McCoy included) could lay claim to him as an ancestor.[30]

As intriguing as these recollections of the radicalising power of local history and folklore might be, however, they must be treated with caution. As Augusteijn has observed, factors such as these were often attributed significance with hindsight, despite the probability that they were insignificant in their causal effect.[31] Indeed, it is likely that many of Aiken's contemporaries in

Newry and south Armagh grew up with these tales without acquiring republican leanings, or becoming actively involved in the politics or violence of the revolutionary period.

Perhaps a more plausible influence on Aiken's early ideological develop-ment during these years was his educational experience. Having first attended the local national school in Camlough, Aiken subsequently went on to study at the Abbey Christian Brothers' School (CBS) in Newry. Contemporaries and historians alike have frequently observed the influence of a Christian Brothers education in the development of the Irish revolutionary generation. Teaching a curriculum which promoted a strong nationalist outlook, the Christian Brothers did much to instil their pupils with three of the central tenets of revolutionary republican ideology; Catholicism, cultural nationalism and a view of Irish history which emphasised the struggle against English rule.[32] Although Aiken left no recollections of his time at the Abbey CBS, others who attended the school left little doubt as to its importance in aiding the development of their nationalist outlook. Patrick Casey, who was in the year below Aiken, recalled that 'these men did more than anything else to influence and mould my outlook on the national ideal.' In particular, he noted the influence of Peadar McCann, a teacher at the school, and a well-known local advanced nationalist and member of the Irish Republican Brotherhood (IRB), who went on to become a prominent figure in the Sinn Féin movement in Newry in 1917 and 1918.[33]

For Aiken, however, the main ideological contribution of a CBS education appears to have been in the fact that it sparked a life-long passion for the Irish language, which in turn inspired his involvement in the Gaelic League. Though it is uncertain exactly when Aiken joined the organisation, we do know that he was appointed as secretary of the Camlough branch in 1914 and remained active in this position until 1920.[34] This branch is likely to have been created in late 1913 amid a resurgence of the organisation in the Newry and south Armagh area, which police reports suggested was being carried out by men of 'advanced views'.[35] As Eoin Magennis has observed, there is also good reason to suspect that it was closely affiliated with the organisation's Newry branch, Craobh an Iúr. The latter was heavily involved in the organisation of summer schools at the nearby Irish college in Omeath, Co. Louth, in which Aiken, along with his sister Nano, became active in 1915 and 1916. Roisín ní Beirne, a neighbour, and a close friend of Nano Aiken, was also on the Newry branch's committee.[36] Given that Craobh an Iúr eventually became a cover for local separatist activity after 1916, such links, however informal, are potentially significant in that they may have offered Aiken a way into the revolutionary movement. As will become clear later, however, it is uncertain what role (if any) this network actually played in facilitating his early activism.

Historians have long recognised the Gaelic League's importance as a 'central institution in the development of the Irish revolutionary elite', with a majority of republican leaders having been members at some point in their youth.[37] Aiken himself gave much credit to his involvement in the organisation, and 'his appreciation of the Gaelic language', for inspiring his early participation in the revolutionary movement; though, like many of his peers, his Irish was far from proficient.[38] Even so, Aiken's involvement in cultural nationalism cannot be considered as an early indication of advanced nationalist idealism. Despite the Gaelic League's deserved reputation as a hotbed of revolutionary activity, it was officially a non-political organisation, and in its early years in particular its membership was drawn from a wide range of social and political backgrounds.[39] Nevertheless, the ethos of the League, with its objectives of reviving the Irish language and Gaelic culture, may have aided the cultivation of separatist ideals; instilling a sense of distinctiveness, a historical justification for nationhood, and a definition of 'Irishness' based on cultural and racialist notions of the Gael. It might also be argued that the organisation helped to nurture the Anglophobic and culturally chauvinistic attitude that became a recognisable feature of the revolutionary republican mind-set.[40]

The importance of such ideals in Aiken's political thinking is certainly suggested by the (admittedly sparse) evidence of his revolutionary beliefs, the most contemporary espousal of which features in his correspondence with Richard Mulcahy shortly after the outbreak of the civil war in 1922. In one letter, for instance, he remarked that 'the only sure test to guide an Irishman was whether or not by taking a particular course he would develop into a clean honourable Irish speaking Irishman.' In another he highlighted the importance of the rejuvenation of Irish civilisation as an objective of the republican struggle:

> Our fight against England since 1916 was simply active expression of the faith always in the Irish people, the love of our country, its language, its traditions, its possibilities for greatness fanned into flames by the sacrifices of the Easter Week heroes, and took the form of organising the Nation under a republican form of government to develop its resources and free it from British rule that was destroying our civilisation.

This correspondence also exhibited a degree of Anglophobia on Aiken's part, with quips about provisional government soldiers becoming 'as rotten and British as the British themselves.'[41]

Cultural nationalist ideals clearly formed an important element of Aiken's revolutionary outlook, but this was not necessarily typical of those individuals who became involved in the republican movement locally after 1916. Such influences are rarely mentioned in the recollections of those local men who joined the IRA in Armagh and south Down during this period. Though there are occasional references to membership of either the Gaelic League or the GAA, few of Aiken's comrades appear to have attached the same significance to cultural nationalism as an explanation for their involvement in the revolution as he later did.

The Gaelic League was not the only organisation that Aiken joined at this time, however. In 1914 – at the height of the third home rule crisis – he also enrolled in the Camlough Company of the Irish Volunteers, becoming both its secretary and lieutenant.[42] At this time, Irish nationalists were on the cusp of achieving what had been their primary goal since the 1870s, an Irish parliament with limited powers of self-governance. In opposing the move, however, unionists had made clear their intention to resist the extension of the measure to Ulster. Under the leadership of Sir Edward Carson, plans were laid for the establishment of a provisional government for the province, and impressive displays of defiance were staged, the most notable of which came in September 1912 when 447,197 unionists signed the Ulster Covenant (or a parallel declaration for women) affirming their determination to oppose home rule by all necessary means.[43] Across Armagh and south Down there were 52,228 signatories, the vast majority of whom (33,997, or 65 per cent) were based in the constituencies of North and Mid. Armagh. The figures were considerably lower in South Armagh (4,941, or 9.5 per cent) and South Down (13,299 or 25.5 per cent).[44] As might be expected, this reflected the variations in the respective strengths of the Catholic and Protestant communities in the region. North and Mid. Armagh had Protestant majorities of 67.5 per cent and 55.5 per cent respectively. In contrast, South Armagh and South Down had Catholic majorities of 68 per cent and 53.5 per cent respectively.[45]

In 1913 and 1914, unionist resistance went a step further with the formation of the Ulster Volunteer Force (UVF) – a paramilitary organisation boasting 100,000 members – and the procurement of large quantities of arms.[46] It was not long before this unionist example had inspired the creation of a nationalist counter-force, the Irish Volunteers, in November 1913, and by the following summer it seemed as though the country was standing on the brink of civil war. Locally, UVF companies began to appear almost immediately after the force was founded in January 1913. By the following September, Royal Irish Constabulary (RIC) estimates suggested that the organisation had 2,015 members in Newry and approximately 6,000 across Armagh.[47] The presence of the force, and its open performance of parades and military drills, clearly held the potential to generate conflict in the region. Throughout 1913 and early 1914, however, local nationalists offered little in the way of an organised reaction.

Though police reports often remarked that 'party feeling was running high', up until as late as April 1914 there was no Irish Volunteer presence in either Armagh or Down. Existing nationalist organisations, such as the Ancient Order of Hibernians (AOH) and the United Irish League (UIL), were also routinely described as offering no response to the unionist resistance.[48] Indeed, it was a similar story throughout the province. In January 1914, the RIC Inspector General could report that 'the nationalists of Ulster remained passive', despite the first stirrings of the Irish Volunteers in Donegal and Tyrone.[49]

It was only in May and June 1914 that Irish Volunteer companies began to form in Armagh and Down. This came shortly after the Irish Party had managed to wrest a degree of control over the organisation, and had made clear its newfound support for it. Within the space of two months 32 companies had been established across Armagh, with an estimated membership of 5,000. In Down, in the same period, 52 companies were formed with a membership of 6,667. Although there is no firm evidence to suggest when or how Aiken's local company in Camlough was formed, it is likely that it also emerged at this time. Consequently, while it might be tempting to look upon his involvement in the organisation as the first step on his path to revolution, this was not necessarily the case. There is nothing to suggest that he was any different from the thousands of other constitutional nationalist men who swelled the organisation's ranks in this period, once the Irish Party had signalled that it was acceptable to do so. At most, his youthful involvement in the Irish Volunteers suggests that, like many of his generation, he was influenced by the prevailing trend of popular militarism current throughout Europe in the opening decades of the twentieth century. Such ideals were readily visible in Ireland during this period with a rising number of 'pseudo-military youth groups' such as the Baden Powell scout movement, its Irish equivalent Fianna Éireann, and more significantly with the creation of the UVF, the Irish Volunteers and the Irish Citizen Army (ICA). As Fitzpatrick has observed, the 'common rhetoric of militarism transcended political divisions', and for 'unionists, nationalists and republicans alike, soldiery was an ideal to be extolled rather than a menace to be confronted.'[50] There are certainly hints of such militarism in some of Aiken's political pronouncements in later years. During a speech at an Easter rising commemoration in Dundalk in 1925, for instance, he stated his belief that the young should 'train in arms and be prepared to defend the rights of the country in arms.'[51] Nevertheless, although his brief flirtation with the Irish Volunteers in 1914 certainly suggests an emerging nationalist outlook, and perhaps an attraction to the perceived values of military life, it can by no means be considered as an early expression of revolutionary tendencies or ideals.

Despite the fact that there were now two opposing paramilitary formations operating openly across Armagh and south Down, the region remained peaceful for the duration of the crisis. Leaders on both sides actively sought to avoid confrontation. In Newry, for instance, Day has observed that 'marches and drills tended to take place in defined areas or at pre-set times in order to avoid clashes'. Other areas 'were considered "neutral" and it was understood that neither side would enter them.'[52] This peaceful, if somewhat tense, co-existence continued throughout the early summer months until, on 28 July 1914, Irish issues were eclipsed by the advent of the Great War. The implementation of the Government of Ireland Act, which was finally enacted on 18 September, was put on hold for the duration of the conflict with the proviso that an accommodation must be reached with the unionists of Ulster. As military reservists were called up for service, incidents of drilling involving both UVF and the Irish Volunteers declined, and tensions eased considerably.[53] Indeed, over the next two years, with the region experiencing something of a boom as a result of rising agricultural prices and wartime demands for local linen, the as yet unresolved issue of Ulster's potential exclusion from home rule melted into the background, and community relations returned to some kind of normality.[54]

For Aiken, the outbreak of the Great War marked the end of his first stint in the Irish Volunteers. With the split in the organisation over the Irish Party's support for the British war effort, most companies in south Armagh appear to have either affiliated with the Redmonite faction – the Irish National Volunteers (INV) – or to have simply ceased functioning. The latter was the fate of the Camlough Company, but this can certainly not be read as an indication that Aiken or his comrades had become any more advanced in their nationalist ideals. Though they may not have integrated in to the INV, there also appears to have been no attempt to affiliate with the anti-Redmondite Irish Volunteers. This was not for lack of opportunity. Indeed, an organiser from Belfast was noted to have visited Camlough in June 1915 to encourage recruitment for the organisation, though he appears to have made little headway.[55] The company's collapse likely reflected a degree of ambivalence concerning the Irish Party's support for the war effort – particularly in light of the nationalist leadership's encouragement for enlistment – or perhaps a degree of disillusion in the aftermath of the split.

Following the demise of the Irish Volunteers in Camlough, Aiken showed no further signs of political activity until 1917. Instead he channelled his energies into his cultural nationalist pursuits with the Gaelic League and the Irish college in Omeath. In 1914, following his graduation from the Abbey CBS, he also took over the management of the family farm, though it seems likely that there was plenty of opportunity for him to pursue further study, if he had so wished. The Aiken family was in a comfortable position financially, and his older siblings, James and May, had both progressed to higher education,

James becoming a doctor and May obtaining a Bachelor of Arts degree. According to family lore, however, Frank was not a particularly enthusiastic student. His performance was satisfactory enough. In 1913, for instance, he had obtained seven passes in the middle grade of the intermediate examinations.[56] Yet his attendance was erratic, particularly after the death of his mother, and earned him the nickname 'corr lá' (or 'odd day'). As Magennis suggests, institutional learning appears to have held little appeal for him, and he was more inclined towards self-education.[57] For that reason, it is likely that he was quite content to leave formal education behind, and to instead assume the role of the quintessential 'strong farmer'.

By the spring of 1916, therefore, there was little to suggest that Aiken was on a path towards revolutionary activism. Though politically aware – and ever so briefly active through his involvement in the Irish Volunteers – there is no reason to suspect that he was anything other than a constitutional nationalist in this period. Likewise, there was little indication that over the next seven years his native south Armagh, and its surrounding environs, were in any way likely to emerge as a site of significant revolutionary republican activity, or indeed as a theatre of considerable political and inter-communal violence. Despite the region's reputation, and the troubles of its past, the preceding three decades had been largely peaceful, and even amid the intense pressures of the third home rule crisis, local nationalists and unionists had ultimately avoided violent confrontation. For Aiken personally, as for the wider Armagh-Louth border region in general, the events of the years to come were neither predictable nor inevitable, as news of a rebellion emanated from Dublin.

NOTES

1. I am extremely grateful to Dr Eoin Magennis for sharing with me his knowledge and research on the Aiken family history and Frank Aiken's early years. Unless otherwise stated, the details related here have been provided by him; interview with Dr Eoin Magennis, 19 May 2010; E. Magennis, 'Frank Aiken: Family, early life and the revolutionary period, 1898–1921' in Evans and Kelly (eds), *Frank Aiken: Nationalist and Internationalist* (Dublin, 2014).

2. *Census of Ireland, 1901, Volume III, Part I, Province of Ulster, No.2 County of Armagh (Dublin, 1902)*; Census returns for Carrickbracken, Co. Armagh, http://www.census.nationalarchives.ie/pages/1901/Armagh/Camlough/Carrickbracken (accessed 11 Dec. 2013).

3. For the United Irishman anecdote see, transcript of conversation with Packy McGrath, 5 Dec. 1979, University College Dublin Archives Department (hereafter, UCDAD), Aiken papers, P104/457.

4. Liam Skinner, *Politicians By Accident* (Dublin, 1947), p. 153.

5. Indentures for land purchases, 7 June 1881, UCDAD, Aiken papers, P104/203–8; Map of lands in Carrickbracken and Derrymore, undated, UCDAD, Aiken papers, P104/210.

6. Annual land valuation revision list for Camlough, 1909–20, Public Record Office Northern Ireland (hereafter, PRONI), VAL/12B/15/6H.

7. Figures based on annual land valuation revision lists for, Camlough, *c.*1909–20, PRONI, VAL/12B/15/6H; Ballybot, 1909–20, PRONI, VAL/12B/15/1J; Newry West Urban, 1911–19, PRONI, VAL/12B/22/18C; Newry South Urban, *c.*1911, PRONI, VAL/12B/22/17B.

8. 'Statistical Appendix', in D. Fitzpatrick, 'The geography of Irish Nationalism 1910–1911', in *Past and Present*, 78 (Feb. 1978), pp 138–9.

9. Details from the Aiken family gravestone, St Malachy's Catholic Church, Camlough; see also Magennis, 'Frank Aiken: Family, early life and the revolutionary period', p. 2.

10. Two of the children died; Annie (in infancy) in 1892, and Gertrude in 1908, aged 14; see List of family members, undated, UCDAD, Aiken papers P104/751.

11. K. Madden, *Forkhill Protestants and Forkhill Catholics* (Liverpool, 2006) p. 73; G. Moran, '"The advance on the north": The difficulties of the home rule movement in south-east Ulster, 1870–1883', in O'Sullivan and Gillespie (eds), *Borderlands: Essays on the History of the Ulster-Leinster Border* (Belfast, 1989), pp 129–30.

12. Moran, 'The advance on the north', pp 129–42; C. Murphy, 'Franchise, elections and parliamentary representation', in A. J. Hughes and W. Nolan (eds), *Armagh: History and Society: Interdisciplinary Essays on the History of an Irish County* (Dublin, 2001), p. 930.

13. *Freeman's Journal*, 22 July 1881.

14. J. Bradley, 'Canon Charles Quin and the Bessborough Commission', in *Seanchas Ard Mhacha: Journal of the Armagh Diocesan Historical Society*, 16: 1 (1994), pp 135–6, 176.

15. *Freeman's Journal*, 18 Feb. 1881.

16. See, for example, *Belfast News-Letter*, 12 Jan. 1885, 17 Dec. 1888, 19 and 26 Aug. 1889.

17. Ibid., 16 Aug. 1889, 28 July 1896, 1 Feb., 22 Mar. and 24 May 1897.

18. For examples see, *Freeman's Journal*, 26 July 1887, 27 Sept. 1888, 18 June 1892, 5 Nov. 1894.

19. J. Privilege, *Michael Logue and the Catholic Church in Ireland* (Manchester, 2009), pp 80–3.

20. *Freeman's Journal*, 18 June 1892; Bradley, 'Canon Charles Quin and the Bessborough Commission', pp 135–6.

21. For factionalism in the selection of election candidates see *Freeman's Journal*, 28 Sept. 1900. Following the 1892 election, only two of the six elections to occur in South Armagh featured more than one nationalist candidate; see Murphy, 'Franchise, elections and parliamentary representation', p. 942; *Irish Times*, 13 Oct. 1900.

22. *Freeman's Journal*, 8, 18 Apr. 1899; *Newry Telegraph*, 14 Aug. 1900.

23. Magennis, 'Frank Aiken: Family, early life and the revolutionary period', p. 2.

24. See Madden, *Forkhill Protestants and Forkhill Catholics*, pp, 5, 10, 18–28, 83–120; though this violence – the attacks at Forkhill in particular – is typically viewed in terms of sectarianism, Madden offers a compelling argument to the contrary.

25. R. English, *Ernie O'Malley: IRA Intellectual* (Oxford, 1998), pp 96–8.

26. 'Transcript of interview notes', 16 Aug. 1972, UCDAD, Aiken papers, P104/450.

27. John McCoy, Irish Military Archives (hereafter, IMA), Bureau of Military History Witness Statement (hereafter, BMH WS) 492.

28. S. J. Connolly, 'O'Hanlon, Redmond (*c.*1640–1681)', *Oxford Dictionary of National Biography* (hereafter, *ONDB*), www.oxforddnb.com.ezproxy.qub.ac.uk/ (accessed 10 Jan. 2010).

29. See serialised biography of Redmond O'Hanlon in *Frontier Sentinel*, 29 Mar.–12 Apr. 1913.

30. John McCoy, IMA, BMH WS 492.

31. J. Augusteijn, *Patrick Pearse: The Making of a Revolutionary* (Basingstoke, 2010), p. 216.

32. English, *Ernie O'Malley*, pp 89–98, 124; see also, P. Hart, *The IRA at War* (Oxford, 2003), pp 56–7.

33. Patrick Casey, IMA, BMH WS 1148.

34. 'Chronology', *c.*1933, IMA, Bureau of Military History Contemporary Documents (hereafter, BMH CD) 6/36/22.

35. *Newry Telegraph*, 1 Nov. 1913; County Inspector's report (hereafter, CI), Armagh, Dec. 1913, The National Archives Kew (hereafter, TNA), Colonial Office (hereafter, CO) 904/91.

36. Tony Woods, a student at the college in 1917, recalled that Aiken was a governor there and often allowed him to stay with the family at Carrickbracken; see U. MacEoin, *Survivors* (Dublin, 1980), p. 312; Magennis, 'Frank Aiken: Family, early life and the revolutionary period', p. 4.

37. T. Garvin, *Nationalist Revolutionaries in Ireland, 1858–1928* (Dublin, 2005), p. 80.

38. C. S. Andrews, *Dublin Made Me: An Autobiography* (Dublin, 1979) p. 242.

39. For a discussion of this see T. G. McMahon, *Grand Opportunity: The Gaelic Revival and Irish Society, 1893–1910* (New York, 2008), pp 85–126.

40. For a discussion of cultural nationalist influences on republican ideology see, English, *Ernie O'Malley*, p. 96; M. Laffan, *The Resurrection of Ireland: The Sinn Féin Party, 1916–1923* (Cambridge, 1999), p. 218.

41. Aiken to Mulcahy, 20 July 1922, UCDAD, Aiken papers, P104/1248; Aiken to Mulcahy, 15 July 1922, UCDAD, de Valera papers, P150/1749.

42. 'Chronology', *c.*1933, IMA, BMH CD 6/36/22.

43. R. Fanning, *Fatal Path: British Government and Irish Revolution, 1910–1922* (London, 2013), p. 71.

44. Figures obtained using the Public Record Office of Northern Ireland's database of Ulster Covenant signatories; 'Search the covenant', www.applications.proni.gov.uk/UlsterCovenant/Search.aspx, (accessed 27 Dec. 2012). The figure for South Down includes Newry.

45. See Appendix II, Table I.

46. For a detailed discussion of the UVF's membership and military capabilities see, T. Bowman, *Carson's Army: The Ulster Volunteer Force, 1910–22* (Manchester, 2007), pp 45–75, 135–62.

47. RIC County Inspectors' Reports (hereafter, CI), Armagh and Down, Sept. 1913, Colonial Office (hereafter, CO) 904/91.

48. CI, Armagh and Down, Jan. 1913–Apr. 1914, CO 904/89–93.

49. Inspector General's report (hereafter, IG), Jan. 1914, CO 904/92.

50. D. Fitzpatrick, 'Militarism in Ireland 1900–1922', in T. Bartlett and K. Jeffery (eds), *A Military History of Ireland* (Cambridge, 1996), p. 379.

51. *Irish Independent*, 13 Apr. 1925.

52. C. S. Day, 'Political violence in the Armagh/Newry area, 1912–1925' (PhD, Queen's University Belfast, 1998), p. 18.

53. CI, Armagh and Down, Aug.–Nov. 1914, CO 904/94–5.

54. Day, 'Political violence in the Armagh/Newry area', pp 22–3; for more on Armagh's wartime economy see C. Cousins, *Armagh and the Great War* (Dublin, 2011), pp 101–33.

55. See Cousins, *Armagh and the Great War*, p. 40. Despite this attempt, by 1916 there was no anti–Redmonite Irish Volunteer presence in Camlough or the wider south Armagh region; CI, Armagh, Mar. 1916, CO 904/99; 'Chronology', c.1933, IMA, BMH CD 6/36/22.
56. The results were reported in the local press, see *Frontier Sentinel*, 16 Sept. 1913.
57. Magennis, 'Frank Aiken: Family, early life and the revolutionary period', p. 3.

THREE

EMERGENCE

—

Though opinions often differ as to when the Irish revolution truly began, there can be little doubt that the Easter rising in 1916 marked a turning point. As Peter Hart has observed, this was 'Ireland's 1789 or 1917, the Dublin GPO its Bastille or Winter Palace.'[1] In its aftermath, the rebellion, and more importantly the executions of its leaders, became an emotional focal point for a monumental shift in popular nationalist opinion. The formerly marginalised minority of separatists and advanced nationalists from which the defeated rebels were drawn came to the fore of a new mass political movement, and the longer-standing nationalist objective of an all-Ireland home rule settlement was superseded by the demand for an Irish republic. Although these developments were much less pronounced in six-county Ulster, where unionism and constitutional nationalism retained their political dominance, they were readily apparent across Armagh and south Down. It was in this climate of republican mobilisation, between 1916 and 1918, that Aiken took his first steps towards revolutionary activism, and gradually established himself as both a prominent Sinn Féin figure in his native south Armagh and a key player in the revitalised Irish Volunteer movement across south-east Ulster.

Aiken's only recollections of Easter week are recorded in a brief chronology of his political activities composed in the early 1930s: 'no organisation locally and completely out of touch. Procured cartridges for shotgun in readiness to join up if fighting spread outside Dublin.'[2] In the event, the violence of the rebellion did not spread. With a few minor exceptions the fighting was confined to the capital, and Irish Volunteer companies in the provinces remained inactive amid the confusion prompted by a last-minute countermanding order from the chief-of-staff, Eoin McNeill. In Dublin, meanwhile, the British army soon quelled the insurrection, shelling the various city centre buildings that had been seized by the rebels, and quickly securing their unconditional surrender.[3]

Leaving aside the obvious question of whether Aiken's professed enthusiasm to participate in the rising was genuine, or whether it was, perhaps, a retrospective addition to his revolutionary credentials, such revolutionary fervour was certainly not typical of the local response to the rebellion across Armagh and south Down. Here, as in most other parts of the country, the episode was generally greeted with shock and condemnation. The nationalist *Frontier Sentinel* branded the rebels as 'criminal and insane'. Meanwhile, its unionist counterpart, the *Armagh Guardian*, used the occasion to attack the Irish administration in Dublin Castle: 'there is not the slightest doubt the authorities were caught napping, but it is somewhat of a consolation that the rebellion had to be dealt with by the military authorities and not by the mollies of the castle.'[4] There is some evidence of a more mixed reaction amongst the nationalist population in Aiken's native south Armagh, however. As John McCoy later recalled,

> The prevailing opinion was the unbelievable madness of the whole affair [. . .] I heard a great many people saying 'weren't they great men, it's a pity there were not more of them' – others saying – 'of course they were mad to attempt such a thing – if they were so keen to fight why did they not join the Army'.[5]

Nevertheless, the bulk of popular opinion was critical of the rebels. Indeed, it is telling of local responses to the rising that the most significant occurrence in the region during Easter week was the co-operation of the UVF and the INV in taking turns to guard the GPO at Newry, an act more noteworthy for its symbolism than its practical value.[6]

Such negative reactions to the rising were hardly surprising. Separatism and advanced nationalism were marginal viewpoints in the region, though they did have an organisational presence. This was due primarily to the efforts of local members of the IRB, the oath-bound revolutionary society that had been the driving force behind the rising. Founded in 1858, the IRB was dedicated to securing an independent Irish republic. Having attempted an insurrection in 1867, and pursued a bombing campaign in England in the 1880s, it had fallen into decline by 1900. As the new century dawned, however, the brotherhood experienced something of a revival under the influence of a new generation of leaders, such as Bulmer Hobson, Denis McCullough and Patrick Thomas Daly. This was particularly true in Ulster where the authorities noted that the IRB had been 'greatly strengthened and reorganised' during 1902 and 1903.[7]

In Newry and south Armagh this resurgence owed much to the efforts of Seamus O'Hanlon, a local carpenter. A native of the area, O'Hanlon had briefly lived in Dublin where he appears to have first become involved in the separatist movement. Upon returning home in 1903, he set about reorganising the moribund IRB presence in the locality, swearing in new recruits and establishing other nationalist organisations through which to promote separatist ideals. The latter included a branch of Cumann na nGaedheal, a pre-cursor to Arthur Griffith's original dual monarchist Sinn Féin party. In 1905, he also established a cultural nationalist group called the Irish Ireland Society, which later morphed into a branch of the pre-1916 Sinn Féin. When O'Hanlon emigrated in 1906, this work was continued by his two most dedicated recruits; Robert Kelly, a stone mason, and John Southwell, a van driver, both of whom were based in Newry. By 1916, the pair had been appointed to the IRB's Ulster Council, and together they continued with their attempts to further expand the movement through the infiltration of other local nationalist organisations. Kelly, in particular, became a prominent figure in the local GAA, the Newry branch of the Gaelic League, and the Newry Trades Council.[8]

This slow but steady conspiratorial approach produced little visible separatist activity, beyond occasional meetings and sporadic protests against British army recruitment or the influence of 'foreign dances'.[9] It also attracted relatively few followers. RIC reports suggest that ten years on from O'Hanlon's return the IRB in Armagh had 22 circles (branches) with an estimated 350 members. The testimonies of John Southwell and Jack Shields (an IRB organiser from Tyrone), suggest that the organisation was particularly strong in the Camlough and Bessbrook districts in the south of the county and in Blackwatertown in the north.[10] In Down, meanwhile, it was believed that the brotherhood had four circles with an estimated 102 members, though special branch intelligence from 1914 suggested that there were perhaps as few as 22 active members in Newry.[11] Other advanced nationalist organisations in the region, namely the pre-1916 incarnation of Sinn Féin and the Ancient Order of Hibernians Irish American Alliance (AOHIAA) – a more radical version of the larger constitutional nationalist AOH – fared no better. On the eve of the Easter rising it was estimated that across Armagh and Down they had memberships of 127 and 152 respectively. To put these figures into perspective, the two main constitutional nationalist organisations, the AOH and United Irish League (UIL), had a combined membership of 12,371 in the same period. The Orange Order, moreover, could boast 15,659 brethren across the two counties, while the Ulster Unionist Clubs – re-established in 1911 as part of the resistance to home rule – had an estimated 11,254 members.[12]

Given their prominence within the IRB in Ulster, Kelly and Southwell were well aware of the plans for the Easter rising, and were intent on participating alongside their small cadre of followers in Newry. Unlike their comrades elsewhere in Ulster, who were under orders to mobilise at Coalisland, Co. Tyrone, in the expectation of fighting in the west of the country, the Newry men were told to join up with the Irish Volunteers at Dundalk.[13] In the event, however, they failed to mobilise. Confusion regarding their vague instructions from Dublin was compounded by McNeill's countermanding orders. Kelly, moreover, was reluctant to serve with the Volunteers in Dundalk because their commanding officer – Paddy Hughes – was not a member of the IRB. As a result, the only local man to actually take part in the rising was Patrick Rankin, another Newry IRB figure, and leader of the local sluagh (company) of Fianna Éireann, the republican equivalent of the Baden-Powell Boy Scout movement. Having received news on Easter Monday that the rising had gone ahead, he set off for Dublin and eventually joined the fighting at the GPO.[14]

It is telling of the limits of Aiken's own nationalism at this time that he was clearly unaware of the radical networks that were operating around him. Indeed, this is particularly striking when it is considered that his home townland of Carrickbracken was situated in the middle of the reputed IRB hotspots of Camlough and Bessbrook, and that as a member of the Gaelic League he likely came into contact with members of the brotherhood. Yet this was not particularly surprising. As has already been shown, although Aiken may have had certain radical inclinations prior to 1916, there was little to suggest that he was an advanced nationalist, and he was not especially politically active. What is striking, however, is that his detachment from the existing local separatist and advanced nationalist scene apparently continued well into 1917, despite the first clear signs of his emerging republicanism, and his initial attempts to engage in the activism surrounding the new Sinn Féin movement.

In many respects, this reflected the limitations of the initial efforts to re-organise the separatist movement in Newry and south Armagh immediately after the rising. As might be expected, Kelly, Southwell and Rankin were the main figures behind this endeavour. All three had been arrested in the aftermath of the insurrection; Rankin upon the surrender of the rebels in Dublin, Kelly and Southwell in the nationwide round-ups of suspects that followed.[15] By July 1916, however, all three men had been released, and upon returning to Newry they began to plot the rejuvenation of the local movement. By this time, similar initiatives were already underway elsewhere in Armagh. As early as August 1916 a new Irish Volunteer company had been formed in Armagh city. One of those who joined the new unit, James Short, later recalled that the preliminary meeting consisted primarily of IRB men, with only five or six attendees having no previous affiliation with the brotherhood. Indeed, the creation of such companies in the region, which continued on a modest scale for the duration of 1916 and 1917, was primarily the work of the IRB. As Short's testimony suggests, the recruits to these units tended to be individuals who were already members of the brotherhood, or who already had considerably advanced separatist views.[16] This was typical of the initial reorganisation of the Irish Volunteers elsewhere in Ulster, notably Tyrone and Derry, though in these areas the initiative usually came from younger, recently recruited IRB members, rather than the older, more established, figures.[17]

In Newry and south Armagh, the efforts of Kelly, Southwell and Rankin were similarly limited in scope. In attempting to reinvigorate the movement, they reverted to the usual IRB methods of infiltration; using other local nationalist groups as both a recruiting ground and a cover for their conspiratorial activities.[18] In January 1917, the RIC observed that Kelly and Rankin were becoming particularly active in the Gaelic League in Newry, and that they were probably using these meetings to 'spread Sinn Féin ideas'.[19] Indeed, at this time there had been a marked increase in activity at the branch, and it is clear from Bureau of Military History witness statements that it was being used as a cover for meetings of Rankin's Fianna Éireann company.[20] Increased activity was also reported within the GAA in Armagh during this period. In Camlough, a new club named 'the Sons of Pearse' was formed, and the RIC began to report more frequently on meetings and matches. In February, the county inspector for Armagh also observed that 'there has been some little development of the GAA within the past few months on more advanced lines.'[21] It is unclear, however, if the IRB were involved in these efforts.

As in earlier years, these infiltrationist tactics produced meagre results. By July 1917 – a full year on from their release – Kelly, Southwell and Rankin had made little progress. This was particularly true beyond Newry, in the rural districts of south Armagh, where Aiken's first efforts at republican activism appear to have been driven entirely by personal initiative, and owed little to the guidance or direction of any local advanced nationalist organisation. In late April 1917, he hoisted a number of Sinn Féin flags around Camlough, something of which he was immensely proud as they had been the first to appear in the district and he had taken the rather daring step of placing one in a tree directly opposite the village RIC barracks.[22] This was most likely intended as a show of support for Sinn Féin's by-election campaign in South Longford, which was underway at the time, but may also have been timed to commemorate the anniversary of the rising. During the next by-election contest that year, in East Clare in July, he went a step further in his support for the party, travelling to the constituency to assist in the republican campaigning.[23] Yet despite his enthusiastic support for the new Sinn Féin movement – and the separatist republican ideal for which it now stood – it appears that he was not yet a member of the party. Nor, indeed, was he a member of the IRB, and there is little to suggest that he was even approached as a potential recruit in this period. This is a telling indication of the local IRB's limited organisational efforts at this time. Aiken was surely a prime candidate for their overtures, and given his presence in the same cultural nationalist circles that Kelly, Southwell and Rankin had endeavoured to infiltrate, he cannot have been unknown to them. This was particularly true in the winter of 1916–17, when Aiken was appointed as a Gaelic League organiser for south Armagh as part of a new promotional initiative. Significantly, he also joined his local GAA club at this time, and was noted as a player on both the football and hurling teams.[24]

By the spring of 1917, the limited organisational efforts of the Newry IRB clique were overtaken by a more general upsurge of sympathy for the republican movement amongst the local nationalist population. This was in keeping with a much broader national trend in which popular nationalist opinion moved away from the constitutional nationalism of the Irish Party and towards the republicanism and separatism of the post-rising Sinn Féin movement, though in Armagh and south Down – as across much of Ulster – the shift was much less pronounced and the Irish Party managed to retain its political dominance. The exact reasons for this transformation in Irish opinion (across southern Ireland at least) are a point of debate. Traditionally, historical narratives of the period attributed it to the public's revulsion at the executions of the leaders of the Easter rising. However, this popular notion has long fallen out of favour with historians who – to quote Fitzpatrick – are now more inclined to turn away from explanations emphasising 'state of mind' in favour of those based upon 'rational calculation' and 'homely logic'.[25] Indeed, the most recent research has suggested that Ireland's revolutionary turn was the result of a complex combination of factors, including the grassroots political impact of Britain's wartime mobilisation policies, the progress of continued negotiations concerning Ulster's exclusion from home rule, and the propaganda activities of groups such as the Irish National Aid Association and Volunteer Dependants' Fund (INAAVDF).[26]

In explaining the gradual emergence of a degree of republican sympathy and support in Armagh and south Down in 1916 and early 1917, the impact of the executions is certainly suspect. Although they undoubtedly provoked a negative reaction amongst local nationalists, this was much more subdued than might be expected. The RIC, for instance, could only note that 'the nationalists have no doubt been upset by the executions in Dublin', but there were few overt signs of discontent.[27] The local nationalist press, meanwhile, was not especially critical of the authorities. Indeed, an editorial published in the *Frontier Sentinel* on 12 May, the final day of the executions in Dublin, was more critical of the rebels themselves for their misguided attempt 'to supersede tried and successful political leaders, especially at so important a juncture of history as we have reached'.[28] Likewise, the influence of separatist propaganda appears to have been negligible. The lacklustre efforts of the local IRB have already been detailed, in addition to which the RIC noted only a handful of isolated seditious incidents throughout 1916. Furthermore, although collections were made for the INAAVDF in the area in July, there were no further references to such activity in the months that followed.[29] There were, moreover, few obvious indications that war weariness, or discontent with Britain's wartime polices, had exerted any particular influence on the radicalisation of nationalist opinion in the region at this stage, though these undoubtedly became a factor later in the 1916–18 period.

Bearing this in mind, therefore, it is fair to suggest that emerging republican sympathy in the region was fuelled primarily by discontent with the Irish Party over the issue of exclusion. In May and July 1916, David Lloyd George (British secretary for war from June 1916, and previously minister of munitions) chaired renewed negotiations with Redmond and Carson in an effort to resolve the issue of Ulster's place in a home rule Ireland. In the course of the talks, Lloyd George gave the two leaders very different impressions of his main proposal; that home rule be given immediate effect, but with the exclusion of the six north-eastern counties of Ulster. Carson was led to believe that the exclusion would be permanent, while Redmond was under the impression that it would be temporary. Redmond agreed to the principle of the temporary exclusion, and won support for the measure at a tense conference of the Irish Party's Ulster delegates at St Mary's Hall in Belfast on 23 June 1916. The deal collapsed, however, when Lloyd George's contradictory promises became apparent, and as Ronan Fanning has observed, although the 'ensuing welter of recriminations did little damage to Lloyd George or Carson', it nonetheless 'corroded the authority of Redmond in nationalist Ireland because it made his acceptance of partition common knowledge.'[30]

The Lloyd George negotiations took precedence in the minds of local nationalists in the immediate aftermath of the rising. Indeed, in June the RIC could note that any lingering bitterness over the executions had been distracted by the talks, adding that, in general, there was 'a great deal of anxiety' over the proposed settlement of the home rule issue.[31] This was hardly surprising given that Armagh and Down – as two of the six counties facing exclusion – would be so directly affected by the final outcome of the negotiations. It was also no surprise, therefore, that the Irish Party's acceptance of the principle of exclusion at the St Mary's Hall conference in June did much to foster discontent within local nationalism. Indeed, it was a similar story elsewhere in the six counties, such as Tyrone, where the decision prompted a number of disillusioned former Irish Party supporters to create a new (albeit short-lived) organisation called the Irish Nation League.[32]

An illustrative example of the effects of the exclusion issue in radicalising local nationalist opinion in Armagh and south Down was the changing political outlook of the *Frontier Sentinel*. As has already been discussed, the paper's editorials had expressed no particular sympathy with the rebels, even amidst the executions in early May, and continued to faithfully support the

Irish Party line. It was only in the aftermath of the June conference that it began to show signs of more advanced nationalist views. Denouncing Redmond, it concluded that the compromise of exclusion was the end result of a 'process of national demoralisation which set in when the Irish Party allied itself with the British Liberal Party and became involved in imperial politics.'[33] Over the course of the next year the paper became increasingly hostile to the constitutional nationalist position, and by the beginning of 1918 it was decidedly pro-Sinn Féin; a reflection of the changing ideological position of its editor, Joseph Connellan.[34]

Although there is little contemporary evidence of Aiken's thoughts and opinions at this time, it seems likely that the exclusion issue significantly influenced his own emergent republicanism. This is not to diminish the un-doubted emotional impact of the Easter rising, or to question his recollections of his enthusiasm to participate in the fighting if it had spread. Indeed, Irish revolutionaries very often cited the rising as the inspiration for their involve-ment in the republican campaign.[35] Yet for young northern nationalists, in particular, the lessons of the rising were closely tied to the continuing uncertainty over home rule.

John McCoy's recollections are informative in this regard. Though complicated somewhat by the fact that they were recorded in later life, and thus subject to hindsight and after-the-fact rationalisation, they nevertheless provide a useful insight into how Aiken and his peers are likely to have interpreted both the rising and the broader political situation at this time. In discussing the executions, McCoy emphasised the perception of a lack of parity in how the British government treated the rebels and the Ulster unionists, who were themselves armed, organised and using the threat of violence to ensure their exclusion from a home rule Ireland: 'it appeared that rebellion entailed the extreme punishment in Dublin and was a means of preferment and elevation in Belfast.' McCoy also recalled his belief that the Ulster unionists' successful use of the threat of violence as a 'means of attaining certain objectives' had thoroughly discredited the Irish Party and demonstrated that the 'doctrine of physical force was an essential part of any future effort to achieve the freedom of the country from British domination.'[36] Sympathetic nationalists throughout the country undoubtedly shared such sentiments. Yet in areas such as Armagh and Down, which were actually facing the prospect of exclusion, they were particularly intense. Although it is impossible to say for certain if Aiken shared McCoy's views on these issues, it seems likely that his rather abrupt engagement in republican activism from early 1917 onwards reflected a similar development in his own political outlook.

Growing local dissatisfaction with the Irish Party over the issue of exclusion, however, did not immediately translate into support for Sinn Féin or republicanism. As Phoenix has observed, reactions to the St Mary's Hall conference among nationalists in Armagh proved more complicated in the immediate term. At an Irish Party conference in Armagh city, for instance, supporters simultaneously applauded the wise leadership of John Redmond while declaring their determination to 'oppose exclusion in any shape or form.'[37] The Irish Party retained a strong hold over nationalism in the region, and action was quickly taken to try to stem the developing discontent there. By the autumn a paid UIL organiser was noted to be active in both Armagh and Down.[38]

In Newry and south Armagh, local discontent with the Irish Party finally began to translate into increased support for the republican movement in April 1917. This was possibly the result of the growing momentum of the Sinn Féin organisation at a national level, with its by-election victories early that year. Similar effects were noticed elsewhere in the country. In west Cork, for example, the RIC attributed the rapid growth of the local Sinn Féin organisation in July 1917 to the party's election victories in South Longford and East Clare.[39] Yet the effects of these by-election victories are by no means clear in Newry and south Armagh, or indeed in the wider Armagh and south Down area. Sinn Féin's successes in North Roscommon and South Longford, for instance, provoked little comment locally. The *Frontier Sentinel*, despite its increasing opposition to the Irish Party, made no mention of the victories in its editorials. Remarkably, the only local newspaper to make any significant comment on the republican successes as they occurred was the unionist *Armagh Guardian*.[40] There is also little indication that local republicans made any use of the by-election victories to generate publicity or support. It was only during the South Longford campaign that any visible sign of Sinn Féin sympathy emerged. Yet this was primarily the result of Aiken's flag hoisting efforts in Camlough during April. Indeed, in May 1917 the RIC in Armagh reported that 'a good many Sinn Féin flags were hoisted last month, principally in S. Armagh [. . .] though I believe sympathy with Sinn Féinism is on the increase there is still no organisation.'[41]

The following month, however, as a third by-election contest got underway in East Clare, the first of the new generation of Sinn Féin clubs was formed in Armagh city. It attracted around one hundred members.[42] Elsewhere in the country, these clubs had been forming from as early as January 1917, and at the organisation's height they came to number around 1,200 nationwide.[43] Across Armagh and south Down, new clubs continued to appear throughout 1917 at a rate of one or two per month. By November, there were 23 branches operating in counties Armagh and Down, with a combined membership of 1,064.[44]

The formation of Aiken's local Sinn Féin branch in Camlough on 6 August 1917 provides a typical example of the way in which these new clubs were created. A meeting was held in the village at which Thomas Woods, an IRB man from Bessbrook, took the chair. Eamon Donnelly, a prominent Armagh city Sinn Féiner, and Sean Brown, a party organiser from Dublin, addressed the crowd. Together, they set out the party's objectives and policies, paying particular attention to its principle of abstention from Westminster. As new members were enrolled a group of supporters arrived from Belfast, one of whom briefly addressed the crowd. The new club was then formed with a membership of around 150. It was initially named in honour of Irish Volunteer leader Eoin MacNeill, although it was later renamed to com-memorate the hunger striker Thomas Ashe after his death by force-feeding in September 1917.[45] One local later explained the apparent enthusiasm for Sinn Féin in Camlough in a letter to the *Newry Telegraph*: 'ten or eleven years ago a very flourishing S. F. Club existed in Camlough and though most of the pioneers of the S. F. policy in Camlough are abroad or dead their teachings have remained with the people.'[46]

The establishment of the Camlough Sinn Féin club marked the beginning of Aiken's formal association with the party, and it is likely that he joined at this initial meeting. He may also have been directly involved in the events surrounding its creation, given his involvement in the East Clare by-election campaign the previous month, and the fact that he was soon appointed as the club's treasurer. Despite this position, however, he received no mention in the early reports of its meetings and activities. This suggests that he was still something of a marginal figure in the local organisation, though this was hardly surprising. He was, after all, only 19 years old, and still a relatively new face in a movement that continued to be dominated by older separatists.

Although lagging behind national events somewhat, Sinn Féin was begin-ning to build momentum in Armagh and south Down. This progress was further encouraged throughout the second half of 1917 by visits from organisers and figures from the party's national leadership. In July, Michael Collins and J. J. Byrne addressed meetings in Armagh and Mullinary.[47] Various events held during the autumn were also addressed by prominent separatist figures such as the new Sinn Féin president, and only surviving leader of the Easter rising, Eamon de Valera, the former independent nationalist MP and repub-lican covert Laurence Ginnell, the Ulster IRB leader Denis McCullough, and the Belfast republican Seán MacEntee. The most significant meeting of the year, however, occurred near Newry on 16 September and was addressed by Sinn Féin founder Arthur Griffith. The event had been organised, in part, by Kelly, Southwell and Rankin, and it was estimated that around 4,000 people attended.[48]

This growing support for Sinn Féin, particularly in Newry and south Armagh, was met with a renewed effort by the Irish Party to reinforce its support base in the region. In the autumn of 1917, Dr Charles O'Neill, the Scotland-based Irish Party MP for South Armagh, conducted a tour of the area to encourage the reorganisation of the UIL. During his various engagements, however, growing hostility to the Irish Party was often evident. At a meeting in Dromintee, shortly after the death of Thomas Ashe, for instance, O'Neill was interrupted by republicans who proposed 'a resolution expressing sympathy with the late Commandant Thomas Ashe' and criticised the attempt 'to hold a meeting on an occasion when Ireland was mourning the loss of one of her noblest sons'.[49] On 10 November, a UIL organiser experienced similar problems at a meeting in Keady where he was mercilessly heckled by the crowd and eventually drowned out by 'loud cheering for de Valera'.[50] Yet incidents such as these should not be read as an indication of any sea change in local nationalist opinion. Rather, they were evidence of a growing, and extremely vocal, minority. Republicanism remained relatively weak in the region, and in November 1917 the RIC in Armagh could still confidently report that the movement was 'not making headway'.[51]

THE SOUTH ARMAGH BY-ELECTION

As 1918 opened, however, the situation changed dramatically. On 14 January, Dr Charles O'Neill died at his home in Coatbridge, North Lanarkshire, after a short illness, and speculation was soon rife as to the possibility of yet another by-election contest; a first test for Sinn Féin in Ulster. For republicans, the South Armagh constituency was an uncertain prospect. Although Sinn Féin had enjoyed some growth locally, the Irish Party remained the dominant political force in the area. Addressing the Sinn Féin standing committee on 17 January, Sean Milroy observed that the party had only eight branches in the constituency and that 'it would be a hard fight.'[52] Nevertheless, the contest was soon confirmed. The Sinn Féin candidate, Dr Patrick McCartan, was a native of Tyrone with a long association with both the IRB and its Irish-American counterpart, Clan na Gael.[53] The Irish Party candidate, Patrick Donnelly, was a solicitor from Newry, and a well-known local nationalist. He was also a favourite of Canon Charles Quin, whose influence in the area had waned little since Aiken's father's days in local politics. Quin had previously tried to secure Donnelly's nomination for the constituency in 1909, but O'Neill had prevailed.[54] The ensuing campaign illustrated the importance of the contest for both parties. As Laffan has observed, 'it was claimed that the election provoked more activity than Roscommon or Longford had done the previous year.'[55] In the process, it provided a significant boost to the organisational efforts of local republicans, and presented fresh opportunities for young activists like Aiken to acquire new roles and responsibilities within the movement.

The election was a purely nationalist affair. As part of a 'political truce' connected with continuing home rule negotiations, no unionist candidate was fielded. Indeed, the attitude of local unionists was that, as they were unlikely to win, it was better they 'should not vote, leaving the nationalists to decide their own quarrel.'[56] An independent unionist temperance candidate, Thomas Richardson, did briefly step forward, but quickly withdrew from the contest amid protests that his nomination was 'a breach of the political truce'.[57] His withdrawal, however, came too late to have his name removed from the ballot papers.

For local republicans, it quickly became clear that the organisation of the Sinn Féin campaign was to be dominated by figures from Dublin. Kelly later recalled that 'a committee from headquarters arrived to run the election (no local men, as far as I know) [. . .] a lot of things were done that we locals never knew of.'[58] This committee first set up its headquarters at Dundalk, but soon moved to Newry. Aiken provided one of his family's properties in Monaghan Street for the party's use, one of his few traceable contributions to the campaign. As supporters from across the country flocked to the constituency there were few duties for local activists aside from the creation of leaflets and posters.[59] The notable local republican figures that had dominated Sinn Féin meetings in the previous months – primarily established IRB figures from Newry, such as Robert Kelly, Peader McCann and Patrick Lavery – were noticeably absent from the platforms. Instead, republican leaders such as de Valera and Countess Markievicz preached the republican manifesto. Furthermore, in the absence of any significant Irish Volunteer organisation in the region, volunteers from various parts of the country were brought into the constituency to provide protection for republican leaders, and act as stewards at meetings. The Clare Irish Volunteer leaders, Patrick and Michael Brennan, were placed in charge of this force, which police reports suggested numbered somewhere in the region of 600 to 700 men.[60]

Outsiders thus dominated the Sinn Féin campaign. This was further compounded by the fact that the republican candidate, McCartan, was not a local, and was not physically present to address the electorate. He was, at that time, working for Sinn Féin in the United States. Indeed, he later stated that he had been unaware of his nomination until he read about it in a New York newspaper, and learned nothing of the actual campaigning until after the results were announced.[61] In contrast, the Irish Party candidate was present to contribute to his own campaign. The constitutional nationalists also bene-fitted from a well-organised support base in the form of the AOH and UIL. Outside support was, however, an important feature of the Irish Party's by-election campaign in South Armagh. The nationalist leaders John Dillon and Joseph Devlin both addressed a series of meetings in the area. Meanwhile, party supporters from Belfast arrived in the constituency to canvass, and to provide additional muscle for the local AOH in the brawls that developed with the Irish Volunteers.

Overall, the Irish Party campaign benefitted from a much greater level of local involvement. It was also clear that the party had learned lessons from its previous by-election defeats during 1917, and was determined to counteract Sinn Féin's aggressive electioneering methods. As the campaign opened, Patrick Donnelly warned that if republicans attempted to use the forceful tactics evident in their earlier campaigns 'they would most assuredly be met by their own weapons.' At meetings, local supporters were also warned of the aggressive methods they could expect to encounter. Indeed, Irish Party supporters in Corran were so successfully briefed that within days of being addressed by their leaders it was reported that the women of the district had confronted a group of Sinn Féin canvassers and chased them from the area.[62]

National issues dominated the campaign. Sinn Féin vigorously attacked the Irish Party on matters such as home rule, the prospect of conscription and their participation in the Irish Convention, yet another British initiative aimed at settling the constitutional question in Ireland. It was claimed that the party's MPs were supporters of extending conscription to Ireland as 'only half a dozen' of them had voted against a recent motion on the issue in the House of Commons. The policy of home rule was also roundly criticised, with appeals to the electorate to 'seize the opportunity which world politics and the crisis of the Great War was offering to her'; specifically the chance to press for self-determination at an eventual peace conference.[63] Meanwhile, republican election pamphlets placed a strong emphasis on the burden of wartime taxation, and its consequences for the farming community in particular. They also carried appeals to sentiment regarding the murder of Francis Sheehy Skeffington while in British custody during the Easter rising, and the execution of Roger Casement, alongside denouncements of the Irish Party's responses to the events.[64] The substance of the Sinn Féin campaign in South Armagh was, therefore, much the same as it had been in North Roscommon, South Longford and East Clare. As Laffan has observed, it was primarily concerned with criticising the Irish Party over various national issues rather than straight-forward ideological concerns such as the demand for an independent republic.[65]

For South Armagh nationalists, however, the most important issue was undoubtedly that of their potential exclusion from a home rule Ireland, or partition in the event of an independent Ireland. Sinn Féin made good use of this issue during the campaign, primarily through its allegations that Donnelly, the Irish Party candidate, had voted in favour of exclusion at the St Mary's

Hall conference in June 1916 in return for the patronage of Joseph Devlin, the party's most influential figure in Ulster. The republicans also appeared to offer a defiant and uncompromising line on the issue of unionist resistance to self-government in Ireland, though the issue only surfaced sporadically during the campaign. The most forceful pronouncements came in two speeches delivered by de Valera. In the first, at Bessbrook, he declared that unionism was a position 'that must be stormed from at home', and that nationalists 'must make up their minds not to be peddling with this rock. They must if necessary blast it out of their path.' More ominous were his comments at a further meeting in Newry when he asserted that 'in the past unionists knew they were perfectly safe because they were met only by ignorant shouting', but that 'if Nationalist Ireland was consolidated they would soon drive the unionists out of the "two race" fortress on which they were depending – a fortress which had no terrors for Sinn Féin.'[66] It is difficult to ascertain the electorate's reception of such statements. Given the discontent within the region over the Irish Party's acceptance of the principle of exclusion in 1916, however, it is likely that this would have appealed to a significant section of the population.

The Irish Party's campaign was fought on similar lines to that of Sinn Féin. Republican policies faced equally vigorous attacks. At Crossmaglen, Joseph Devlin poured particular scorn on Sinn Féin's position of abstention, describing its strategy for fighting land taxation as 'to remain away from parliament and let the British government play fast and loose with every economic and industrial interest in the country.' This was coupled with appeals for the retention of the political status quo, such as Devlin's plea at a further meeting in Mullaghbawn that 'the people would have to decide between the new-fangled politics of intruders and the tried and effective policy of the Irish Party.' There were also personal attacks on the Sinn Féin candidate. In a scathing address delivered during a meeting in Newry, for example, John Dillon asked 'where was Dr MacCarten [sic] in Easter Week?' McCartan's mission to the USA, where the Irish Party's own T. P. O'Connor was also touring to raise funds, was depicted as a 'brutal insult to the United States Government'.[67] He was also criticised for allegedly having loaned his car to the UVF in 1912 to assist in their gunrunning operation at Larne.[68] With regard to the issue of exclusion, however, the Irish Party was less vocal, though it did criticise Sinn Féin for attempting to disrupt the essential nationalist unity in Ulster, and for preaching a 'doctrine of hate'.[69]

The campaigning was often volatile. Rival supporters frequently disrupted each other's meetings. Speakers were shouted down and pelted with missiles. At a meeting in Bessbrook, de Valera faced xenophobic taunts about his father's Spanish ancestry. Various figures on both sides were attacked as they travelled through the constituency. In Meigh, a policeman was wounded during fighting between rival supporters at an Irish Party meeting. In Newry, meanwhile, a large crowd of Irish Party supporters attacked an Irish Volunteer 'barracks', and some adjoining Sinn Féin committee rooms, in William Street.[70] Involvement in such violence was usually limited to rival nationalist and republican factions, though on one occasion a group of Sinn Féin supporters, led by the prominent republican organiser Harry Boland, did become involved in clashes with unionists in Newtownhamilton. According to Kevin O'Shiel, who witnessed the ensuing riot first-hand, this came about as the result of the RIC's unwillingness (or, more accurately, their inability) to repel an attack on a Sinn Féin meeting in the town; a version of events that was corroborated elsewhere.[71] In general, however, unionists remained aloof from the campaign, and its accompanying violence.

Aiken's contribution to the by-election campaign is obscure. He was, of course, too junior a figure to receive any attention in the local or national press coverage of the contest. Nevertheless, there are indications that he threw himself into the campaigning with enthusiasm and vigour, and although it is likely that he contributed to more mundane activities such as canvassing, or the production and distribution of election literature, it was his involvement in the stewarding duties of the Irish Volunteers which gained most attention. Andrew McDonnell, a Dublin volunteer sent to Newry to assist with the Sinn Féin campaign, recalled that 'the big man in that political fight was Harry Boland, with Frank Aiken a good second, who was on his own doorstep so to speak.'[72] A tall and athletic youth, with an imperturbable and often intimidating persona, he was perfectly suited to the type of defensive functions which were required of the Volunteers during the campaign.[73] What is more, he was evidently taken with the role. Indeed, on a personal level the most significant outcome of the by-election was his renewed involvement in the Irish Volunteers and his resulting efforts to promote the resurgence of the organisation locally.

Prior to the by-election there was virtually no Irish Volunteer organisation in Armagh and south Down. As has already been observed, the IRB had been forming companies in an ad hoc fashion throughout 1917, but these had engaged in little activity after their initial creation. Indeed, the RIC was unaware of the existence of any Irish Volunteer companies in Armagh prior to the by-election. The first references to the organisation in local police reports did not appear until after February 1918. This may have reflected a tendency within the RIC – noted by one district inspector – to consider organisations as being of no real consequence unless they were led by 'people of importance'; specifically people with political or local standing.[74] It was, however, also a genuine indication of the weakness and irrelevance of the organisation locally.

The by-election exposed this weakness very effectively, and demonstrated the need for competent local Irish Volunteer units to counter the opposition of the AOH, particularly in the event of a general election, which was expected to occur once the war in Europe had come to an end. It also provided the impetus for the creation of new companies, partly through local initiative, but more often through the efforts of visiting volunteer elements that made good use of the opportunity presented by the campaign. Of the latter, the most notable efforts were those of Michael Brennan, George Plunkett and James McGuill, who travelled throughout the constituency giving speeches and enrolling companies into the North Louth Brigade.[75]

Aiken's actions provide a good example of the local initiatives that contributed to the creation of the Irish Volunteer organisation in the region during this period. During a particularly rowdy meeting in Bessbrook, he and some other local men were forced to intervene to hold back an Irish Party mob during a speech by de Valera.[76] On the same day, also in Bessbrook, Canon Charles Quin had succeeded in disrupting and dispersing a smaller meeting addressed by Laurence Ginnell.[77] Spurred on by this aggressive opposition to republicanism in the district, Aiken approached Jack McElhaw, a like-minded relative, about creating an Irish Volunteer company in Camlough and establishing a Sinn Féin hall in the village. Together they called a meeting and enrolled 19 members. Aiken was subsequently elected as company captain.[78] It was partly as a result of such initiative, and his instrumental yet obscure role in the agitation surrounding the campaign, that Aiken emerged as the main Irish Volunteer organiser in the months that followed.

Polling took place on 1 February 1918, and the press coverage of the event was dominated with stories of the questionable tactics used by both sides. Most striking was an attempt by republicans to confuse voters with a circular purporting to be written by the withdrawn unionist candidate, Thomas Richardson. It announced his last minute intention to contest the election and appealed to unionists for their votes. This attempt to divert any potential unionist votes for the Irish Party candidate ultimately failed. The bogus circular proved remarkably unconvincing – referring to Richardson by the wrong name – and was effectively counteracted by a hastily distributed rebuttal. Personation was also reportedly rife throughout the polling districts, with several arrests made on both sides.[79] The Irish Volunteers were on duty throughout the constituency and John Grant, a new recruit, recalled that they were charged with providing transport, getting the voters out to the polls and taking charge of the booths.[80] Throughout the day, with confidence remaining high, de Valera was reported to have been touring the constituency in a car bearing a banner declaring 'McCartan is winning.'[81] By the following day, however, it was clear even to Sinn Féin that the Irish Party was the victor.

When the results were announced they confirmed a substantial victory for the Irish Party. Donnelly topped the poll with 2,324 votes, defeating McCartan (who received 1,305) by a surplus of 1,019.[82] Sinn Féin was quick to offer excuses for its defeat. The Irish Party was accused of having rushed the election, and much was made of the importance of unionist votes in securing Donnelly's victory.[83] The Sinn Féin newspaper, *Nationality*, claimed that 'had the unionists remained neutral, Mr. Donnelly would have been in minority of 46.' Elsewhere in the press, views differed as to the importance of the unionist vote. The *Belfast News-Letter* claimed that 'more than half, probably three fourths of his [Donnelly's] majority is due to the support given him by the unionists of the division.' The *Armagh Guardian*, however, believed that 'about 800 [unionists] polled, therefore without what unionists say was their protest against Sinn Féin methods, Mr Donnelly would have been elected.'[84]

There is certainly little doubt that Donnelly received unionist votes. The *Newry Telegraph* reported that at Newtownhamilton a unionist meeting of 500 'decided in favour of solidly voting for Mr Donnelly in order to keep Sinn Féin out.' Similar views were expressed at meetings in Mount Norris and Clady, and it was even claimed that in one district 'a large Union Jack floated over an Orange Hall, bearing the inscriptions – 'up Donnelly' and 'to [hell] with the Pope.'[85] It was also alleged that the Irish Party had intentionally courted the unionist electorate. The *Armagh Guardian* observed that nationalist speakers had been careful throughout the campaign to refrain from 'their usual sarcastic or abusive attacks on Sir Edward Carson.'[86] Charles McGleenan, an Irish Volunteer from Blackwatertown, also recalled that Irish Party supporters had removed the green flags from their vehicles in order to bring unionist voters to the polls.[87] It would seem, however, that unionist votes were not decisive. Figures compiled by the *Newry Telegraph* in the weeks after the election suggest that in areas with a significant unionist population the voter turnout was considerably lower than elsewhere. In Newtownhamilton, which had a unionist population of around 40 per cent, for example, there were only 650 votes cast out of a possible 1,014.[88] Similar figures presented for other districts indicated that the majority of unionist voters simply did not vote. This corresponded with the RIC's conclusions on the issue: 'about one-third of the unionists voted for Donnelly, and the remainder together with a good many nationalists, abstained from voting.'[89]

A more pertinent factor in Sinn Féin's defeat, perhaps, was the fact that the party was drawing most of its support from the younger generation. Press coverage frequently commented on the youth of Sinn Féin's support base in the constituency, with condescending references to 'young men without the vote' and 'youths of servant boy class'.[90] These observations were corroborated, to an extent, by RIC reports. In Armagh it was noted that 'the Sinn Féin doctrine has been instilled in the young people in the hope that they would influence the older [generation].'[91] In Newry, meanwhile, it was reported that 'the Sinn Féiners have developed a strength amongst the young people of Newry which has been a surprise to everybody.'[92] Such observations must be treated with caution. Hart has noted, for example, that dismissals of republican supporters on the basis of age and class were extremely common throughout the revolutionary period.[93] Yet in this instance, republicans themselves appear to have been aware of the youth of many of their supporters, and made concerted attempts to exploit it. Sean MacEntee, for instance, appealed to the young men of south Armagh 'not to plough, sow or reap for fathers who would be so base as to betray Ireland.'[94] Given that the election was fought on a register compiled in November 1913, however, the prevalence of young men amongst Sinn Féin's support base in the constituency was not particularly fortunate.[95]

Another factor which may have influenced the result was the attitude of the local Catholic clergy. On the whole, the constituency's senior clergy were opposed to the republicans. Canon Charles Quin was the most obvious example. Aside from denouncing Sinn Féin and disrupting republican meetings, he was vocal in his support of both the Irish Party and Donnelly, whose nomination he had been so instrumental in securing.[96] The attitude of Cardinal Logue was also important. The constituency lay within his archdiocese, and there was little doubt as to his disapproval of the republicans. Only a few months earlier, in late November 1917, he had denounced the Sinn Féin movement in a pastoral letter to the local clergy, the details of which were subsequently reported in the national press. In it he described republicanism as 'ill-considered and utopian' and ridiculed the notion of gaining independence through either a post-war European peace conference or by force of arms. During the by-election campaign itself, he also refused a request from de Valera for a meeting. It is impossible to say how this may have influenced the local electorate's decision, but the RIC could later report it was 'probably effective' in at least preventing some of the younger clergy in the area from taking an active part in the contest.[97] This deprived Sinn Féin of an important and influential source of support that had proven extremely useful during previous campaigns in North Roscommon and South Longford, where some curates had even gone so far as to address Sinn Féin meetings.[98]

Although Sinn Féin ultimately lost the election, it did succeed in boosting its profile in the region. Clubs throughout South Armagh experienced significant increases in membership in the month after the campaign. The Bessbrook club was reported as having enrolled around 150 new members.[99] Aiken's branch in Camlough boasted that it had 'almost doubled its membership.'[100] There were also signs of increased activity within the movement locally, with the first reported meetings of a South Armagh constituency executive (comhairle ceanntair) and the creation of new clubs.[101] Observing these developments, the RIC in Armagh could report that 'there is no real doubt [. . .] that the election for S. Armagh with the influx of suspects and rebels generally has given a considerable impetus to Sinn Féin.'[102]

Yet the growth in support for Sinn Féin at this time should not be overstated. Constitutional nationalism retained its dominance in the region, just as it did throughout six-county Ulster. This was further demonstrated only two months later by another Sinn Féin by-election defeat in nearby East Tyrone, a contest which bore striking similarities to that in South Armagh, with its intra-nationalist brawls, allegations of a nationalist-unionist alliance, and an overt lack of support for Sinn Féin amongst the local clergy.[103] In north-east Ulster, the Irish Party did not suffer anything like the type of decline observed throughout southern Ireland, where the growing popularity of Sinn Féin resulted in large-scale defections from organisations such as the UIL and the AOH.[104] In Armagh, the effects of the by-election fell far short of this type of monumental shift in local politics. Defections, for instance, were remarkably rare, though local press reports did note one AOH branch's overnight transformation into a Sinn Féin club during the campaign.[105] Police reports, meanwhile, indicate no great decline in the memberships of either the AOH or the UIL. By October 1918, the two organisations could still boast a combined membership of 4,913 in the county. This represented only a 4.2 per cent decline from their combined membership in 1916, and was still much more substantial than that of Sinn Féin, which now stood at 1,731.[106]

In the aftermath of the by-election, Aiken became a more visible figure within the local republican movement. As Sinn Féin and the Irish Volunteers sought to consolidate the considerable organisational gains achieved during the two weeks of intense campaigning, a variety of new roles and responsibilities emerged within the political and military spheres of the movement. Aiken was well placed to benefit from these opportunities, and whether driven by ambition, ideological commitment, or the social aspects of such activities, he accepted those that came his way with enthusiasm.

His first new appointment came at the end of February 1918, when he became director of plebiscite for the South Armagh constituency. In this role he was responsible for the local implementation of a nationwide petition in favour of Irish independence. In part a Sinn Féin propaganda exercise, the plebiscite also had ulterior motives, with the RIC noting that it was used both as an opportunity to make 'a house-to-house collection of funds' and a 'register for election purposes'.[107] In early March, Aiken also began to appear in reports of the meetings of Sinn Féin's South Armagh constituency executive as the local representative to the central committee (ard chomhairle). As such, he attended meetings in Dublin and reported back to the local executive on their proceedings.[108] Beyond the announcement of these appointments, however, there is very little specific evidence of his performance in either role.

A slightly better impression can be gained of Aiken's activities within the Irish Volunteers at this time, however. Following the formation of the Camlough Company, and his election as its captain, Aiken began to act as a local organiser for the force in south Armagh. In the months that followed he established further companies in the surrounding area, a task that typically involved drawing together interested parties and presiding over the election of officers. There is also some evidence to suggest that his organisational efforts may have extended to encouraging the development of the republican women's organisation, Cumann na mBan, with members of his Camlough Company placed in charge of putting the local branch through military drill.[109]

Aiken was typical of the 'opinion makers' and 'self-appointed organisers' within the Irish Volunteers in this period, who used social and familial networks to draw recruits into the movement. As Hart has observed, these individuals 'would recruit from among their trusted "pals" – relatives, school-mates, neighbours, co-workers, teammates and so on.'[110] Jack McElhaw's testimony concerning the creation of the Camlough Company certainly suggests that Aiken used such methods. So too, perhaps, does the emergence of the Aikens as a prominent 'revolutionary family' in the area during the by-election. Although it is far from certain, it does seem probable that Frank's connections to the movement may have influenced the republican politics of his siblings, James and Nano, both of whom (to varying degrees) became active in the movement during and after the by-election campaign. James, for instance, was noted as a signatory on Patrick McCartan's nomination paper. He also became involved in a public spat with Canon Quin over the Aiken and McElhaw families' support for Sinn Féin. Nano, meanwhile, became treasurer of the South Armagh District Council of Cumann na mBan, and later acted as a courier, regularly travelling to Dublin and partaking in risky tasks such as the transportation of weapons.[111]

The Aikens were not unique in this respect. The emergence of such 'revolutionary families' – where multiple siblings, and even parents, became involved in various aspects of the republican movement – was not uncommon in the region during this period. Another notable example was the Quinn family in Newry. The Quinns were well known in the town for their grocery business in Hill Street, and during the revolutionary period they became heavily involved in the local republican movement. Of the four sons in the family who were of appropriate age, three became prominent in the IRA; Padraig, Seán and Malachi. Their father, John, was also active in Sinn Féin, becoming a county councillor, chairman of the Harbour Board, and later a district judge for the Dáil courts.[112] Examples such as these offer a striking indication of the importance of familial networks in determining revolutionary involvement during the period.

Aiken's advancement within the movement at this time provides an insight into the variety of factors that influenced the formation of the provincial republican elite in Armagh and south Down during the early stages of revolution. As has already been observed, his attainment of new roles was partly a result of the dramatic increase in local republican activity following the by-election. Yet, on an individual level, it also owed much to his willingness to seize such opportunities as and when they arose. His record of organisational involvement prior to 1918 is a testament to this character trait. Aside from his aforementioned roles in the Gaelic League, the original Irish Volunteer organisation in 1914 and the GAA, he had also helped to found a co-operative flax scutching society in 1917, serving as both its chairman and its representative to the Ulster Agricultural Organisation Society.[113]

Such a prolific involvement in local organisations and societies was not uncommon for a young and upcoming revolutionary figure. McGarry, for example, has noted the same tendency in the Monaghan republican leader, Eoin O'Duffy. Yet, whereas O'Duffy was driven by 'voracious appetite for public life' and an obsessive 'craving for public exposure', Aiken does not appear to have harboured any such desire for the limelight.[114] This is clear enough from his lack of visibility in the local press, and there is little to suggest that he actively schemed or jostled for promotion or advancement within any of the organisations in which he was involved. He seems to have lacked any particularly grand political ambitions. Indeed, in many respects his involvement in such roles could be viewed as little more than an attempt (conscious or unconscious) to preserve the Aiken family's status within the community by emulating the success and local standing attained by his late father. Now that he was running the family farm, and his elder brother James had decided to leave Ireland to work in England (departing at some point after the by-election), he may have felt a sense of duty in doing so. This does not detract from the fact that he was ideologically committed to republicanism, however. If the attainment of status or local influence had been his only concern the constitutional nationalist movement would likely have been a safer bet at this early stage.

Aiken's track record of organisational experience and attainment suggests that his advancement within both Sinn Féin and the Irish Volunteers owed much to his own abilities. His peers clearly perceived him to be a capable figure. He was also better educated than most, having completed his intermediate examinations at a time when relatively few children progressed to secondary education.[115] Furthermore, he had become involved in the movement at a relatively early stage, prior to the by-election and the resulting influx of new members. As such, his republican credentials were well established. Within the Irish Volunteers, moreover, his past involvement in the organisation in 1914, as well as his initiative in founding a new Camlough Company, were likely factors in his selection as a leadership figure. Taken together, these experiences suggested both the necessary aptitude and, perhaps, some semblance of military ability (however slight). His prominence in the local Sinn Féin club, however, may also have been an influence. Indeed, regional studies have frequently observed a high level of overlap between the membership of Sinn Féin clubs and local Irish Volunteer companies, particularly at leadership level.[116] In Camlough the extent of dual membership is less clear. At the very least, however, Aiken's existing position within Sinn Féin would have marked him out as a credible local leadership figure.

Yet there are other factors, beyond his actual abilities, which may have influenced his rising prominence in the movement during this period. Within both Sinn Féin and the Irish Volunteers appointments to positions of authority were decided democratically. In Irish Volunteer companies, the rank and file elected their own officers. In Sinn Féin, positions in bodies such as the constituency executive were decided by a vote within the local club. As a result, it was often the case that local officers or officials would be selected on the basis of popularity or local standing rather than ability.[117] This was particularly true in the case of the Irish Volunteers where, as Ernie O'Malley later recalled, an officer might be chosen because 'he was from the town, a strong farmer or a neat hurler.'[118] Bearing this in mind, the local standing of the Aiken family – in terms of their relative affluence, property holdings, and the legacy of James Aiken as a prominent nationalist – was likely of some influence on Frank's emergence as a member of the local republican elite. As is clear from O'Malley's observations, this was more than enough to ensure an individual's initial selection as an Irish Volunteer officer, and it is probable that such status would also have had some influence within the local Sinn Féin clubs.

Historians have long recognised the prominence of individuals from a 'rural bourgeois' background amongst Ireland's revolutionary elite. Tom Garvin, for instance, using a sample of 157 notable republican figures from across Ireland, has noted that over three quarters came from such a background.[119] In socio-economic terms, therefore, Aiken was certainly typical of the revolutionary elite at the national level. Yet how representative was he of the republican leadership more locally in Armagh and south Down? In the absence of detailed membership lists for the party's local clubs, it has only proven possible to identify and subsequently trace the backgrounds of 31 prominent officials from the region with any degree of accuracy. Nevertheless, this small sample does indicate that those with a degree of wealth and social status dominated the local leadership.[120]

The majority (around 70 per cent) were members of the agricultural, professional or commercial classes. Accounting for 29 per cent of the sample, agriculture was the largest sector represented and consisted primarily of independent farmers and those making their living from a family farm.[121] Those within this group tended to be living or working on holdings with greater value than that of the rank and file of the republican movement. Using annual rateable land valuations as a guide, the farms belonging to members of this group had a median valuation of £15.1s in 1918. By way of comparison, the same figure for a sample of local rank and file members of the Irish Volunteers was just £8.10s. Therefore, although a direct comparison is not possible, it is plausible to suggest that members of the farming class that became prominent within the local Sinn Féin movement were slightly wealthier than those within the party's regular membership.

Agriculture was followed closely by the professional classes, a group more readily identified as enjoying a degree of wealth and status, and which accounted for 25.8 per cent of the sample.[122] Particularly prevalent were those involved in the legal profession, which accounted for half of those represented. They were joined by two teachers and a dentist. Taken together, this group can be seen to consist of the types of figures who traditionally held a significant degree of influence in provincial Irish society. Similar in this respect were those represented in the commercial classes, who accounted for 16.1 per cent of the sample.[123] While this category could cover a range of occupations from low-level clerks to local businessmen, it was the latter that were most prevalent. Publicans and grocers were particularly well represented. Like those in the professions, as well as being relatively wealthy, these figures could often hold a considerable degree of influence within the local community.

Another noteworthy feature of the emerging Sinn Féin elite in Armagh and south Down was the presence of a significant number of former constitutional nationalists. At least nine per cent of the individuals traced had previously been members of the UIL or AOH. This figure must be treated with caution, however, due to the limited nature of the sample and the absence of detailed local membership lists for Sinn Féin, the UIL or the AOH. Such continuity between the constitutional nationalist movement and the newly emerging republican movement was not particularly uncommon. Indeed, it was a natural result of the often large-scale defections from the AOH and UIL to Sinn Féin that occurred throughout the country in 1917 and 1918.[124] In many areas, to borrow Fitzpatrick's oft quoted analogy, the 'old wine' of the home rule movement was simply 'decanted into new bottles'.[125]

Yet this was not always the case. In Galway, for example, Fergus Campbell has demonstrated that Sinn Féin drew a much greater proportion of its membership from the local separatist and radical agrarian traditions. McCluskey has noted a similar trend in East Tyrone, where pre-rising Irish Volunteers and IRB members were more prevalent than former UIL or AOH supporters amongst local Sinn Féin committee members. In north Louth, meanwhile, Donal Hall has observed that support of the republican movement reflected long-standing factional divisions between Redmondite and Healyite nationalists, with the latter group emerging as the core of the local Sinn Féin organisation after 1916.[126] In Armagh and south Down, the extent to which the emerging Sinn Féin elite represented a line of continuity with the constitutional nationalist movement is also somewhat questionable. As has already been discussed, defections from the AOH and UIL were not particularly common in the region. Although a few high profile individuals changed their allegiance in late 1917 – notably three former secretaries of the UIL – local constitutional nationalist organisations experienced only a very slight decline in membership.[127] Furthermore, although there was insufficient evidence to trace the political histories of all 31 individuals within the sample, the small number of those whose past affiliations could be accurately traced presented an even mixture of former constitutional nationalists, existing members of the IRB and younger men like Aiken with no significant history of political activism.[128]

Aiken was, therefore, somewhat representative of the Sinn Féin elite in Armagh and south Down, though at only 20 years of age in 1918 he was younger than the average local party official, who would have been around 36. Yet how did he compare to his peers within the Irish Volunteers? More substantial observations can be made in this regard. As a greater amount of local membership information is extant, it has proven possible to construct a larger sample of 203 individuals, consisting of 180 rank and file members and 23 officers. Occupational information, however, is somewhat problematic for this set. The average volunteer was 24 years old in 1918, and was too young to have an occupation listed in the 1911 census. As a substitute, therefore, where no distinct occupation is provided for an individual, the occupation of the household's primary breadwinner has instead been considered as a broad indication of socio-economic background.[129]

As with Sinn Féin, the agricultural sector was heavily represented within the Irish Volunteers, accounting for 58.6 per cent of the total sample. The professional classes were almost entirely absent, at just one per cent, and the commercial sector, trades and unskilled labour were quite evenly represented at 13.3 per cent, 10.3 per cent and 12.9 per cent respectively.[130] Amongst officers, however, a similar pattern emerges to that within the local Sinn Féin elite. Here the agricultural and commercial classes accounted for over 70 per cent of those individuals traced. In order to consider the relative wealth of those officers and men from agricultural backgrounds, it is again best to consider the annual rateable land valuations for their farms. Using a subset of 33 men from four rural companies in the region, it can be suggested that, as with the Sinn Féin elite, those in positions of authority tended to be more prosperous than those who served under them. While the farms of the rank and file held a median farm value of £8, the three officers in the sample came from farms valued at £43, £32.15s and £28.7s. It is a similar story with those volunteers from the commercial classes. For officers, a commercial occupation was more likely to denote the ownership of a business. For the rank and file, it usually indicated less prosperous occupations, such as shop work.

Broadly speaking, therefore, those obtaining positions of authority within the local Irish Volunteer movement tended to come from slightly more affluent backgrounds than those they commanded. Yet this was not always the case. Individuals from a background of unskilled labour formed a very significant minority amongst the officers' sample, accounting for 17.4 per cent of those traced.[131] Indeed, at the local level, socio-economic differences between the elite and the rank and file membership appear to have been less pronounced within the Irish Volunteers than within Sinn Féin. Given the lack of detailed information regarding Sinn Féin membership in this period, however, and the relatively small sample of Irish Volunteer officers that could be traced, it is impossible to draw any firm conclusions in this regard. At best, the figures presented here can provide only a very broad impression of the social structure of the local republican movement and its various component parts.

Socio-economic background aside, there were other criterion by which an individual might be judged as a 'local notable', particularly within the Irish Volunteers. As O'Malley's quote suggests, other factors such as sporting prowess could also prove influential when selecting company captains. Indeed, John McCoy recalled that the captain of the Mullaghbawn Company 'was selected for his fine physique, football ability and his decency of character'.[132] Such qualities were often tied up with republican perceptions of masculinity. Beyond the occasional anecdotal reference, however, it is impossible to assess the extent to which such perceptions may have impacted on the selection of local leadership figures. In Aiken's case, for example, it can certainly be said that he was athletic, given that he was active in both his local gaelic and hurling teams. He also exuded certain desirable leadership traits, notably a cool head, and an unexcitable demeanour. Yet there is little way of knowing what influence (if any) such considerations had in his selection as a local officer.

Indeed, regardless of whatever influence such superficial considerations may have had on the initial selection of a local leader, such appointments rarely lasted if an individual proved incompetent. In the Mullaghbawn Company, for instance, the footballer with the fine physique was soon replaced by John McCoy when it became clear that he had not the 'organising ability or sense for discipline' to make a good officer.[133] This ousting of officers who were ill-suited or inefficient (or merely perceived as such) became particularly noticeable as the separatist campaign progressed. While men such as Aiken may have been chosen for reasons that did not directly relate to their appropriateness for a given role, therefore, their continuation in such positions, and their further advancement, ultimately depended on their actual performance.

DEFIANCE

The establishment of a functional Irish Volunteer organisation in Armagh and south Down in early 1918 set the stage for what Augusteijn has described as a campaign of 'public defiance'.[134] This consisted of open displays of illegal drilling and public parading by local companies. Such activities had begun elsewhere in the country in late 1917, following the death of the hunger striker Thomas Ashe. The demonstration at his funeral provided the precedent for such displays. In Armagh and south Down, the first instances of illegal drilling were recorded by the RIC in February 1918, in the aftermath of the South Armagh by-election. These activities greatly perturbed the local authorities. Up until that point, they had apparently been unaware of the existence of the Irish Volunteers in the region.[135] Generally speaking, local republicans had engaged in few provocative acts prior to the by-election, aside from the occasional hoisting of Sinn Féin flags and posting of seditious literature. The by-election itself, with its party affrays, had brought a certain level of unrest to Newry and south Armagh with offences including 'incendiary fires, malicious injury, and one case of assault', but such trouble was not uncommon during electoral contests.[136] Now, however, the RIC were faced with an orchestrated campaign designed to challenge their authority.

In March 1918, there was an intensification of such activity nationwide. The RIC inspector general reported 456 incidents of illegal drilling across the country. In Ulster, Donegal and Armagh were noted as the worst affected counties.[137] This national escalation was due to a direct order from the newly established Irish Volunteer general headquarters (GHQ) in Dublin. John McCoy recalled that 'an order was issued to all companies to take part in open drilling in public places, and to resist the authorities if they attempted to stop such work.'[138] In Armagh and south Down, while some futile attempts were made to break up displays, the local police chose to adopt a strategy of observation, avoiding confrontation and instead identifying local ringleaders that could be arrested later. As Augusteijn has observed, there was a naive belief that 'all Volunteer activity could be stopped if they singled out and discouraged the few "bad apples".'[139]

It was as a result of this policy that Aiken was arrested on 30 March 1918 at his home in Carrickbracken. Two weeks earlier he had led his local company in military drill near Camlough, and had been identified by the police. Aiken's arrest was the first in the region for such an offence. Consequently, he briefly became a local celebrity. His day in court was exploited to full effect by the movement. Sinn Féin supporters converged on Newry courthouse and packed the gallery. As the trial proceeded, Jack McElhaw drilled an Irish Volunteer company on the street outside.[140] The trial itself was a short affair. Aiken, in keeping with both his republican sensibilities and Irish Volunteer policy, refused to recognise the court. No defence was offered and he said little while in the dock. Legal counsel, of a sort, was present in the form of the Newry solicitor, and Sinn Féin supporter, John Henry Collins, although he stressed he was there merely as a friend of the defendant. The case was quickly presented and judgement passed. Aiken was found guilty and sentenced to one month's imprisonment without hard labour. In passing sentence, James Woulfe Flanagan, the Resident Magistrate, remarked that he felt bound to tell the accused that 'if he were brought up again on a similar charge they would have to give him a very heavy sentence'. He then proceeded to lecture Aiken on the futility of any attempt to effect a campaign against the might of the British Empire. As the trial ended Aiken broke his silence to address the court, first in Irish and then again in English, only to be interrupted and removed on the orders of Woulfe Flanagan, who was determined that no political statements would be made. In a statement to the press Aiken claimed that, having observed other republican trials, he believed that there would have been no objection to his speaking at that point. He was removed from the court to the cheers of supporters, the singing of republican songs and the waving of tricolours. After the trial, the Irish Volunteer and Cumann na mBan contingents, which had remained outside, marched through Newry with little interference from the police. [141]

Imprisonment has often been identified as a key formative experience in the lives of many prominent revolutionary republicans. Much has been made in the literature, for example, of the importance of Frongoch Camp (often nicknamed Frongoch University) in the development of figures such as Michael Collins, Richard Mulcahy and Terence MacSwiney after the Easter Rising.[142] A parallel more fitting to Aiken's experience is that provided by the Monaghan republican leader, Eoin O'Duffy, who was arrested and imprisoned for a similar offence later that year. As McGarry has observed, Duffy's incarceration had 'seen him join the revolutionary elite on the inside, while bestowing him with popularity and notoriety on the outside.'[143] The same can undoubtedly be said of Aiken who, like O'Duffy, served his time in Belfast only a few months before the latter's arrival. On a more personal level, however, Aiken's first spell in prison seems to have made little impression on him. He served his time when the regime in Belfast Prison was relatively lax. This is suggested by a contemporary account written by fellow prisoner, Charles Kenny, who arrived in late April as Aiken's sentence was coming to an end. Although Kenny recalled that conditions in the gaol gradually became more oppressive and restrictive in early May 1918, he observed that his first few weeks were relatively comfortable. Prisoners serving sentences for political offenses, such as drilling, were allowed to associate freely. They could wear their own clothes, and have food, tobacco and newspapers sent in from the outside. They also received a better quality diet than regular inmates.[144] This special treatment for political prisoners – who like Aiken did not have hard labour attached to their sentences – was the result of a set of concessions known as the 'September rules', which had been granted by the authorities after Thomas Ashe's death by force-feeding in September 1917.[145] Against this backdrop, it is a little less surprising that Aiken left few recollections of his time in prison, good or bad. A rare exception was a brief remark in a letter to Ernie O'Malley in 1923 in which he revealed, 'I was never in jail very long myself but while I was there I was absolutely fed up with the way men used to lounge around.'[146] For the energetic young farmer, who was accustomed to hard work, and whose spare time was dominated by his various social and political activities, the slow pace of prison life was clearly little more than a frustration.

Further convictions for illegal drilling in the region swiftly followed. On 17 April, Jack McElhaw was sentenced to two months with hard labour for drilling volunteers in Camlough, presumably having taken charge in Aiken's absence. Again, this trial was used to good effect by local republicans, with supporters in the court providing disruption with cheering and singing. Before the end of April three men from Crossmaglen had also been arrested for the offence.[147] These instances were accompanied by a degree of unrest in their localities. In Camlough, already tense after Aiken's imprisonment, a republican mob attacked the local police barracks with stones.[148] In Crossmaglen, mean-while, the initial news of the arrests drew an aggressive republican crowd that eventually had to be dispersed with a bayonet charge by the RIC.[149] There were also more positive shows of support and solidarity, however. At a ceilidh (traditional dance) organised by his local Sinn Féin club, for instance, Aiken was praised in a song specially composed for the occasion. Perhaps more remarkably, however, shortly after his incarceration, close to a hundred men with horses and ploughs were reported to have converged on Aiken's farm at Carrickbracken to plant his crops in his absence.[150]

Public defiance through illegal drilling was clearly producing results in Armagh and south Down. Arrests of figures such as Aiken and McElhaw not only generated further sympathy and support amongst the local population, they also fostered a degree of hostility towards the authorities. On 18 April 1918, however, national political developments suddenly changed the republican movement's priorities. On that day, the Military Service Act was passed in Westminster. Contained within it were provisions for the extension of conscription to Ireland. Increasingly feared as the war in Europe wore on, the measure prompted widespread nationalist indignation, uniting Sinn Féin, the Irish Party, the Catholic Church and the labour movement in opposition. It also served to strengthen the republican movement at a national level, prompting huge increases in membership and the creation of numerous new Sinn Féin clubs.[151]

In Armagh and south Down, the nationalist agitation was typical of that experienced elsewhere in the country. As was the case in most areas, an anti-conscription committee, consisting of representatives of each of the main opposition bodies, was formed to take charge of local opposition activities.[152] The clergy took charge of administering the anti-conscription pledge throughout the region's Catholic churches. In Newry, meanwhile, nationalists and republicans observed a nationwide one-day strike organised by the labour movement, though many working for unionist employers lost their jobs as a result.[153] In accordance with the views of their leaders, the majority of local unionists appear to have accepted the principle of extending conscription to Ireland, viewing it as a means of further strengthening their bond with Britain and implying 'the maintenance of the United Kingdom.'[154] Nevertheless, the RIC in Down could report that some unionists had signed the anti-conscription pledge.[155] Though not particularly common, this was by no means a unique occurrence in Ulster. Indeed, in some parts of the province there were reports of grand displays of cross-community solidarity on the issue. Perhaps the most exceptional occurred in Ballycastle, Co. Antrim, where members of the Orange Order, the AOH and Sinn Féin took turns marching around the town to songs such as 'The Boyne Water' and 'A Nation Once Again'.[156] Such incidents were exceedingly rare, however.

Numerous protest meetings were also held locally, the largest of which was a Sinn Féin rally in Newry that attracted between 8,000 and 10,000 people. Sharing the platform with an array of local clergymen, including the bishop of Dromore, Robert Kelly addressed the crowd, and used the opportunity to criticise the local anti-conscription committee for its failure to organise a public meeting that was representative of all parties. Such an event, he remarked, had instead to be called 'under Sinn Féin auspices.'[157] The incident highlighted the tensions that continued to exist between local constitutional nationalists and republicans so soon after the South Armagh by-election. It was also illustrative of the way in which Sinn Féin sought to portray itself as Ireland's saviour in the face of conscription; a claim that later came to the fore in propaganda after the crisis in the lead up to the 1918 general election.[158]

Throughout the crisis, the republican movement also made its own arrangements for opposing conscription, independent of those agreed by the broader based anti-conscription committees.[159] Sinn Féin co-ordinated republican propaganda efforts and made arrangements for a nationwide campaign of passive resistance in the event that attempts were actually made to enforce the policy. Meanwhile, the Irish Volunteers made preparations for military resistance. Regional units were ordered to cease drilling and parading, and to instead conduct an inventory of 'goods and skills' in all company areas.[160] There was little sign of such activity in Armagh and south Down, however. Discussing the role of Irish Volunteers at this time, John McCoy recalled that local companies did little more than swell the attendance at various demonstrations.[161] Units throughout the region did at least benefit from an influx of new recruits during the crisis. Yet these increases in membership were often fleeting, and the majority of men that joined in response to the conscription threat soon drifted away once it had passed.

Aiken was released at the height of the crisis, and appears to have quickly resumed his activities within both Sinn Féin and the Irish Volunteers.[162] His trial and imprisonment had clearly boosted his profile in the local movement. For the first time his name began to appear in reports of local political meetings. In June, for example, his attendance was noted at a protest meeting in Camlough prompted by the arrests of members of Sinn Féin's national leadership for involvement in an alleged 'German plot'.[163] Yet Aiken's time was increasingly dominated by his role in the Irish Volunteers. In his capacity as an organiser he became heavily involved in the efforts to develop the local structures of the organisation. Although companies were functioning in the region, they were not yet part of any battalion or brigade network. In response to this, shortly after his return, Aiken established the Camlough Battalion and was elected as its leader. Although evidence is scarce, it is also likely that he was involved in the creation of many of the other battalions that emerged in the region in the months that followed, and which finally came together in the winter of 1918–19 with the creation of the Newry Brigade. This new unit covered the Armagh and south Down area, with battalions based in Newry, Kilkeel, Camlough, Newtownhamilton, Ballymoyer, Armagh and Lurgan.[164] Aiken was elected as its vice-commandant. Patrick Rankin became its leader, out of respect for his status as the area's only veteran of 1916. Aiken later claimed that he was originally elected as brigade commandant, but refused the appointment in favour of Rankin.[165]

The concentrated effort to develop battalion and brigade structures in Armagh and south Down ensured that there was little outward Irish Volunteer activity for the duration of 1918. Indeed, in September, the RIC in Armagh could report that 'the various Volunteer Corps are practically only "on paper".'[166] Instead, republican activity was concentrated in the political sphere in preparation for the much anticipated general election. Pursuing such activism had become increasingly difficult at this time, however. On 3 July 1918 Sinn Féin was proclaimed a dangerous organisation, alongside the Irish Volunteers, Cumann na mBan and the Gaelic League. The move was part of a fresh initiative by the administration in Dublin which also included the prohibition of assemblies except by permit.[167] As was the case throughout the country, local republicans used this situation to engage in further acts of public defiance. In August, for example, Robert Kelly and Peadar McCann flouted the restrictions to address crowds at an aeraíocht (cultural festival) and were subsequently arrested and imprisoned. In the absence of Kelly, the most active republican orator in the wider Newry area, larger public meetings effectively ceased. Sinn Féin activity did continue, but demonstrations became increasingly impromptu and were most often accompanied by arrests.[168]

The suppression of public meetings stifled one of the more traditional methods by which Sinn Féin could continue its attempt to build a popular following. By the second half of 1918, however, it began to compensate for this by positioning itself at the centre of nationalist social activity. This was most visible in the rural villages of south Armagh, and Aiken's native Camlough is a particularly illustrative example. In terms of overtly political organisations, both men and women, young and old, were catered for. The men of the village could join the Sinn Féin club or the Irish Volunteers. Women had the local branch of Cumann na mBan, and for children there was the movement's youth wing, Fianna Éireann. Yet the republicans also had a strong presence in other organisations, such as the local Gaelic League branch, of which Aiken was still secretary.[169] In February 1918, the Sinn Féin club formed its own GAA team in the village, a common occurrence in the months that followed the by-election when tensions between republicans and constitutional nationalists led to 'the almost complete break-up of the GAA organisation in Co. Armagh and Co. Louth'.[170] Later in the period further additions came in the form of a Cumann na mBan camogie league and the 'Thomas Ashe' cycling club.[171] Significantly, these organisations were the primary organisers of events such as ceilithe (traditional dances) and aeraíochtaí (festivals or concerts) in the area. In dominating the primary social outlets, the republican movement had acquired a useful means by which to influence the local population, and the youth in particular.

The notoriety that Aiken had enjoyed after his arrest and trial proved short-lived. By the summer of 1918 he was once again absent from reports of Sinn Féin meetings. With the prohibition of public meetings, and the increased likelihood of arrest, it is possible that he was intentionally keeping a low profile. He was now known to the authorities, and at his trial in April he had been warned that a repeat offence would incur a harsher sentence.[172] His activities with the Irish Volunteers were also beginning to dominate his time. Yet he was still active in promoting Sinn Féin in the region. Indeed, his continued importance as an organiser in the period was highlighted at a Sinn Féin event honouring the Newry solicitor, and local party official, P. J. McQuaid. In his acceptance address McQuaid graciously expressed his belief that he had 'been given too much credit' and instead attributed the strength of Sinn Féin in south Armagh to the efforts of 'Mr James McGuill of Dromintee and Mr Frank Aiken of Camlough.'[173] Indeed, although Aiken's role as a regional political activist was somewhat overshadowed by his activity as a militant, it is clear that he was capable of balancing the demanding responsibilities of both roles. In this he differed from many militant republican figures, who shunned politics and often displayed a deep mistrust of politicians.[174] Speaking in 1972, Aiken made clear that at the time he had no such feelings: 'as far as I was concerned I perceived no difficulty in handling both the political and military roles and activities simultaneously.'[175]

By October 1918, Sinn Féin activity in Armagh and south Down was once again beginning to build momentum. Eamon Donnelly, a prominent republican from Armagh city, was appointed as the party's organiser for Ulster. On 8 November, a Sinn Féin conference in Newry was addressed by Fr O'Flanagan, the party's joint-vice president, and proved one of the most significant republican events in the region since the introduction of restrictions on public meetings in July.[176] When the First World War finally ended days later, and the much anticipated general election was announced, the republicans were the first to spring into action. The RIC in Armagh reported that 'the Sinn Féin organisation is the only one showing much activity but that consists in organising for the approaching election'.[177] Yet these exertions were soon rendered ineffectual. Republicans did not contest either South Armagh or South Down, the only two constituencies in the Armagh and south Down region with nationalist majorities. In a compromise brokered by Cardinal Logue and the northern bishops, Sinn Féin and the Irish Party divided the northern seats for fear that a split in the nationalist vote might benefit the unionists, and thus strengthen the case for exclusion or partition.[178] The decision was unpopular with local republicans. Robert Kelly later recalled that 'we lost South Down, which we could have easily won.'[179] Likewise, John McCoy reflected that 'the agreement of Sinn Féin to such an allocation of seats was bad policy as it gave the parliamentarians a representation which they could not otherwise obtain'. He also expressed his belief that Sinn Féin's support of such an overtly 'sectarian policy' had alienated potential republican supporters from within the northern Protestant community.[180]

On the day of the election itself, with no Sinn Féin contests locally, Irish Volunteer units from Armagh and south Down were ordered to perform duty elsewhere. They ended up serving in nearby Carlingford, Co. Louth. Armed with hurling sticks, they spent the day defending republican supporters in the rowdy affrays that developed with rival nationalists.[181] The eventual result of the election was an overwhelming victory for Sinn Féin, which won 73 of a possible 105 seats, and thus replaced the Irish Party as the voice of nationalism throughout southern Ireland. Yet it was a different story across six-county Ulster. Here the republicans only managed to win two seats; South Fermanagh and North West Tyrone. Unionist candidates dominated, winning 23 of a possible 29 seats. The remaining four – including South Armagh and South Down – went to the Irish Party.[182]

The results of the general election in December 1918 were a striking reminder of the uphill struggle that the republican movement faced in Ulster in the period of revolutionary mobilisation between 1916 and 1918. Nevertheless, through the efforts of Aiken and his ilk, there was now a confident and growing separatist presence across Armagh and south Down. Both Sinn Féin and the Irish Volunteers were firmly established locally, and although their organisational progress could not compare with that across southern Ireland, it represented a significant feat in the unique social and political context in the six counties. For Aiken, meanwhile, the two years and nine months between the Easter rising and the general election had also been a period of rather impressive achievement. He had come a long way since his first minor act of defiance in hoisting the Sinn Féin flag in Camlough and, in proving both his dedication and his worth as an organiser and activist, was fast establishing himself as the coming man of the republican movement in south-east Ulster.

NOTES

1.   P. Hart, *The IRA at War* (Oxford, 2003), p. 12.
2.   'Chronology', *c.*1933, Irish Military Archives (hereafter, IMA), Bureau of Military History Contemporary Documents (hereafter, BMH CD) 6/36/22.
3.   For the most recent historical perspectives on the rising, see C. Townshend, *Easter 1916: The Irish Rebellion* (London, 2005) and F. McGarry, *The Rising: Easter 1916* (Oxford, 2010).
4.   *Frontier Sentinel*, 12 May 1916; *Armagh Guardian*, 28 Apr. 1916.
5.   John McCoy, IMA, Bureau of Military History Witness Statement (hereafter, BMH WS) 492.

6.   *The Times*, 1 May 1916.

7.   R. Lynch, *The Northern IRA and the Early Years of Partition* (Dublin, 2006), pp 9–12; M. J. Kelly, *The Fenian Ideal and Irish Nationalism, 1882–1916* (Woodbridge, 2006), pp 141, n. 48.

8.   Robert Kelly, IMA, BMH WS 181; John Southwell, ibid., 230.

9.   For accounts of the separatist scene in Newry and south Armagh in the decade before 1916 see, Robert Kelly, ibid., 181; John Southwell, ibid., 230; Peadar McCann, ibid., 171; Patrick Rankin, ibid., 163; for examples of typical activities see, RIC Chief Inspectors' reports (hereafter, CI), Armagh, Jan. 1913, The National Archives, Kew (hereafter, TNA), Colonial Office Papers (hereafter, CO) 904/89; Special Branch précis, Sept.–Nov. 1914, TNA, CO 904/94–5.

10. CI, Armagh, Jan. 1913, TNA, CO904/89; Kelly, *The Fenian Ideal and Irish Nationalism, 1882*, p. 224, n. 181; John Southwell, IMA, BMH WS 230; John (Jack) Shields, ibid., 928.

11. CI, Down, Mar. 1916, TNA, CO904/99; Special Branch précis, Nov. 1914, TNA, CO 904/95.

12. CI, Armagh and Down, Mar. 1916, TNA, CO 904/99.

13. For details of the Coalisland mobilisation see Lynch, *Northern IRA and the Early Years of Partition*, pp 13–14; F. McCluskey, *Fenians and Ribbonmen: The Development of Republican Politics in East Tyrone, 1898–1918* (Manchester, 2011), pp 180–1.

14. For more see Robert Kelly, IMA BMH WS 181; John Southwell, ibid., 230; Peadar McCann, ibid., 171; Patrick Rankin, ibid., 163. These statements sometimes refer to the group of would-be rebels based around the Newry IRB circle as an Irish Volunteer company, but this appears to be a retrospective label and there is no evidence to suggest that such a company was in operation in Newry at this time.

15. Patrick Rankin, IMA, BMH WS 163; CI, Down, May 1916, TNA, CO904/100.

16. James Short, IMA, BMH WS 534; see also James McCullough, IMA, BMH WS529.

17. For Tyrone see, McCluskey, *Fenians and Ribbonmen*, pp 212–3; for Derry see J. Augusteijn, 'From Public Defiance to Guerrilla Warfare: The Radicalisation of the Irish Republican Army – a Comparative Analysis' (PhD Thesis, Leiden University, 1994), pp 61–2.

18. Robert Kelly, IMA, BMH WS 181; Peadar McCann, ibid., 171; for more on the IRB's infiltrationist tactics see T. Garvin, *Nationalist Revolutionaries in Ireland 1858–1928* (Dublin, 2005), p. 37.

19. CI, Down, Jan. 1917, TNA, CO904/103.

20. Edward Fullerton, IMA, BMH WS 890.

21. CI, Armagh and Down, Feb.–Mar. 1917, TNA, CO904/103.

22. 'Chronology', *c.*1933, IMA, BMH CD 6/36/22.

23. L. Skinner, *Politicians By Accident* (Dublin, 1946), p. 153.

24. 'Chronology', *c.*1933, IMA, BMH CD 6/36/22; E. Magennis, 'Frank Aiken: Family, early life and the revolutionary period, 1898–1921', in Evans and Kelly (eds), *Frank Aiken: Nationalist and Internationalist* (Dublin, 2014), p. 4.

25. D. Fitzpatrick, *Politics and Irish Life, 1913–1921: Provincial Experience of War and Revolution* (Cork, 1977), p. 108.

26. J. Borgonovo, *The Dynamics of War and Revolution: Cork City, 1916–1918* (Cork, 2013); see also, C. Nic Dháibhéid, 'The Irish National Aid and the radicalisation of public opinion in Ireland, 1916–1918', *The Historical Journal*, 55: 3 (Sept. 2012), pp 705–29.

27. CI, Armagh and Down, May–June 1916, TNA, CO 904/99–100.

28. *Frontier Sentinel*, 12 May 1916.

29. CI, Armagh and Down, May–Dec. 1916, TNA, CO 904/100–1.

30. R. Fanning, *Fatal Path: British Government and Irish Revolution, 1910–1922* (London, 2013), pp 145–7.

31. CI, Armagh and Down, May–June 1916, TNA, CO904/99–100.

32. McCluskey, *Fenians and Ribbonmen*, pp 184–7.

33. *Frontier Sentinel*, 8 July 1916.

34. J. Rouse, 'Connellan, Joseph', from *Dictionary of Irish Biography* (hereafter, *DIB*), www.dib.cambridge.org (accessed, 3 Mar. 2010).

35. J. Augusteijn, 'Motivation' in ibid. (ed.), *The Irish revolution, 1913–1923* (Basingstoke, 2002), p. 110.

36. John McCoy, IMA, BMH WS 492.

37. E. Phoenix, *Northern Nationalism: Nationalism, Politics, Partition and the Catholic Minority in Northern Ireland, 1890–1940* (Belfast, 1994), p. 25.

38. CI, Armagh and Down, Oct.–Nov. 1916, TNA, CO904/99–101.

39. M. Laffan, *The Resurrection of Ireland: The Sinn Féin Party 1916–1923* (Cambridge, 1999), p. 144.

40. *Armagh Guardian*, 9 Feb. 1917, 18 May 1917, 13 July 1917.

41. CI, Armagh, May 1917, TNA, CO904/103.

42. Ibid., June 1917, TNA, CO904/103.

43. Laffan, *Resurrection of Ireland*, pp 204–5.

44. CI, Armagh and Down, Nov. 1917, TNA, CO904/104.

45. *Frontier Sentinel*, 11 Aug. 1917; for references to the branches various names see Ibid., 1 Sept. 1917, 1 Dec. 1917.

46. *Newry Telegraph*, 26 Jan. 1918.

47. CI, Armagh, July 1917, TNA, CO 903/104.

48. For details of the event see *Frontier Sentinel*, 22 Sept. 1917. Estimates of attendance varied considerably, the figure of 4,000 is that suggested by the RIC; CI, Down, Sept. 1917, TNA, CO 904/104.

49. *Frontier Sentinel*, 6 Oct. 1917.

50. Ibid., 10 Nov. 1917.

51. CI, Armagh, Nov. 1917, TNA, CO904/104.

52. Sinn Féin Standing Committee Minutes, 17 Jan. 1918, National Library of Ireland (hereafter, NLI), P.3263 (microfilm).

53. M. Coleman, 'McCartan, Patrick', from *DIB*, www.dib.cambridge.org (accessed, 4 Jan. 2010).

54. *Freeman's Journal*, 21 Oct. 1909.

55. Laffan, *Resurrection of Ireland*, p. 123.

56. *Armagh Guardian*, 1 Feb. 1918.

57. *Irish Independent*, 29 Jan. 1918.

58. Robert Kelly, IMA, BMH WS 549.

59. Ibid.

60. RIC Inspector General's Report (IG), Jan. 1918, TNA, CO 904/105; John McCoy, IMA, BMH WS 492; M. Brennan, *The War in Clare 1911–1921* (Dublin, 1980), p. 33.

61. Laffan, *Resurrection of Ireland*, p. 124.

62. *Irish Independent*, 21 Jan. 1918; for the events in Corran see *Irish News*, 23 Jan. 1918, 26 Jan. 1918.

63. *Irish Independent*, 28 Jan. 1918.

64. South Armagh By-Election Pamphlets, *c.*Jan. 1918, IMA, BMH CD 227/7/c1 (a–u).

65. Laffan, *Resurrection of Ireland*, pp 98–9, 101.

66. *Irish Independent*, 28 Jan., 1 Feb. 1918; *Newry Telegraph*, 28 Jan. 1918.

67. *Irish Independent*, 28, 29 Jan. 1918; *Newry Telegraph*, 29 Jan. 1918

68. Laffan, *Resurrection of Ireland*, p. 124.

69. *Irish Independent*, 1 Feb. 1918.

70. Ibid., 28 Jan. 1918; *Irish Times*, 28 Jan. 1918; *Newry Telegraph*, 29 Jan. 1918.

71. *Armagh Guardian*, 1 Feb. 1918; Kevin O'Shiel, IMA, BMH WS 1770; see also D. Fitzpatrick, *Harry Boland's Irish Revolution, 1916–1922* (Cork, 2003), p. 99.

72. Andrew McDonnell, IMA, BMH WS 1768.

73. For character sketches of Aiken during the revolutionary period, see Padraig Quinn memoir, Kilmainham Gaol Museum (hereafter, KGM), McCann Cell Collection, 20/M5/IP41/08; C. S Andrews, *Dublin Made Me: An Autobiography* (Dublin, 1979), pp 241–2.

74. J. M. Regan, *The Memoirs of John M. Regan: A Catholic Officer in the RIC and RUC, 1909–1948*, ed. J. Augusteijn (Dublin, 2007), p. 113.

75. James McGuill, IMA, BMH WS 353; not to be confused with his cousin, also James McGuill, a prominent Sinn Féin figure from Dromintee.

76. Skinner, *Politicians By Accident*, p. 154.

77. *Irish Times*, 28 Jan. 1918.

78. The exact details surrounding the formation of the company are uncertain. McElhaw recalled that it was created before the by-election, after Canon Quin had disrupted a meeting addressed by Herbert Moore Pim. Yet all other evidence points to the company having been created during, or shortly after, the by-election campaign, and that the incident involving Quin was that involving Ginnell in Bessbrook; Jack McElhaw, IMA, BMH WS 634.

79. *Newry Telegraph*, 2 Feb. 1918.

80. John Grant, IMA, BMH WS 658.

81. *The Times*, 2 Feb. 1918.

82. B. M. Walker (ed.), *Parliamentary Election Results in Ireland, 1801–1922* (Dublin, 1978), p. 329.

83. *Frontier Sentinel*, 2 Feb. 1918.

84. *Nationality*, 9 Feb. 1918; *Belfast News-Letter*, 4 Feb. 1918; *Armagh Guardian*, 8 Feb. 1918.

85. *Newry Telegraph*, 31 Jan. 1918; *Irish Independent*, 1 Feb. 1918.

86. *Armagh Guardian*, 1 Feb. 1918.

87. Charles McGleenan, IMA, BMH WS 829.

88. *Newry Telegraph*, 5 Feb. 1918.

89. IG, Jan. 1918, TNA, CO 904/105.

90. *Armagh Guardian*, 25 Jan. 1918; *Irish News*, 26 Jan. 1918.

91. CI, Armagh, Jan. 1918, TNA, CO 904/105.

92. Ibid., Down, Feb. 1918, TNA, CO 904/105.

93. See, for example, P. Hart, *The IRA and its Enemies: Violence and Community in Cork, 1916–1923* (Oxford, 1998), pp 165–70.

94. Laffan, *Resurrection of Ireland*, p. 124.

95. *Armagh Guardian*, 25 Jan. 1918.

96. See, for example, *Irish Independent*, 23 Jan. 1918.

97. *Irish Times*, 1 Dec. 1918; IG, Armagh, Jan. 1918, TNA, CO904/105; see also J. Privilege, *Michael Logue and the Catholic Church in Ireland, 1879–1925* (Manchester, 2009), pp 118–19.

98. M. Coleman, *County Longford and the Irish Revolution* (Dublin, 2003), pp 54–5.

99. IG, Feb. 1918, TNA, CO904/105.

100. *Frontier Sentinel*, 23 Feb. 1918.

101. Ibid.

102. IG, Mar. 1918, TNA, CO 904/105.

103. For more on the East Tyrone election see McCluskey, *Fenians and Ribbonmen*, pp 223–39.

104. See, for example, Fitzpatrick, *Politics and Irish Life*, p. 138; Coleman, *County Longford and the Irish Revolution*, p. 74; F. Campbell, *Land and Revolution: Nationalist Politics in the West of Ireland 1891–1921* (Oxford, 2005), pp 167–8.

105. *Irish Independent*, 30 Jan. 1918.

106. CI, Armagh, Oct. 1918, TNA, CO 904/107.

107. *Frontier Sentinel*, 23 Feb. 1918; IG, Jan. 1918, TNA, CO 904/105.

108. *Frontier Sentinel*, 16 Mar. 1918, 15 June 1918.

109. Jack McElhaw, IMA, BMH WS 634; Eileen MacCarvill, ibid., 1752.

110. P. Hart, 'Youth culture and the Cork IRA', in D. Fitzpatrick (ed.) *Revolution? Ireland 1917–1923* (Dublin, 1990), p. 18.

111. Interview with Dr Eoin Magennis, 19 May 2010; for more on Nano's activities later in the period see Nano Aiken (file), *c.*1923–25, Public Record Office of Northern Ireland (hereafter, PRONI), HA/5/2303; for position in Cumann na mBan see 'South Armagh District Council', IMA, Military Service Pension's Collection (hereafter, MSPC), CMB/59.

112. Padraig Quinn memoir, KGM, McCann Cell Collection, 20/M5/IP41/08.

113. 'Chronology', c.1933, IMA, BMH CD 6/36/22. In an undated biographical sketch amongst Aiken's papers it states that Aiken was appointed as the co–operative's representative to the 'Ulster Federation of such societies', which was presumably a reference to the Ulster Agricultural Organisation Society; see Biographical sketch, undated, University College Dublin Archive Department (hereafter, UCDAD), Aiken papers, P104/447.

114. For more on O'Duffy, see F. McGarry, *Eoin O'Duffy: A Self-Made Hero* (Oxford, 2005), pp 13–14, 30.

115. D. Ferriter, *The Transformation of Ireland, 1900–2000* (London, 2004), pp 88–9.

116. Coleman, *County Longford and the Irish Revolution*, pp 78–9; Hart, *The IRA and its Enemies*, pp 232–3; Laffan, *Resurrection of Ireland*, pp 196–7.

117. M. Hopkinson, *The Irish War of Independence* (Dublin, 2002), p. 15.

118. E. O'Malley, *On Another Man's Wound* (Dublin, 1990), p. 127.

119. Garvin, *Nationalist Revolutionaries in Ireland*, p. 53.

120. For a detailed overview of how this information was compiled, see Appendix I.

121. See Appendix II, Table II.

122. Ibid.

123. Ibid.

124. See above, p. 41.

125. Fitzpatrick, *Politics and Irish Life*, pp 127–8.

126. Campbell, *Land and Revolution*, p. 224; D. Hall, 'Violence, Political Factionalism and their Effects on North Louth' (PhD, National University of Ireland Maynooth, 2010), p. 50; McCluskey, *Fenians and Ribbonmen*, p. 216.

127. The defections of the three former secretaries of the UIL were highlighted in the coverage of Griffith's appearance in Newry in *Frontier Sentinel*, 22 Sept. 1917. For details on how past political history was compiled see Appendix I.

128. Each accounted for around 9–10 per cent of the total sample.

129. For a detailed overview of how this information was compiled, see Appendix I.

130. See Appendix II, Table III.

131. Ibid.

132. John McCoy, IMA, BMH WS 492.

133. Ibid.

134. J. Augusteijn, *From Public Defiance to Guerrilla Warfare: The Experience of Ordinary Volunteers in the Irish War of Independence* (Dublin, 1996), pp 55–87.

135. CI, Armagh and Down, Feb. 1918, TNA, CO 904/105.

136. IG, Feb. 1918, TNA, CO 904/105.

137. Ibid., Mar. 1918, TNA, CO 904/105.

138. John McCoy, IMA, BMH WS 492.

139. Augusteijn, *From Public Defiance to Guerrilla Warfare*, p. 66.

140. Jack McElhaw, IMA, BMH WS 634.

141. *Frontier Sentinel*, 6 Apr. 1918; Jack McElhaw, IMA, BMH WS 634.

142. See, for example, P. Hart, *Mick: The Real Michael Collins* (London, 2005), pp 96–111; Hopkinson, *Irish War of Independence*, p. 16.

143. McGarry, *Eoin O'Duffy*, p. 40.

144. Statement of Charles Kenny, 19 July 1918, National Library of Ireland (hereafter, NLI), Moore papers, Ms 10,556/6.

145. S. McConville, *Irish Political Prisoners 1848–1922: Theatres of War* (London, 2003), pp 610–18.

146. Aiken to O'Malley, 27 June 1923, IMA, Captured Documents, Lot 130.

147. *Frontier Sentinel*, 20 Apr. 1918; *Irish Times*, 27 Apr. 1918. In the report of the ceilidh Aiken was referred to as the Sinn Féin Club's president. This was possibly an error, as there is no corroborating evidence to suggest he ever held that post.

148. *Irish Times*, 15 Apr. 1918.

149. *Weekly Irish Times*, 27 Apr. 1918.

150. *Frontier Sentinel*, 6 Apr. 1920.

151. Laffan, *Resurrection of Ireland*, p. 137.

152. Robert Kelly, IMA, BMH WS 549.

153. CI, Armagh and Down, Apr. 1918, TNA, CO 904/105.

154. Fanning, *Fatal Path*, p. 171.

155. CI, Down, Apr. 1918, TNA, CO 904/105.

156. Laffan, *Resurrection of Ireland*, p. 135.

157. *Frontier Sentinel*, 20 Apr. 1918.

158. Laffan, *Resurrection of Ireland*, p. 163.

159. Robert Kelly, IMA, BMH WS 549.

160. Augusteijn, *From Public Defiance to Guerrilla Warfare*, p. 75.

161. John McCoy, IMA, BMH WS 492.

162. 'Chronology', *c*.1933, IMA, BMH CD 6/36/22.

163. *Frontier Sentinel*, 22 June 1918.

164. John McCoy, IMA, BMH WS 492.

165. Skinner, *Politicians By Accident*, p. 154.

166. CI, Armagh, Sept. 1918, TNA, CO 904/107.

167. C. Townshend, *The British Campaign in Ireland 1919–1921: The Development of Political and Military Policies* (Oxford, 1975), p. 10.

168. See, for example, CI, Armagh and Down, Sept. 1918, CO 904/107.

169. 'Chronology', *c.*1933, IMA, BMH CD 6/36/22.

170. John McCoy, IMA, BMH WS 492.

171. *Frontier Sentinel*, 29 May 1919.

172. See above, p. 49.

173. *Frontier Sentinel*, 18 Oct. 1919.

174. R. English, *Ernie O'Malley: IRA Intellectual* (Oxford, 1998), p. 98.

175. 'Transcript of interview notes', 16 Aug. 1972, UCDAD, Aiken papers, P104/450.

176. *Frontier Sentinel*, 16 Nov. 1918.

177. CI, Armagh, Nov. 1918, TNA, CO 904/107.

178. For more on the pact see Laffan, *Resurrection of Ireland*, pp 160–161; Privilege, *Michael Logue and the Catholic Church in Ireland*, pp 131–2.

179. Robert Kelly, IMA, BMH WS 549.

180. John McCoy, ibid., 492.

181. Patrick Rankin, ibid., 671; Jack McElhaw, ibid., 634.

182. For a complete list of the results see, 'The Irish Election of 1918', www.ark.ac.uk/elections/h1918.htm (accessed, 3 Jan. 2013).

FOUR

WAR FOR INDEPENDENCE

—

In accordance with their policy of abstention, Sinn Féin's newly elected MPs refused to take their seats in Westminster, and duly created their own revolutionary assembly in Dublin, Dáil Éireann. Coincidentally, on the day of its opening, 21 January 1919, a group of Irish Volunteers ambushed and killed two RIC constables at Soloheadbeg, Co. Tipperary, while stealing a consignment of gelignite en route to a local quarry.[1] It was an ominous start to the year, and an early indication of the changing nature of the republican struggle. Whereas the years 1917–18 were characterised by an aggressive and defiant brand of political activism, the period 1919–21 would be marked by the steadily escalating violence of the war for independence.[2] For Aiken, the shifting emphasis of republican activity had important repercussions. Though Armagh and south Down did not experience anything like the levels of violence witnessed in the most disturbed areas of southern Ireland, it was one of the few hot spots of militant republican activity in Ulster throughout the period. As the violence escalated, and republican political activity declined, his role in the Irish Volunteers – or Irish Republican Army (IRA) as it became known from 1919 onwards – increasingly came to monopolise his time.

For the greater part of 1919, however, political activism remained the primary focus of activity throughout Ireland, and the situation in Armagh and south Down was no exception. In the elation that accompanied Sinn Féin's monumental general election success (in southern Ireland at least), political protests and demonstrations once again became common locally, and exhibited a newfound confidence and aggression. This was particularly true in Newry and south Armagh where such events usually took the form of protest meetings or celebratory processions to welcome home recently released republican prisoners.[3] The most noteworthy of such occasions occurred on 7 March when a crowd of Sinn Féin supporters succeeded in disrupting a meeting of the Irish Centre Party (ICP) at Newry Town Hall. Founded by Stephen Gwynn, a former Irish Party MP, the ICP endorsed a federalist or dominion-based solution to the problem of Irish self-government. It had no organisational presence in the area; the event was merely a lecture aimed at promoting its policy. Nevertheless, a group of local republicans, headed by Patrick Rankin, succeeded in interrupting the proceedings, and launched a vitriolic verbal attack on Gwynn about his Irish Party past. After 45 minutes of such disruption the lecture was abandoned and a triumphant Sinn Féin counter-demonstration was held in its place. As was the case with republican demonstrations in late 1918, however, four of those involved in the commotion were later arrested and imprisoned.[4]

Such displays aside, the establishment of Dáil Éireann also created a range of new opportunities for provincial activists to engage in political work. For the most part, these centred around attempts to develop the institutions of the nascent republican counter-state, such as the Dáil courts, or efforts to promote non-violent resistance against the existing British administration in Ireland, through initiatives such as the boycott of the RIC. It also included the fund-raising efforts of the Dáil Loan, a bond buying scheme directed by the new Department of Finance under Michael Collins. In Armagh and south Down, these types of activities were often limited because of the hostility of a large section of the local population, both unionist and nationalist. As a result, initiatives such as the courts or the boycott were not much in evidence, though there were at least attempts to collect the Dáil Loan. This was typical of the situation throughout six-county Ulster at this time. In Derry, for example, Augusteijn has noted that a similar lack of popular support restricted republican activity to little more than the registration of voters during the same period.[5]

For Aiken, this fresh wave of political activity brought new roles and new responsibilities within the local Sinn Féin organisation, and as in early 1918 he readily accepted them. Though the exact dates are unclear, in the course of 1919 he was promoted to the chairmanship of the party's South Armagh constituency executive. With the launch of the Dáil Loan in August, he was also appointed as the constituency's director for the initiative, a logical enough decision given his past experience as treasurer of both the Camlough Sinn Féin club and his local Gaelic League branch.[6] As with his earlier Sinn Féin appointments, there is little evidence of his precise activities in these roles. By 1919, the local press was no longer reporting the minutes of the constituency executive's meetings, and there is little in the way of contemporary correspondence or documentation relating to either appointment. Nevertheless, there is some indication of his performance with regard to the Dáil Loan. Dáil records show that under his direction the constituency managed to raise £1,665 by the time the initiative ended in late 1920.[7] This was no mean feat in the context of north-east Ulster, where Sinn Féin was at its weakest. Indeed, eight other constituencies across the six counties – among them both North and Mid Armagh – failed even to reach the £1000 mark. Yet neither was South Armagh particularly exceptional. It was outperformed by its immediate neighbour, South Down, which raised £1,845 10s. Nearby North-East Tyrone, meanwhile, managed £2,307 10s.[8] Aiken's achievement, therefore, was a relatively modest one. There is also evidence that the Irish Volunteers were prominently involved in conducting the local collections, a situation that was likely facilitated by Aiken in his dual positions as director of the Dáil Loan and vice commandant of the Newry Brigade.[9]

The involvement of the Irish Volunteers in political work was typical throughout the country during 1919, and serves to highlight both the slow pace at which military activity developed throughout the year, and the degree to which it continued to be subordinated to politics.[10] Despite sporadic incidents such as the Soloheadbeg ambush in January, or the assassination of detectives from the Dublin Metropolitan Police's G Division during the summer, the official policy of the GHQ in Dublin remained one of preparedness and restraint. All military style operations were forbidden, unless explicitly sanctioned. Preparatory works, such as training, organisation and the acquisition of arms continued to be the primary focus of Irish Volunteer efforts. Only rarely was this low-level activity punctuated by violent attacks on the authorities.[11] Indeed, as Michael Hopkinson has observed, 'the extremely limited and episodic nature of the hostilities during the rest of 1919 scarcely merits the term "war".'[12]

Events in Armagh and south Down conformed to this broader national trend. Locally, there were few acts of violence committed by republicans during 1919. Indeed, aside from occasional disturbances at political demonstrations, there were only two notable violent incidents that year. The first occurred in July when two policemen were attacked and beaten by a group of men returning from a GAA match at Crossmaglen.[13] Although those involved in the attack were volunteers, the incident does not appear to have been planned and was most likely an opportunistic attempt to disarm the constables. The second occurred in November when a Protestant clergyman, Reverend Edward Foy, was the victim of a non-fatal shooting during an alleged republican arms raid on his home in Lisnadill. UVF rifles had previously been stored at the property, and the attack was apparently carried out by a lone assailant. Responsibility for the incident is unclear, however. In a report to GHQ in Dublin, Rankin claimed that local Irish Volunteer units were not involved in the incident. Rather, he alleged that the shooting was the result of a domestic dispute between Foy and his son, and that the story of the arms raid had been concocted by the family to cover-up the incident.[14] Significantly, the RIC also appeared somewhat sceptical about the incident, describing it as 'very mysterious' and conceding that 'there was no evidence of a raid as usually done.'[15] Whatever the truth, such episodes were certainly not common.

Aside from an occasional involvement in political work, arms raids were the Newry Brigade's primary activity throughout 1919. In some parts of the country, notably Cork, such operations had begun as early as 1917, and became particularly intense during the conscription crisis the following year.[16] In Armagh and south Down, the late beginnings of the Irish Volunteer organisation ensured that they did not commence until early in 1919. Although there were numerous small scale raids on private houses throughout the year, with searches on the homes of anyone suspected of possessing a gun or ammunition, the most promising local targets were the arms caches of the UVF, which included large quantities of rifles smuggled into the country during the home rule crisis. In the hunt for this elusive bounty, local units – occasionally with the guidance of GHQ and assistance from Irish Volunteer officers from nearby north Louth – forcibly searched a number of suspect properties; among them an Orange hall, the country manors of three prominent unionists (among them a UVF regimental commander), and possibly the home of the Reverend Foy at Lisnadill; though as has already been observed, republican responsibility for the latter incident is far from clear.[17] The most significant of these raids occurred at Ballyedmond Castle, near Rostrevor, in May, and Loughgall Manor, in August. These were operations of a significant scale, involving large numbers of local volunteers and meticulous planning on the part of brigade leaders. In the case of Ballyedmond Castle, support was also provided by officers from north Louth and Dublin.[18] In each case the raids failed to capture any significant quantity of weaponry, but they did illustrate the increasing capabilities of the brigade, as well as its growing boldness and military potential. For the average volunteer, however, involvement in an occasional arms raid was the very most that could be expected in terms of military activity at this time, and the majority of men continued to be occupied with little more than routine organisational work. As Edward Fullerton, a Newry volunteer, later recalled, 'training practices, drills, manoeuvres and dispatch work were "orders of the day" with me up to the end of 1919.'[19]

Republican military activity in the region may have remained somewhat subdued throughout 1919, but activities such as arms raids nevertheless added a new dimension to Aiken's existing Irish Volunteer duties. Although his time continued to be dominated by routine organisation matters, such as the maintenance of discipline, and further expansion of the organisation in north Armagh and (to a lesser extent) west Down, he now faced the task of commanding actual operations.[20] He was particularly visible in this capacity during the raids at Ballyedmond Castle and Loughgall Manor, and played a very direct and active role in both their planning and implementation; an early indication of the hands on leadership style for which he became known later in the period. Prior to the Ballyedmond operation, for instance, he and Rankin had personally carried out the necessary reconnaissance of the area. On the night itself, he also led the party that searched the premises, and was apparently responsible for locating the head of the household – Major Arthur Nugent, a former British army officer and regimental commander of the south Down UVF – and dragging him out from his hiding place underneath a bed.[21] He performed a similar role in the Loughgall raid three months later, where a more determined resistance was offered by the lady of the house, and her butler, who managed to open fire on the party before being disarmed and tied up.[22] Significantly, Aiken's initial operational outings appear to have attracted some positive attention from his superiors at GHQ, Michael Collins in particular. A few months after the Loughgall raid, Aiken was ordered to assist Ernie O'Malley with a further (unsuccessful) GHQ led search for UVF arms in Derry.[23] This was, perhaps, an early indication that he was coming to be considered as one of the more competent officers in Ulster.

It was only in the winter of 1919–20 that violence began to gain momentum throughout the country. This came as a consequence of various measures introduced by the authorities that served to stifle republican political activity and weakened the position of those within the movement who wished to avoid violent confrontation.[24] Most important among these were the suppression of Dáil Éireann in September, and the nationwide proscription of Sinn Féin and all associated organisations – the Irish Volunteers, Cumann na mBan and the Gaelic League – in November following a series of regionally-based bans earlier in the year.[25] In Armagh and south Down, the proscription of Sinn Féin merely formalised the existing situation. From August 1919 onwards, republican demonstrations and events had increasingly faced disruption from the RIC.[26] With the suppression of Dáil Éireann the following month, the local police also began to place prominent local republicans under greater scrutiny. In Newry, for instance, the introduction of the measure coincided with a series of raids on the homes and businesses of well-known Sinn Féin leaders.[27] The Armagh Sinn Féin organiser Eamon Donnelly was also arrested and imprisoned at this time for addressing an event in Tynan in October 1919 as part of the local Dáil Loan effort.[28] In this repressive atmosphere, political meetings declined significantly. The dramatic decrease in Sinn Féin's public presence, combined with the increased risk of arrest for all those associated with the party, also resulted in the departure of many less dedicated rank and file members. In December, the RIC could report that 'some supporters of Sinn Féin in Armagh have re-joined the AOH.'[29] A month later, it was further observed that 'the AOH has been putting a better grasp on nationalists than it had some time ago.'[30]

Declining republican political activity was soon accompanied by an increase in violence, both locally and nationally. The suppression of Dáil Éireann prompted GHQ to formally adopt a policy of aggression. This ushered in a new phase of activity by the Volunteers – or the IRA as they were now known –

with the first authorised attacks on RIC barracks in January 1920, and the destruction of numerous smaller police posts that had been vacated as a result of the rising violence throughout 1919.[31] The Newry Brigade quickly followed the example set elsewhere and, as might be expected, Aiken was in the thick of the action.

On the night of 12–13 May 1920 the Newry Brigade carried out a prolonged attack on Newtownhamilton RIC Barracks. A few months previously a small group of IRA men under Aiken's leadership had attempted to capture the building by ruse, disguising themselves as British soldiers from Dundalk and requesting entry. When this plan failed it was decided to plan a full-scale attack. On the night of the operation, all roads leading to Newtownhamilton were blocked and secured by armed outposts. The IRA attacking party then entered the town, taking up positions directly opposite the barracks, and in a field behind the building. Aiken, meanwhile, took charge of a smaller group of men who entered a neighbouring public house and set about mining the wall; the plan being to create a large breach through which a small force could enter and capture the building. Having been alerted by the noise of this endeavour, the RIC opened fire on the IRA positions opposite the barracks and the attack commenced.

Aiken and his companions were inexperienced with explosives, and despite their best efforts they were unable to create a substantial breach in the thick stone walls between the pub and barracks. With any hope of storming the building thwarted, they instead shifted their attentions to destroying it. After making a series of calls for the RIC garrison's surrender, each of which was steadfastly refused, Aiken gave the order to burn the barracks. His mining party poured paraffin through the small openings created by their earlier endeavours, and set it alight. Before the attack had commenced, a potato sprayer had also been used to soak the façade with flammable liquid. The building was soon engulfed in flames and the IRA contingent departed the town with the small RIC force maintaining their resistance from an outbuilding in the rear yard of the premises.[32]

Although the Newtownhamilton operation represented a partial success, another large-scale attack of its kind was not attempted until December 1920. In the meantime, lower-level operations were the greater focus for local IRA activity. These included actions such as the theft and censorship of mail and further arms raids.[33] More significant, however, was the growing frequency of arson attacks. The first occurred in April when GHQ issued a nationwide order for the burning of vacated police posts and government offices. Despite the relatively low levels of violence in six-county Ulster at this time, barracks closures nonetheless occurred in south Armagh and south Down.[34] This initial operation targeted vacated posts at Whitecross, Rostrevor, Mayobridge,

Loughbrickland and Cullyhanna. In Newry, meanwhile, Aiken led a party of men who entered the local customs house and set fire to record books and documentation.[35] After this first series of attacks, arson became a staple of local activity, and another six such operations occurred in the region during 1920. These typically targeted further vacated police posts, and other symbols of government authority such as courthouses.[36]

By November 1920, the local IRA's newfound aggression had produced the first fatalities of the conflict in Armagh and south Down. In two separate incidents, neither of which appears to have been sanctioned by the Newry Brigade leadership, two policemen and a volunteer were killed. The first occurred in June 1920 at an aeraíocht at Cullyhanna in south Armagh, when an RIC constable and a local volunteer were killed during a brief confrontation. A second policeman and a visiting IRA officer from Dundalk were also wounded in the incident. The shooting was apparently the result of a botched attempt to disarm the constables.[37] The second, in November 1920, was a much more determined and aggressive attack on a policeman in Newry. The target was RIC Head Constable John Kearney. As one of those involved in the killing later explained, Kearney was viewed as being 'most aggressive' in his pursuit of members of the republican movement. Operating without the knowledge of their battalion officers – who were evidently considered to be too timid in their approach to the conflict – a handful of local volunteers decided to kill Kearney to 'ease the enemy pressure' in the town.[38] He was shot at the corner of Needham Street shortly after leaving mass. The killing provoked an aggressive response from the authorities, with 'uniformed men' (presumably police) ransacking the local Sinn Féin hall and Gaelic League offices. A number of houses were also raided and one man arrested.[39]

While the IRA campaign in Armagh and south Down was clearly gaining momentum during 1920, republican political activity continued to decline. Sinn Féin demonstrations and events were increasingly sporadic. The main exception was the participation of local nationalists and republicans in a nationwide general strike in support of the hunger strikers in Mountjoy Prison in April. The action was reasonably well observed in nationalist areas, Newry in particular, where there were also some 'lively scenes' when republicans picketed unionist businesses that had continued to trade. When the protests proved successful, and the hunger strikers were released, a celebration was also held in the town to welcome back a number of local prisoners who had been incarcerated in the gaol.[40] For the most part, incidents such as these remained uncommon, most likely as a result of the continued risk of arrest and imprisonment. Yet there was also a noticeable absence of initiatives for underground political activity within Sinn Féin. Elsewhere in the country this was provided by the operation of the Dáil courts. In Armagh and south Down, however, the open hostility of local unionists, and the majority of local nationalists, ensured that these did not appear on any significant scale until after the truce.

Indeed, the only noteworthy republican political activity to occur in the region during 1920 came as a result of local government elections in January and June. Sinn Féin performed reasonably well locally. In the county council contests, the party held its own against its constitutional nationalist rivals. In Armagh, it won three out of the eight seats claimed by nationalist candidates. In Down, meanwhile, it managed to capture four out of five.[41] Sinn Féin candidates also performed well in the contests for those urban and rural district councils with a predominantly Catholic-nationalist population. Across eight such council districts republicans won outright majorities in two – Newry No. 2 RDC in south Armagh and Kilkeel RDC in south Down – and claimed the highest number of seats in a further three. In two others they drew with constitutional nationalist candidates, and only in Keady Urban District Council (UDC) did they face a solid defeat, scoring one seat against the constitutional nationalists' nine.[42]

The extent of republican electioneering during the local government contests is unclear. As Laffan has observed, there was an 'absence of extensive coverage or comment' regarding the elections. This was due to the fact that many candidates were returned without contest. As Sinn Féin was a banned organisation, much of the press coverage of its activities may also have been suppressed through government censorship.[43] In Armagh and south Down, however, RIC reports also made no reference to any particular election activities on the part of republicans. Indeed, even amongst Bureau of Military History witness statements there is no indication that Sinn Féin engaged in any significant election activity in the region, although the announcement of the results did occasion a few celebratory processions.[44]

Nationally, Sinn Féin gained control of the vast majority of local government bodies. In January it captured 72 out of 127 urban councils and county boroughs. This was followed in July with the accession of 28 out of 33 county councils and 172 out of 206 rural councils.[45] Those that remained beyond republican control were primarily those unionist dominated local authorities in six-county Ulster. Councils with Sinn Féin majorities were soon requested to pass resolutions declaring allegiance to Dáil Éireann. In the Armagh and south Down region, Newry No.2 RDC and Kilkeel RDC, the only two councils with sufficient republican majorities, duly did so. Generally speaking, however, there was little scope for the movement to use its newfound position in local government to further Dáil policy in the region in any meaningful way, and Aiken's experience provides a striking example of this.

In June 1920, Aiken stood as a candidate for both Armagh County Council and Newry No.2 RDC. The latter was the same body in which his father,

James, had served two decades earlier, the former that to which he had failed to get elected in the same period.[46] Aiken's entry into local politics was a logical progression of his Sinn Féin activities, and, as suggested earlier, his readiness to pursue such a role could be viewed as a natural outgrowth of a latent sense of family duty or a desire to emulate his father. He received an impressive personal result in this electoral debut. In the contest for Armagh County Council he topped the poll in the Forkhill district, receiving 1,427 out of 5,953 first preference votes and exceeding the quota by 434. He also topped the poll in the contest for Newry No. 2 RDC, receiving 522 out of 2,387 first preference votes and exceeding the quota by 212.

Unlike many IRA officers elected to local government positions in 1920, and despite his busy schedule, Aiken proved an active member in both bodies, though he and his colleagues ultimately achieved little. In Armagh County Council, this was due to Sinn Féin's miniscule presence and the opposition of both the constitutional nationalists and a sizeable unionist majority. The republican councillors were outspoken in meetings, and occasionally proposed resolutions, but their motions were usually quickly defeated.[47] In Newry No. 2 RDC, with its Sinn Féin majority of five, they enjoyed greater success in · pushing their agenda, but even here their achievements were limited.[48] In accordance with republican policy, Aiken proposed on 10 July that the council pledge its allegiance to Dáil Éireann. The motion was quickly passed by seven votes to two. Following the example of republican councils elsewhere in the country, he and his colleagues also passed resolutions to block compensation claims relating to IRA activity. On 14 August, speaking on Aiken's behalf, James McGuill proposed that 'in future no steps be taken to defend claims for damages to buildings used (of family hold) as police barracks or courthouses and that any resolutions or orders on the books to the contrary be rescinded.'[49] At that same meeting a series of existing claims arising from IRA activity were allowed to go unopposed, but thereafter the new policy was rigorously enforced. On 9 October, for instance, Aiken successfully moved that 16 claims for malicious injury be 'destroyed'. Aside from these more deliberate policies, however, the only other republican resolutions passed by the council were largely symbolic in nature, such as Aiken's motion, on 11 September 1920, to adjourn a meeting in protest at the treatment of the hunger striker Terence McSwiney.[50]

Throughout southern Ireland, republican control of county and district councils led to financial issues. Those local government authorities that pledged allegiance to Dáil Éireann soon found themselves in dispute with the LGB, the body in charge of distributing government grants. Financial support was withdrawn from any council that failed to provide assurances that its accounts would be submitted to the LGB for audit, and that all necessary regulations would be obeyed. Republican councils, unsurprisingly, refused to provide these assurances, and as a result they lost around 15 per cent of their revenue.[51] Although, in some areas, this led to a serious decline in the quality of public services, in Armagh and south Down it did not have so detrimental an effect. In the majority of local government bodies, unionist and constitutional nationalist councillors joined forces and easily defeated Sinn Féin on the issue. Even in Newry No. 2 RDC, with its secure republican majority, it proved possible to undermine the policy when attendance was low. In December 1920, Aiken and a number of colleagues were forced to go 'on the run' as a result of escalating IRA violence and the subsequent response of the authorities. With the council's republican majority seriously weakened, nationalist and unionist members introduced a resolution to submit to the LGB's demands. The motion passed by one vote. In the face of continued violence and suppression, Aiken and his other absent colleagues never returned to their council duties, and after six months of non-attendance they were finally disqualified from their seats in line with council procedures.[52]

ESCALATION

Throughout the country, the final six months of the war for independence proved to be the most intense and bloody of the conflict. As Hopkinson has observed, 'deaths rose from forty-four in the first six months of 1920 to 171 in the second half of the year, and 324 in the next six months.'[53] Armagh and south Down conformed to the national trend. Conflict related deaths rose from eight in 1920 to 27 in the first six months of 1921, and the figures for the wounded as a result of such violence jumped from nine to 35. This escalation of the local conflict was driven by two factors. The first was the increasingly aggressive tactics adopted by the police (and, to a lesser extent, the military) in response to republican violence. The second was the emergence of a small band of full-time IRA guerrilla fighters in the Newry and south Armagh area. The spark, however, was provided by an attack on Camlough RIC Barracks as 1920 drew to a close.

The Camlough attack took place on 12 December, and was the local IRA's second large-scale assault on a police barracks. The planning for the operation had begun in the early autumn with the assistance of GHQ. In accordance with new security measures, introduced in response to barracks attacks throughout the country, the post had been reinforced with a variety of defences including steel shutters, barbed wire and sandbags.[54] Realising that there was little chance of successfully entering the building, it was decided instead to set fire to it in order to secure the surrender of the garrison. On the advice of Peadar Clancy, a GHQ officer, it was also decided to combine the attack on the barracks with an ambush on the main road between Newry and Camlough at a railway bridge known locally as the Egyptian Arch. This would intercept any relief party from Newry and, as John McCoy later noted, would provide the 'best chance of inflicting losses on the enemy.'[55]

Despite such high hopes, however, the operation proved disastrous. As at Newtownhamilton, Aiken commanded the operation and took charge of its most dangerous task; setting fire to the building. This was to be achieved using an elaborate device that would pump a mixture of petrol and paraffin through a first floor window whilst simultaneously igniting it with a piece of burning flax tow. Aiken's efforts were quickly frustrated, however, when this contraption was damaged by gunfire. Realising the futility of the situation, he ordered that the attack be abandoned. Meanwhile, at the Egyptian Arch, the IRA ambush party was insufficiently armed. Earlier that evening, an attempt to transfer weapons and ammunition to the ambush site from a dump on the opposite side of Newry had failed due to heavy police activity in the town. When a relief party of British military from Newry reached the bridge, having been alerted to the attack by flares discharged by the beleaguered RIC garrison, they quickly overwhelmed the small IRA force with machine-gun fire. The inexperience of the volunteers involved brought further misfortune, when William Canning, a young draper's assistant from Newry, dropped a live grenade, killing himself and wounding three others, two mortally.[56] The ambush lasted a mere five minutes, and resulted in no military casualties.[57] There were also no reported casualties amongst the RIC garrison at Camlough Barracks, although one IRA officer was wounded in the leg during the attack there.

In the aftermath of the operation the military, with the assistance of recently deployed members of the Ulster Special Constabulary (USC), carried out a series of reprisals in Camlough. The USC was a newly created paramilitary force recruited from the unionist population in Ulster to reinforce the RIC; a northern equivalent of the notorious temporary constables ('black and tans') and auxiliary cadets deployed throughout southern Ireland. It consisted of a full-time force (A class), a part-time reserve in which members helped to police their own districts (B class), and a further emergency reserve (C class). This was the first significant outing of the newly arrived A class in Newry and south Armagh, and their actions set an ominous precedent for the months, and indeed years, to come. Working with the military, they first burned down a number of houses opposite the police barracks that had been occupied by the IRA during the attack. This was in keeping with an emerging policy of 'official reprisals' that was formally instituted by the authorities later that month.[58] They later returned to carry out further burnings, targeting homes and businesses belonging to prominent republican figures. The Aiken family homestead at Carrickbracken was destroyed, as was a pub owned by Jack McElhaw's uncle.[59]

The reaction of the authorities contrasted sharply with their response to the Newtownhamilton attack earlier in the year. As John McCoy recalled, 'the surprising aftermath of this attack [Newtownhamilton] was the casual manner in which the affair was allowed to blow over', in the apparent belief that it had been the work of southerners, rather than local republicans.[60] By December, however, the situation had changed considerably. Locally, tensions were high on account of the shooting of Head Constable Kearney in Newry a few weeks earlier.[61] Elsewhere in the country, the IRA had scored two shocking victories, with the executions of 15 suspected intelligence officers on Bloody Sunday (21 November), and the Kilmichael ambush (28 November); two of the most ruthlessly efficient republican operations of the conflict.[62] Furthermore, only a day before the Camlough attack, British forces had committed one of their most destructive reprisal attacks, with the burning of Cork city centre. Against this backdrop of heightened tension – and perhaps instructive precedent – the reprisals at Camlough are much more comprehensible.

The Camlough attack prompted a significant increase in activity amongst the authorities in Newry and south Armagh. As McCoy later recalled, 'raids and roundups were of daily occurrence and every effort was made by them to round up all active IRA men.'[63] January 1921 also witnessed the first large-scale military sweeps in the region. In one such operation an estimated 300 men were detained, although the vast majority were released shortly afterwards once processed.[64] The threat of arrest and imprisonment, meanwhile, was increasingly overshadowed by the understandable fear that capture might result in summary execution. On 28 December, in circumstances that would become all too common in the months that followed, the USC shot two republican suspects during searches in the townland of Beleek, just outside Camlough. The victims were Peter Mackin and Michael Smyth. Smyth, an IRA man, was killed, while Mackin, a civilian, was badly wounded but ultimately survived. It was claimed that the men were shot whilst trying to escape. Mackin later testified, however, that the constables involved had told him that his life would be spared if he ran, but that before he could move he was shot twice.[65]

As a result of this pressure, Aiken and his most active officers across Newry and south Armagh – such as John McCoy, Séan Quinn, Patrick Casey, Ned Fitzpatrick and Andy O'Hare – had little other option than to go 'on the run', and effectively become full-time IRA fighters. As with various earlier developments in the local conflict, this followed the precedents established elsewhere in the country, where active service units (ASUs), or 'flying columns' had started to form as early as the spring of 1920. In the autumn, when increasingly successful British counter-insurgency measures forced a growing number of men to leave their homes, the creation of these units had become an official policy, with GHQ ordering that they be established in all brigade areas.[66] In Armagh and south Down, the conflict had lacked the necessary intensity to force such a transition, until the attack on Camlough Barracks and the subsequent crackdown. And although there is no evidence to suggest that the Newry Brigade formally established an ASU at this time, in practice Aiken and his small cadre of officers operated in the same way as these formations, moving from district to district to plan and carry out attacks, and drawing on whatever local support they could muster.

For Aiken, the personal impact of these developments cannot be overestimated. Homeless, and facing the threat of arrest, or possibly worse if captured by the USC, his previously comfortable existence was now replaced with the constant strain and dislocation of life on the run. His first weeks were mainly spent living rough in a derelict house outside Camlough. Brooding over the destruction of the family home, he was determined to provide some kind of violent response, and eventually settled on an attempt to ambush the USC from its charred ruins. This attack was duly carried out in early January, and though it had little practical value, and inflicted no serious casualties, there was little doubt as to the message it conveyed.[67] Thereafter, the Newry Brigade's headquarters were moved to Mullaghbawn, and Aiken and his companions typically sought food and shelter with various friendly parties in mountainous border areas of south Armagh, south Down and north Louth.[68] Writing shortly after the civil war, he recorded his particular fondness and devotion towards 'several motherly women' in those districts, who had cared and prayed for him and his comrades throughout the period, and whose faith in the republican cause apparently served to strengthen their own determination: 'I need not tell you now that we'd all prefer to die before we'd do anything which would make us ashamed to meet them – some did die.'[69]

Aiken quickly adapted to life on the run. This was, perhaps, aided by the fact that he was a more fortunate fugitive than many of his contemporaries. Though his home had been destroyed, he was not without means. The farming may have ceased, but the family continued to receive an income from its rental properties, and even with the destruction of six small houses in further reprisals during 1921, this was likely a considerable sum.[70] He also had no dependents. Though his sister Nano had still been living at home, other family members were on hand to support her if need be. In the absence of such worries he was relatively free to focus on his IRA duties, though he clearly longed for the comfort and stability of a regular home life. Indeed, as the copies of *House and Garden* among his papers clearly suggest, planning a new home became a means of escapism amid the continuing stress and bloodshed of 1921, and later again amid the political uncertainty surrounding the truce and the Anglo-Irish Treaty.[71]

With the emergence of a makeshift ASU, the local conflict escalated significantly. From January 1921 onwards there was a marked increase in IRA activity. In 1920 there had only been three attacks on the authorities (not including barracks attacks). In the first six months of 1921 there were 17. These usually consisted of small-scale ambushes of RIC or USC patrols. Low-level operations, such as mail raids, the destruction of goods in connection with the Belfast boycott and the trenching of roads, also became more frequent.[72] The most spectacular operation of 1921, however, occurred on 23 June when a group of volunteers under Aiken's command successfully derailed a troop train at Adavoyle, close to the village of Meigh. The train was carrying members of the 10th Hussars who had acted as the King's cavalry escort at the opening of the new Northern Ireland parliament in Belfast one day earlier. The operation was instigated by GHQ and was intended to be one of a series of derailments on the Belfast to Dublin line that day. Aiken's operation was the only one to occur as planned, however. The derailment was achieved very simply by removing the outer rail at a selected spot on the line. The specific location was chosen as it was on a slight bend in the track and sat atop a 15-foot embankment. Four soldiers were killed in the incident, alongside an estimated 80 horses.[73]

The growing frequency of such operations highlights the extent to which the presence of dedicated and proactive local leaders could influence the levels of IRA activity in a region. This is a point that has been disputed in the past by some historians, most notably Fitzpatrick, who has argued that leadership figures were not indispensable and could easily be replaced.[74] Yet in the context of six-county Ulster – now Northern Ireland – this was not necessarily the case. Support for the republican movement was limited amongst the nationalist population, and the pool of active IRA volunteers was remarkably small. Without Aiken, and the handful of dedicated officers that surrounded him – most notably, perhaps, John McCoy and Seán Quinn – it is unlikely that the region would have experienced the levels of republican activity that it did in 1921. It was their initiative that fuelled the local campaign, and they were responsible for the planning and execution of the vast majority of the IRA attacks in the area. In this they were no different to those other tiny IRA elites in other parts of the embryonic Northern Irish state, whose commitment and ability was often the deciding factor in the IRA's success or failure at a local level.[75]

One of the more significant features of the escalating violence that occurred throughout Ireland in the first six months of 1921 was the rising civilian death toll. As Eunan O'Halpin has observed, the proportion of civilian deaths during the conflict increased from 39 per cent in 1920 to 45 per cent in 1921.[76] Events in Armagh and south Down conformed to this national pattern. Between

January 1919 and July 1921, a total of 10 civilians were killed as a result of conflict related violence in the region. All but two of these deaths occurred in the first six months of 1921.[77] At least two of the victims – along with numerous wounded – were the largely unintended casualties of the IRA and the USC as they recklessly went about their respective operations in the area. In January, Patrick Kirke, a 23 year old postman, was killed near Cullyhanna when an ambush party under Aiken's command attacked the USC escort that accompanied him.[78] Shortly before the truce in July, Teresa McAnuff, a 30 year old schoolmistress on a brief visit home, was accidently shot dead when a party of USC constables crowded into her mother's house and compelled her brother to sign a spurious declaration to the effect that he would not engage in attacks on the police.[79] Most often, however, civilian deaths in the region resulted from one of two relatively recent developments in the conflict. The first was a gradually escalating cycle of reprisal and counter-reprisal pursued by members of the IRA and USC. The second was the IRA's increasingly aggressive attitude towards suspected informers.

Given the political and religious geography of the Armagh and south Down area, it was always a likelihood that the IRA would come into conflict with the (predominantly Protestant) unionist population. As local IRA officers were often keen to point out, the presence of this large and hostile community acted as a severe constraint on republican operations. In April 1921, for example, the Kilkeel Battalion complained that 'owing to the fact that there are so many unionists in this district, it is hard to carry out an ambush.'[80] An officer of the Lurgan Battalion, meanwhile, later attributed the lack of IRA activity in his district to the 'large unionist and antagonistic population.'[81] These were not mere excuses, though leaders at GHQ often treated them as such. Unlike the unionist minority in southern Ireland, which could offer little opposition to the IRA and could easily be intimidated into quiescence, unionists in Ulster clearly had the potential to offer an effective resistance. They had strength in numbers, competent leadership, the dormant paramilitary structures and networks of the UVF through which to organise, and access to an arsenal that far exceeded that of their republican counterparts.

It was hardly surprising, therefore, that militant republican activity should inspire the creation of armed unionist patrols, which emerged in some districts as early as April 1920.[82] The formation of these bands was, for the most part, a defensive reflex in response to IRA arms raids, the most significant of which in 1919 had struck at targets that symbolised some of the most important elements of the Protestant establishment: the Church of Ireland, the Orange Order, and prominent members of the unionist elite. It mattered little that republicans may not actually have been involved in the shooting of Reverend Foy, or that the raids carried no obvious sectarian intent. As Wilson has convincingly argued, what really mattered was that they could be understood in sectarian terms.[83] Meanwhile, the numerous smaller scale raids on private homes (both unionist and nationalist), which continued throughout 1920, ensured that the perceived threat extended across a much wider section of the population than was actually ever directly affected by such activity.

Although these patrols did not become particularly active until the autumn of 1920, and then all but disappeared with the creation of the USC in November, their existence had an immediate effect on IRA decision making. John McCoy later claimed that the decision to attack Newtownhamilton Barracks in May 1920 was partly influenced by the alleged presence of armed 'Ulster Volunteers' in the district, and a concern that in-fighting amongst local nationalists had distracted their attention from the threat posed by the unionist majority. This was combined with residual ill-feeling from clashes between republicans and unionists in the district during the 1918 by-election, as a result of which 'it was considered advisable to give them [local unionists] a chance to prove their mettle when up against a serious local attack on what they had sworn to defend.'[84] Suspected loyalist volunteers also became a target for further arms raids, the most significant of which occurred in September 1920 as part of a nationwide effort co-ordinated by the republican leadership in Dublin.[85]

This belligerent attitude towards the prospect of armed confrontation with local unionists was curbed somewhat when various events, both local and national, demonstrated the potential consequences of such confrontation. In June 1920, an armed unionist patrol successfully repulsed an attempted IRA arson attack at Lisbellaw, in nearby Co. Fermanagh. At least one IRA volunteer was wounded, but more importantly the authorities took no action against the unionist patrol for its vigilante action.[86] Closer to home, in Kilkeel, local unionists also succeeded in thwarting an attempted IRA arson attack in October, though in this case there were no resulting casualties.[87]

More significantly, however, in July and August 1920, mob attacks and workplace expulsions targeting members of the Catholic-nationalist community in Belfast, Banbridge and Lisburn had demonstrated the devastating potential of reprisal violence arising from IRA operations. These events were sparked by the IRA's assassinations of Lieutenant-Colonel Gerard Smyth, a Banbridge native, in Cork, and District Inspector Oswald Swanzy in Lisburn. The violence in Banbridge had a particular effect on local republicans. The town fell within the operational area of the Newry Brigade and one of the main targets for loyalist aggression was the family of a prominent local IRA officer.[88] The riots were also witnessed first-hand by Aiken and John McCoy when they inadvertently stumbled into the chaos whilst returning home from a battalion meeting in Lurgan.[89]

Organised unionist resistance, and the threat of retaliatory violence, had mixed results in terms of their impact on IRA violence. Local units did begin to confine their operations to those districts with a pronounced republican presence, where there was less threat of interference or reprisals; in particular Newry and the adjacent districts of south Armagh, the Armagh-Monaghan border at Keady, and Armagh city.[90] Yet they ultimately remained indifferent to the largely unintended sectarian significance of many of their actions. In 1921, for example, volunteers in Mullaghbawn burned down a vacant rectory on the suspicion that it was to be commandeered for the use of the army.[91] Attacks and raids on Orange halls, which in many districts served as meeting places and equipment stores for the USC's part-time reservists (the B Specials), also became common as the conflict progressed.[92] Occurring alongside sporadic (though unattributable) acts of vandalism, such as the defacement of a gate post outside Armagh's Church of Ireland cathedral,[93] it is easy to see why such incidents were construed as simple acts of bigotry or religious intolerance.

Prior to 1921, the Newry Brigade avoided engaging in reprisals against the unionist community, though a horrendous arson attack on a department store in nearby Dundalk in August 1920, which claimed the lives of three Protestant shop staff, demonstrated the awful potential for such violence.[94] Local republicans generally viewed themselves as being above petty sectarianism, which in their minds was a trait of constitutional nationalism. John McCoy, for example, decried the AOH for being 'sectarian and anti-Protestant in its policy.'[95] A similar attitude has been observed in IRA units elsewhere in Ulster, particularly in Belfast, where local officers attempted to remain aloof from the sectarian violence in the city during the summer of 1920.[96]

The situation began to change in late December 1920, with the arrival of the USC. As has already been shown, members of this force began to carry out their own reprisals in response to IRA activity. This initially manifested in the destruction of republican property, but very quickly escalated to include the execution of republican suspects during late night raids. The shootings of Smyth and Mackin at Beleek in the aftermath of the Camlough Barracks attack had set the precedent, but in all, nine republican suspects were killed in such circumstances in Newry and south Armagh alone between December 1920 and July 1921. Although evidence is often sketchy, the majority of these shootings appear to have been carried out by members of the USC – perhaps in conjunction with RIC comrades or other elements within the local unionist population – who usually did little to hide their involvement. As Wilson has observed, 'a striking feature of the loyalist death squads that arose in the [USC] is the confidence with which they carried out their operations.' Most often in uniform, on many occasions leaving female witnesses, and then dumping the bodies on the roadside to be found by the public, they did little to hide their involvement.[97]

Although there is nothing to suggest that such shootings were a result of an official clandestine policy, it does seem clear that there were no active attempts to discipline those involved or to curtail their activities. USC constables were arrested and court-martialled during the period for a number of offences, including assault, but there were no prosecutions for the apparently unlawful killings of suspects, even when witnesses could identify those involved.[98]

Initially, the IRA's response to such reprisals was to step up their attacks on members of the USC, in much the same way that Aiken had responded to the burning of his home with an ambush on a USC patrol.[99] The guiding logic was simple enough. Members of the USC were responsible for attacks on republicans, thus the force as a whole was liable for republican retribution. Its communal identity, as a thoroughly unionist, and primarily Protestant organisation, was not necessarily a factor at this early stage. Nevertheless, it surely could not have escaped the attention of Aiken and other local leaders that attacks on members of the USC would, in Wilson's words, 'be perceived by Protestants as an assault on a fellow Protestant.'[100]

Before long, however, IRA reprisals began to radicalise, mimicking the practices of the police and military, and drawing on precedents established by IRA units elsewhere in the country. This was strikingly demonstrated by an attack at Killylea, near Armagh city, in April 1921, the wider context of which is worth recounting in detail as a representative example of how such events could develop. On 10 April 1921, the IRA ambushed a group of USC constables in Creggan, close to the Armagh-Louth border. The attack took place on a Sunday morning, as the constables made their way to church. In making their preparations the ambush party rounded up local church-goers, both Catholic and Protestant, who were held under armed guard at a nearby pub to ensure that there would be no interference, an aspect of the event that has since been misconstrued as a sectarian hostage-taking of a Protestant congregation. It is also often assumed – wrongly – that Aiken was in command of the operation.[101] During the subsequent attack, one constable was killed and another, named Hans Leeman, was seriously wounded.[102] The incident provoked a reprisal in Leeman's home village of Killylea, some thirty miles away on the outskirts of Armagh city. The homes of two local nationalists were burned, and one of the householders was seriously wounded by gunfire. Neither man was linked to the republican movement. Indeed, as members of the AOH it is likely that they were antagonistic to both Sinn Féin and the IRA. Significantly, however, the republicans and the nationalists were co-operating at this time as an anti-partition panel in the upcoming general election (discussed in more detail below). Perhaps out of solidarity, therefore, the IRA carried out a counter-reprisal in the area. The homes of two local unionists were burned. Both victims had connections to the USC; one was a B Special, the other was Leeman's

father. There is some evidence to suggest that the IRA reprisal party was
under orders to kill the two men, but decided not to when they provided
information on those responsible for the earlier attacks on nationalists in the
area. An Orange hall was also set on fire during the reprisal, as was a quantity
of hay and straw at the neighbouring Protestant farm.[103]

Such cycles of reprisal and counter-reprisal were a common feature of the
conflict in the border counties of Ulster. McGarry, for example, has noted a
similar tendency in Monaghan, and the border areas of neighbouring Tyrone.[104]
They were also not uncommon elsewhere in Ireland. As Hart has observed in
Cork, for instance, 'what at first appears as an indistinguishable welter of
shootings, bombings, and house burnings can in many cases be broken down
into sequences of interlocking reprisals.'[105] In Armagh and south Down, such
sequences can be readily identified in early 1921, and then again in early 1922,
and typically consisted of between two and four events before they petered out
or were superseded by a fresh sequence. This supports Augusteijn's assertion
that the 'continuous escalation' of such cycles of violence ultimately had a
'short natural life span'.[106]

The escalation of IRA reprisals in the region owed much to Aiken's own
radicalisation on the issue. This was due, in large part, to his involvement in
an IRA reprisal at Rosslea, Co. Tyrone, in March 1921. This GHQ-sanctioned
operation was a response to USC attacks on nationalist homes in the village
after the IRA attempted to kill a local unionist. It was ordered by Eoin
O'Duffy and ultimately resulted in the burning of 14 houses and the killings of
three unionists, two of whom were USC constables.[107] It is unclear if Aiken,
or any of his men, actually participated in the reprisals, but he did attend the
meeting at which they were planned. As John T. Connolly, captain of the
Rosslea Company, later recalled,

> Frank Aiken did not at first approve of the burnings, as he thought the B. men
> would retaliate by burning double the number of nationalist houses. O'Duffy
> struck the table and said: 'when you hit them hard they will not strike again.' Aiken
> then said: 'well, burn them and their houses'.[108]

The timing of the Killylea operation would suggest that it was influenced by
Aiken's adoption of this harder line on the issue of reprisals. It is also notable
that in early April there were reports that a number of prominent Newry
unionists had received threats, purporting to be from the IRA, notifying them
that they would be targeted as reprisals for any attacks on republicans.[109]

No further reprisals of the kind witnessed at Killylea occurred locally prior
to the announcement of the truce on 11 July 1921. On the penultimate day of
hostilities, however, the IRA did carry out its first retaliatory killing of a

civilian. The victim was a Protestant railway worker named Draper Holmes, and his death ultimately served as a reprisal for the killings of four IRA men who had been rounded up and shot by the USC during late night raids in the townlands of Altnaveigh and Lisdrumliska a week earlier.[110] Holmes was apparently not the IRA's intended target. Rather, he had stumbled upon the reprisal party as they waited for a group of suspected off-duty B Specials who worked with him, and was killed in a frantic and panicked attempt to keep him from warning his unsuspecting colleagues. This ultimately failed, and the IRA ambush party hurriedly made off.[111] Nevertheless, Holmes's death was subsequently rationalised to fit the purpose using a logic of – what Frank Wright has termed – 'representative violence', where 'anyone of a great number of people can be "punished" for the something done by the community they come from'.[112] As one of his killers explained in later years, Holmes 'suffered not for anything he himself had done but for a deadly danger to the lives and freedom of our companions in arms which men of his class represented.' Little regret was expressed, aside from the fact that the incident had left 'our score on the losing side.'[113] There were no attempts to downplay IRA responsibility, and there is no indication that the incident raised any significant internal criticism. As such, it set a dangerous precedent.

Reprisal attacks against members of the unionist community were not the only form of IRA violence through which civilians were targeted. In the final six months of the war for independence the first executions of suspected informers also occurred in the region. Before 1921, the Newry Brigade had taken action against at least two alleged informers, and in both instances it had avoided using the death penalty. The first instance involved a postman named Francis Lappin from Mullaghbawn. He was accused of giving information to the police regarding an arms raid in the area in the autumn of 1920. This had allegedly led to the arrests of a number of local volunteers, among them John McCoy, who was briefly gaoled for his part in the incident. As a result, Lappin was abducted and brought to Camlough where he was tried by an IRA court and banished from the area. Although there is no firm evidence, it is likely that Aiken was responsible for Lappin's expulsion, particularly given the location of the trial and the fact that members of the Camlough Company, including McElhaw, were involved in guarding the accused while he was in their custody.[114] The second instance was a more peculiar affair involving a woman who arrived in Armagh claiming to be the mother of the Tipperary IRA leader Dan Breen. Having made contact with local republican sympathisers, she attempted to organise a meeting with Aiken. Suspicious of her actions, the IRA made various enquiries, and apparently discovered that she was actually a recently released convict named Rafferty who, it was alleged, was sent to Armagh to carry out intelligence work. The matter was reported to Aiken who ordered that she be confronted with the evidence and banished from the area.[115]

In the first six months of 1921, however, a more extreme attitude towards alleged informers developed. This was a nationwide trend and reflected the increasing intensity of the conflict from late 1920 onwards. As Augusteijn has observed, 'the more serious fighting that developed at the end of 1920 made informing increasingly life threatening to volunteers.'[116] It is also frequently observed that in 1921 the authorities began to enjoy much greater success in terms of intelligence.[117] These developments can readily be observed in Armagh and south Down during this period. Not only were the USC killing republican suspects, they were demonstrating a remarkable degree of accuracy in their selection of targets. Of the nine victims of such shootings in Newry and south Armagh there is evidence to plausibly suggest that as many as seven were members of the IRA.[118] Furthermore, even those occasions when civilians were killed tended to follow on from unsuccessful attempts to abduct known republicans. The murder of William Hickey is a case in point. Hickey, a Catholic shop manager with no confirmed connection to the republican movement, was abducted and killed in Newry in early July 1921. It was later alleged that he had been mutilated, and possibly dragged for some distance behind a lorry prior to being shot. On the night of his disappearance, those responsible appear to have first unsuccessfully raided the homes of two known republicans; Robert Kelly and Edward Fullerton.[119] Indeed, the IRA suffered the highest number of fatalities of any group in Armagh and south Down during the war for independence period; 16 in all, in contrast to ten civilians and nine policemen (RIC or USC).[120] Furthermore, in April 1921, the authorities had scored a significant success when John McCoy was once again arrested after being very seriously wounded during police searches in Mullaghbawn.[121] The utilisation of local unionists as a paramilitary police force had not only brought an increased brutality to the fight against the IRA, it had also clearly improved the quality of local intelligence.

Before the truce, two alleged informers were executed in Armagh and south Down. Both killings occurred in the Camlough area in the early hours of 7 June 1921. The victims, Hugh O'Hanlon and James Smyth, were taken from their homes, shot dead and pinned with notices stating that they were informers. Both men were members of the AOH, and the RIC could later report that they had been 'most loyal subjects and on account of their friendly relationship with the police were the recipients of threatening letters to which they paid no attention.'[122] Various, more specific, accusations surfaced for O'Hanlon's execution. It was believed that he provided the police with information leading to the capture of John McCoy in April 1921. It was also claimed that he had given the authorities advance warning of the Camlough Barracks attack in December 1920. Press reports, meanwhile, suggested that the RIC had permitted him to carry a gun for self-protection.[123] The allegations against the second victim, Smyth, are less clear, though he may have been suspected of providing information to the police that had resulted in the killing of another IRA man, Sean Doran, at Keggal in January 1921.[124]

There is very little evidence as to how these executions were ordered and authorised. From 20 April 1921, brigade commandants were empowered to carry out a death sentence on suspected informers without the sanction of GHQ, so it is likely the decision was taken locally.[125] It is also likely that Aiken was involved. Although there is no evidence to directly link him to the executions, it is highly unlikely that they occurred without his sanction. His prominent role in earlier actions against alleged informers in the region testifies to this. His power and status in the organisation, particularly in the Camlough district, also make it difficult to conceive that they were carried out without his knowledge.

There has been much debate regarding the IRA's targeting of alleged informers. In his seminal study of Cork, Hart has argued that allegations of informing were often little more than thinly veiled excuses to target minority elements and individuals viewed as outsiders. This view rests on the fact that a disproportionately high number of those killed throughout the country were Protestants, ex-servicemen or other perceived 'undesirables' such as travellers or the mentally handicapped.[126] Hart's analysis has proven controversial, and his findings have been rigorously challenged, most notably by Borgonovo.[127] Yet for all the heated discussion over the minutiae of individual cases, there is a degree of consensus that social outsiders were more likely to be executed as informers by the IRA. The disagreement comes in regards to whether such individuals were targeted because of their outsider status or whether this simply made them more susceptible to receiving the death penalty for allegations of informing. The implication being that such sentences might not have been so readily passed on men or women with social or familial connections to the republican movement.[128]

This theme is of relevance in the discussion of the executions of O'Hanlon and Smyth as both victims were members of the constitutional nationalist AOH, which with a membership of 5,031 in April 1921 remained the second largest organisation in Armagh and Down after the UIL.[129] As Wilson has observed, the IRA killed as many as nine members of the organisation in the province between 1918 and 1922.[130] Many of the victims were executed for allegations of informing. In Monaghan, for example, McGarry has noted that the IRA executed three Hibernians for such offences during the war for independence years.[131] The continued strength of constitutional nationalism in Ulster had created much bad blood between republicans and the AOH and it might be suggested that the IRA's targeting of Hibernians was a result of this antagonism.

In Armagh and south Down there was certainly evidence of conflict between republicans and constitutional nationalists. This was most obvious during the South Armagh by-election in 1918 when, as has already been observed, there had been numerous factional affrays. These tensions had persisted after the elections, despite the occasional unity such as that achieved in opposition to conscription. There had been occasional violence, notably a republican mob attack on the home of a local nationalist politician amid rowdy celebrations of Arthur Griffith's victory in the East Cavan by-election in late June 1918.[132] The continuing ill-feeling between the two groups was also colourfully illustrated the following October when members of the AOH accused Sinn Féin supporters of poisoning wells in south Armagh.[133]

Locally, there was little further escalation in this conflict between republicans and constitutional nationalists in 1919 or 1920. There is some evidence to suggest, however, that these past antagonisms helped shape the IRA's suspicions regarding informers. John 'Ned' Quinn, a member of the Mullaghbawn Company, later recalled two cases in particular; that of Francis Lappin, the aforementioned postman, and another regarding a local woman named Susie Pyers. The specific allegations that surfaced about Lappin have already been detailed.[134] Those against Pyers appear to have centred on the fact that she was friendly with the RIC, and the suspicion that she may have provided them with information about a group of volunteers that attacked two constables outside Camlough in July 1919. Significantly, however, both Lappin and Pyers had first come to the attention of local republicans during the by-election in 1918, when they had been among a crowd that had attacked a republican convoy, and had apparently been viewed with suspicion ever since.[135] Indeed, Quinn's testimony seems to suggest that allegations of informing were most likely to befall those local nationalists who were forthright in their opposition to either Sinn Féin or the IRA – though whether or not these individuals were actually any more likely to pass information to the police is difficult to substantiate. Furthermore, although evidence of IRA intelligence gathering in the area is decidedly sketchy, basic operational policy on the matter apparently did little to curb the influence of such bias. A rare divisional order on intelligence from late June 1921, for instance, asked that 'a list of all persons suspected of spying shall be kept and their movements closely watched and noted.' Yet there was little indication of how such suspects should be determined, or what type of evidence would be considered sufficient proof of guilt.[136]

The fact that O'Hanlon and Smyth were members of the AOH may have contributed to the belief that they were informers, though the RIC's remarks clearly suggest that the IRA's suspicions may not have been unwarranted. The obvious divisions between constitutional nationalists and republicans may also have influenced the decision to carry out the extreme sentence of execution. Yet this should not be overstated. As Wilson has observed, in highlighting the extent of intra-nationalist conflict in Ulster, historians are 'in danger of obscuring the degree to which rank and file Hibernians and the IRA continued to overlap as products of the same Catholic sub-culture.'[137] Although it is tempting to think of the IRA's executions of Hibernians as another example of the targeting of outsider elements, the truth of the situation was not always so simple. In Monaghan, for example, McGarry has noted that some republicans showed considerable opposition to the execution of certain Hibernians, and that the killings that did occur 'divided the local community for decades'.[138] In the cases of O'Hanlon and Smyth, it must be remembered that both men were as deeply rooted in the close-knit Catholic community of south Armagh as any local republican. Indeed, it is telling that O'Hanlon's body was lifted from the road and prepared for burial by John Cosgrave, a well-known local republican whose wife was O'Hanlon's cousin.

In a somewhat mysterious sequel to the executions, Cosgrave was himself shot a week later, though by whom remains unclear. At the inquest into his death it was claimed that he had been killed by the IRA for his act of kindness in preparing O'Hanlon's body.[139] Other rumours circulated to the effect that he had been killed by Protestant neighbours as part of a land dispute. Yet another theory suggests that he was shot as a reprisal for the earlier executions, possibly by members of the AOH.[140] The latter is perhaps the most likely. Certainly the RIC's original conclusion was that he was killed in retaliation for the deaths of O'Hanlon and Smyth, and this is further suggested by the fact that those responsible appear to have unsuccessfully raided the home of another local republican that same night.[141] Nevertheless, Cosgrave's death is a sobering reminder of just how elusive the truth behind such killings can often be.

PARTITION

Though the escalating violence of early 1921 was broadly in keeping with national events, in Ulster it took place in the somewhat unique provincial context of partition. Severely underestimating the depth of the discontent in Ireland, and assuming that the majority of the population would accept a settlement falling far short of independence, the British government pushed ahead with a policy of home rule tempered by the exclusion of six counties. The result was the Government of Ireland Act, which became law on 23 December 1920. Dividing Ireland into two self-governing entities – Northern Ireland and Southern Ireland – the measure was, in Townshend's estimation, an admission of Britain's 'inability either to find a way through the impasse created by unionist resistance or to give shape to the proposed devolution'.[142]

Remarkably, perhaps, given the mobilising power of the issue of exclusion in the years 1916-18, and the Government of Ireland Act's slow progress through the legislative process during 1920 (it was first introduced into the commons on 25 February), the looming threat of partition appears to have had little influence on republican activity in Armagh and south Down. As Phoenix has observed, this corresponded with a more general conviction amongst the broader northern nationalist population that the proposals 'had little chance of being implemented and, even if they were, would be "foredoomed to rejection".'[143] For republicans in particular, Sinn Féin's landslide election victory in 1918 was viewed as an exercise in self-determination that superseded home rule, and with it, presumably, the whole issue of partition. The movement remained blind to the obvious ethno-religious limitations of its appeal and continued to emphasise, in Laffan's words, 'a geographic rather than a historic or confessional image of the community or the nation.'[144] The poor result in Ulster was dismissed as an irrelevance and, as has already been observed, some local republicans consoled themselves in the belief that Sinn Féin would have performed better had it not been for the electoral pact with the Irish Party.[145]

As a result of this complacency, the first republican initiative aimed at counter-acting the threat of partition did not emerge until August 1920 when the Dáil enacted the Belfast boycott. Introduced at the behest of a number of prominent Belfast republicans, among them Aiken's future Fianna Fáil colleague, Seán McEntee, the boycott was initially intended as a response to the expulsion of Catholic workers from the Belfast shipyards in the summer of 1920. Yet its potential as a means of combating partition was also clearly envisaged, in the belief that the economic pressure exerted by the boycott would demonstrate to northern unionists the importance of the southern market for their continued prosperity and thus the need for Ireland's continued unity.[146] In pursuing the policy, suppliers and consumers alike were encouraged (sometimes through intimidation) to boycott Belfast goods, and to avoid doing business with Belfast based financial institutions, such as banks and insurance companies. The IRA, meanwhile, actively sought out such businesses for direct acts of sabotage and destruction.

Despite the reservations of some Sinn Féin figures – notably the Ulster Protestant Ernest Blythe – the majority of northern republicans, and the IRA in particular, wholeheartedly supported the boycott initiative. This was particularly true in Armagh and south Down where Aiken and his fellow officers enthusiastically pursued the policy between August 1920 and July 1921, and then again in early 1922. Although there is no record of Aiken's own views, they likely corresponded with those of his adjutant, John McCoy, who later stated his belief that it was the republicans' 'strongest weapon [. . .] against British interests in Ireland', and contended that its value in dealing with northern unionism 'could only be appreciated by people living on the spot in Northern Ireland.'[147] Consequently, boycott related activity became relatively common in the region, usually taking the form of arson attacks on bread vans delivering for Belfast bakeries. At least 16 such incidents occurred prior to the truce, and they proved particularly popular in unionist dominated areas where operations of a more ambitious nature were difficult to stage. In Lurgan, for example, J. J. Murray recalled that the boycott was one of the few feasible activities open to his local IRA battalion. As a result, its members not only engaged in attacks on bread vans, but also played a prominent part in canvassing and intimidating local traders to ensure their compliance.[148]

Lynch has argued that the enthusiastic support for the boycott amongst northern republicans displayed the degree to which many were desperate for 'some kind of southern lead' in their efforts to fight partition.[149] This paralysis within the local movement was certainly suggested by its reaction – or, more accurately, its lack of reaction – to the Government of Ireland Act when it finally passed in December 1920. In Armagh and south Down, for instance, the event generated virtually no independent initiatives within either Sinn Féin or the IRA. Although the RIC in Armagh could report that the act had incited 'bitter party feeling', this was not expressed in any meaningful way.[150] There were no protest meetings, strikes or symbolic acts of violence. There is also little to suggest that the timing or motivation of the most significant operation to occur in the region that month, the Camlough Barracks attack, was in any way related to the event.

Nevertheless, the changed situation from December 1920 onwards may have had some influence on the way in which Aiken and his fellow officers viewed the utility of their violent actions. In the aftermath of the Camlough Barracks attack Aiken and his officers began to realise that even those operations that were unsuccessful in the military sense could prove valuable in that they challenged the notion of unionist hegemony and control within Northern Ireland. According to John McCoy, the attacks at Camlough and the Egyptian Arch, though disastrous, were nonetheless a minor success 'in the fact that such elaborate plans should be attempted in an area where British propaganda claimed that loyalty to the empire was an undeniable fact.'[151] Indeed, it seems plausible that the increased frequency of violent attacks in the first six months of 1921 – and the greater appreciation of smaller-scale operations – were influenced by this logic.

Partition may also have influenced GHQ's decision to select Ulster as one of the first provinces to undergo the process of divisionalisation in early 1921. This organisational restructuring was driven by a number of factors. For GHQ, the primary concern was security. With the authorities scoring greater successes against the IRA, particularly in terms of intelligence, it was now thought desirable to delegate a number of functions to regional divisional commandants and thus have fewer units coming into direct contact with the leadership in Dublin.[152] In revolutionary hotspots such as Munster, meanwhile, it was hoped that divisionalisation would facilitate a greater level of co-operation between brigade areas.[153] In Ulster, however, reorganisation along divisional lines was pursued for other reasons. As one GHQ officer later recalled, divisionalisation in the north was undertaken to 'enable local volunteers to tackle their special problems in a more comprehensive way', and to allow GHQ 'to keep in better touch by reason of having fewer units to deal with.'[154] 'Special problems' was presumably a reference to the new situation created by partition, as well as the longer standing difficulties posed by the hostility of the local unionist population.

Divisionalisation is often considered as a turning point for the IRA in Ulster. Lynch, for example, has described the development as having 'signalled the birth of the northern IRA', and observes that it was widely welcomed by local units as a 'sign that GHQ was at last acting positively in prioritising northern issues.'[155] Augusteijn has similarly viewed divisionalisation as the 'main expression of GHQ's growing involvement in northern units', something which he observes only began late in the conflict.[156] For many Ulster units, in areas such as Antrim, Derry and Belfast, this was undoubtedly true. Yet for the Newry Brigade the situation was somewhat different, and it is doubtful that the restructuring had any significant transformative effect.

The common generalisations concerning the state of IRA units in Ulster at this time – that they were disorganised, inactive and out of touch with GHQ – did not really apply to the Newry Brigade. The unit's relations with GHQ were relatively strong. Aiken and Rankin had already forged close ties with the Dublin leadership in 1918, prior to the unit's creation. Effective lines of communication were also well established throughout the period 1918-20. In addition to surviving correspondence between Rankin and Collins, there is also plentiful anecdotal evidence to suggest this. Aiken's sister, Nano, for instance, frequently carried dispatches between Newry and Dublin throughout the period.[157] Aiken and McCoy regularly visited the capital to meet with senior IRA figures.[158] The chief-of-staff, Richard Mulcahy, also appears to have visited Newry at least once in 1919 on IRA business.[159] These connections with GHQ were further strengthened through two local medical students who became active in the Dublin IRA, Padraig Quinn and Mick O'Hanlon. The former was a brother of Seán Quinn, the Newry Brigade's quartermaster. The latter was John McCoy's cousin and a close acquaintance of Aiken. He also played an active part in local operations when at home in Mullaghbawn during the holidays.[160]

Before divisionalisation, GHQ also clearly enjoyed a considerable level of influence over the Newry Brigade, and frequently instigated activity in the region. It had prompted the Ballyedmond arms raid and contributed significantly to its planning and implementation.[161] The wave of arson attacks that occurred in the region in April 1920 was the result of a GHQ order instigating such activity across the country.[162] It is also likely that the Dublin leadership ordered the kidnapping of an RIC man in Armagh in July 1920 in order to disrupt a murder trial relating to the Knocklong ambush in Limerick.[163] The constable was abducted on the evening before the trial and held captive long enough to ensure its adjournment until the next assizes.[164] Furthermore, in addition to directly instigating activity, GHQ was clearly in a position to influence operations conceived locally, such as the Camlough Barracks attack, the plans for which were adjusted on the advice of Peadar Clancy.[165]

In addition, GHQ was apparently quite content with the Newry Brigade's performance before 1921, despite its relatively low levels of activity when compared to some southern units. This was, perhaps, a reflection of the prevailing attitude within both Sinn Féin and the IRA that there was little likelihood of fighting the British to a standstill in Ulster.[166] Yet, it was also an indication of the genuine confidence that the Dublin leadership had in the brigade and its officers. Indeed, this was further demonstrated by the decision to place north Louth under its command in the winter of 1920–21. The latter area had fallen into a state of inactivity and disorganisation during 1920 following the imprisonment of a number of local officers. It was hoped that its absorption by the Newry Brigade might assist in the rejuvenation of the organisation there, and stimulate greater levels of activity. Aside from an attempted ambush at Plaster in early January 1921, however, little progress was achieved on this front prior to the truce.[167]

Divisionalisation offered little prospect of improving the Newry Brigade's already cordial and productive relationship with GHQ. It also did little to assist local officers with the 'special problems' that they faced in Northern Ireland. Contrary to Lynch's assertions regarding six-county Ulster in general, the reorganisation prompted by divisionalisation had no discernable effect on the levels of IRA activity in Armagh and south Down. As already shown, the escalation of violence in the area was driven by factors that predated the initiative.[168] Furthermore, although GHQ did use the opportunity presented by divisionalisation to address the local military situation in each new divisional area, its thinking was far from practical. A strategy document produced for the Fourth Northern Division in April 1921, for instance, spoke of the unit in grandiose terms as the 'spear point' for any general offensive in the six counties.[169] Such notions were far from the realities of the small-scale guerrilla campaign being fought by Aiken and his officers, and ultimately had little influence on their operations prior to the truce.

For the Newry Brigade, therefore, divisionalisation meant little more than a change in title, and the final confirmation of Aiken's displacement of Patrick Rankin as the unit's top ranking officer. This had been a somewhat convoluted process. In April 1920, Rankin had been arrested and briefly imprisoned, and Aiken (as vice-commandant) had dutifully assumed responsibility for the Newry Brigade in his absence. During his incarceration, Rankin was transferred to Wormwood Scrubbs Prison in London and went on hunger strike. After a few weeks, he and a number of other prisoners were admitted to St James Infirmary in Clapham. Here, he apparently managed to obtain a pass for a day's leave to explore the city and simply never returned.[170] He resumed duty in Newry on 17 May 1920. In the six months that followed, however, Rankin appears to have been gradually side-lined by Aiken. The latter had always had a considerable influence in the brigade. Indeed, his relationship with Rankin had often carried the appearance of an equal partnership. Aiken was subsequently promoted to the rank of brigade commandant in October 1920. This was followed in January with his appointment as an Inspection Officer, most likely as part of the process surrounding divisionalisation. Finally, in March 1921, he became divisional commandant of the Fourth Northern Division. Rankin, meanwhile, played no further role in the conflict.[171]

The reasons for Rankin's removal as leader are somewhat vague. John McCoy later claimed that 'Rankin lost his nerves for he wasn't fit' and as a result 'Frank replaced him'.[172] In a similar vein, though the substance of his comments have been redacted from his Bureau of Military History witness statement, Patrick Casey recalled that after returning home from prison Rankin 'had to be escorted from one hiding place to another' by an armed volunteer guard. 'On the formation of divisions', he continued, 'Aiken took over and I cannot recall what happened to Rankin. He just seemed to fade out.'[173] These remarks can be read in one of two ways; either as a comment on Rankin's mental health, or an indication that he was perceived as being too cautious in his approach to the IRA campaign. The former is surely a possibility. The timing, for instance, might suggest that he suffered some kind of nervous breakdown as a consequence of his participation in the hunger strike at Wormwood Scrubbs. Yet the latter is equally likely. Certainly, in a movement that glorified violence and emphasised the supremacy of the 'fighting man', such perceptions would have been reason enough for his removal.[174]

There is good reason to suspect that Rankin was a victim of generational tensions that surfaced within the movement at this time. As one Armagh volunteer later recalled, there was 'a tendency amongst the younger men to get rid of the IRB influence in the Volunteer organisation' as the conflict progressed. This was apparently a result of the younger men's frustration with the cautious attitudes of the older IRB men 'which tended to restrict the younger generation from undertaking any of the activities that most of the young men who had recently joined the volunteers wished to take part in.'[175] This certainly described Rankin. As Magennis has noted, some younger officers later indicated that he had acted as a brake on violence.[176] He was, moreover, seven years older than the average Newry Brigade volunteer, and very much associated with the elder generation of pre-1916 Newry separatists, alongside figures such as Robert Kelly, John Southwell, Peadar McCann and Patrick Lavery. It is also clear that in his role as commandant of the Newry Brigade he had made vigorous – even aggressive – attempts to promote the influence of the IRB. John McCoy, for example, later recalled that Rankin had not so subtly threatened him with demotion should he refuse to join the brotherhood, though he ultimately resisted such pressure due to his strongly held suspicion of secret societies.[177]

Significantly, Aiken appears to have had a good relationship with Rankin up until mid-1920. They had worked together closely throughout the preceding two-and-a-half years, and there is nothing to suggest an unpleasantness in the relationship. Unlike McCoy, Aiken seems to have shown no compunction in accepting Rankin's invitation to join the IRB. He appears to have been sworn into the brotherhood sometime in 1918 or 1919 – around the same time that McCoy was himself approached – and subsequently made good use of its networks to purchase arms in the winter of 1920–1.[178] Indeed there is good reason to suspect that Aiken's relationship with Rankin prior to April 1920 may have been the first of a series of decidedly deferential attachments that he formed with various superiors during the revolutionary period; similar to that which would emerge with Michael Collins in 1921–2 and, more significantly, with Eamon de Valera in 1923. The fact that he may have declined the position of brigade commandant when the unit first formed in the winter of 1918–19, certainly lends weight to this argument.

If Rankin was side-lined for his perceived cautiousness with regard to the armed struggle, the fact that Aiken replaced him was not particularly surprising. Not only was he held in high repute as an organiser, he had also earned a reputation as a 'fighting man'. Having taken charge of the majority of local operations since 1919, and having frequently performed the most dangerous operational tasks himself, he had created a favourable impression amongst his men. Recorded decades later, their Bureau of Military History statements are interspersed with various anecdotes that reinforce this view. How, for example, he had briefly entered Newtownhamilton Barracks during the attack in May

1920 and exchanged shots with one of the RIC garrison. How, in the immediate aftermath of the disastrous Camlough Barracks attack in December
1920, as reinforcements from Newry approached, he had remained behind to
carry out first aid on a wounded volunteer. Or how, during an ambush near
Cullyhanna in January 1921, he had covered the retreat of his men after
weapons malfunctions left him with the only working rifle.[179]

Aiken's willingness to place himself on the front line during IRA operations
was a reflection of his views on leadership. These were best summed up in a
letter to de Valera after the civil war: 'our army is a volunteer army. I have always
believed that its officers should show the example to those under them, that in a
fight they should take the most risk.'[180] Such an attitude was not necessarily
common. Aiken's behaviour contrasted greatly with that of his Monaghan IRA
colleague Eoin O'Duffy, for instance, who despite posturing as a 'man of action'
tended to avoid any direct involvement in violence himself.[181] Aiken's actions,
therefore, earned him a great deal of respect amongst his men. Joe Farrell, a
member of the Fourth Northern Division from Louth, later summed up the
sentiments of many who fought under him: 'he didn't send men out, he went
with them and he was looked up to by everybody.'[182]

Aiken undoubtedly commanded the respect of his men. Yet, while he was
often admired and venerated, he was rarely recalled with warmth or personal
affection. Unlike some revolutionary figures, most notably Michael Collins,
who amassed a loyal following through personal charm and the fostering
of close friendly relationships, Aiken was often distant and aloof.[183] Close
comrades most frequently remarked on his restrained and somewhat uncom-
municative manner. Padraig Quinn, for instance, described him as 'normally
reticent, even taciturn'.[184] This was often unsettling, particularly for those who
were not accustomed to his ways. On recounting his first meeting with Aiken
during the civil war, for instance, Todd Andrews recalled that his 'taciturnity
had totally disconcerted me. I had seen men in all sorts of moods, behaving in
all sorts of ways [...] but never anything that discommoded me like this
seemingly endless silence.'[185] Nevertheless, this austere, even intimidating
persona, may have added to his leadership appeal. It certainly added to his
overall image as a 'hard man'. His lack of emotion and seemingly imperturbable manner, moreover, suggested that he was well suited to the pressures of
military command.

Such considerations aside, however, Aiken's appointment was also a
reflection of the high regard with which he was held by GHQ. He appears to
have had a good personal relationship with figures such as Mulcahy and
Collins at this stage, and in return they clearly viewed him as a competent and
capable officer. Indeed, Seán Mac Eoin, leader of the IRA in Longford
during this period, later claimed that Aiken's promotion was primarily a result

of Collins's patronage, something that Aiken himself acknowledged to an extent.[186] Kevin O'Shiel also later indicated that Aiken was one of 'Collins's men'; perhaps the only six-counties man among a sub-grouping of provincial officers (and 'sworn members of the IRB') that formed an important part of Collins's extended entourage, and which could often be found crowding around him in the back room of Vaughan's Hotel, the popular Dublin IRA haunt.[187] Regardless of such influences in his appointment, however, it must also be acknowledged that Aiken faced no significant competition within the brigade and was arguably the only plausible candidate.

The local IRA's responses to partition prior to the truce were ultimately the result of initiatives determined in Dublin. Likewise, the only republican political activity to occur in the region – that surrounding the elections for the new northern parliament in April 1921 – was determined primarily by the decisions of the southern leadership. In contesting the election, the Sinn Féin leadership quickly decided to negotiate an election pact with Joseph Devlin and prospective northern nationalist candidates. They would join forces on an anti-partition platform of self-determination and abstention. Each party fielded 21 candidates and agreed to encourage their supporters to pass on their lower preference votes to their anti-partition allies.[188] As Lynch has observed, the majority of the republican candidates were southerners, with only one of the six successfully elected Sinn Féin MPs coming from an Ulster background. Michael Collins was nominated for Armagh, with Aiken as his running mate. In Down, meanwhile, de Valera was the main republican candidate alongside Newry man Patrick Lavery.

In Armagh, neither of the Sinn Féin candidates was available to make an active contribution and the burden of the republican campaigning fell upon a number of figures from outside the region, notably the Belfast republicans Desmond Creann and Seán MacEntee, and the republican Mayor of Drogheda, Phillip Monaghan.[189] The nationalist candidate, John Dillon Nugent, a native of Keady and perhaps the second most powerful figure in the AOH after Devlin, also addressed various meetings in the county and espoused the anti-partition position in accordance with the election pact.[190] Nationalist and republican rhetoric during the campaign was characterised by rather generalised statements against partition. At a meeting in Armagh, for example, Creann urged the voters to 'let the world know that Ireland refused to accept the nefarious Partition measure.'[191] Passionate denunciations of partition also appeared in the *Frontier Sentinel* which, in informing the voters of their 'duty' at the election, described the policy as both 'a crime against the Almighty from whom the physical and national unity of Ireland has proceeded' and 'a cruel outrage on those whose interests partition is supposed to serve.'[192] Indeed, only Nugent appears to have forwarded any practical arguments against the policy, remarking that it would be 'inimical to the interests of religion, and ruinous to the economic prosperity of the country.'[193]

The unionist campaign, meanwhile, revolved around a similar set of stock arguments in favour of partition, occasionally interspersed with scaremongering about republican tactics. On the day before the polls, for example, voters were warned by the unionist candidate, Richard Best, that 'a number of roads had been studded with large nails' in an effort to sabotage the motors carrying voters to and from the polls.[194] Much ridicule was also directed at the republicans for their absence from the campaigning. At one unionist meeting, for example, the speaker entertained the crowd in the following manner:

> Was Mr Collins or Aiken present at the nomination proceedings? (Laughter.) He was told that Mr Michael Collins was a 'banshee', and that there was no such man (loud laughter). He was a 'bogey' (renewed laughter). There was such a gentleman as Mr Aiken alright, but he did not think he was at his usual place of residence (laughter). About 150 police were searching for Mr Aiken over his native mountain the other day but could not find him (laughter).[195]

A similar tendency amongst the northern unionist press was commented upon by the *Irish Independent*, which suggested that such taunts were 'symptomatic of the mentality with which the Partitionists regard their opponents.'[196]

Polling took place on 24 May. While in Belfast and other parts of the six counties there were claims of violence and intimidation, all appears to have passed relatively peacefully in Armagh and south Down. Across the province the turnout was an impressively high 89 per cent.[197] The importance of the election was further highlighted in reports by the *Newry Telegraph* that 'many voters, old, decrepit, lame, blind and even sick unto death were conveyed to the various polling stations in traps and other vehicles.'[198] Personation by unionists, nationalists and republicans was also alleged to be rife, with the *Armagh Guardian* dryly remarking that 'the graveyards voted 100 per cent.'[199]

The result in Armagh was, in effect, a draw. Collins and Nugent were both successfully elected, alongside unionist candidates Richard Best and Major David Shillington. Aiken, meanwhile, was quickly eliminated after receiving only 1,301 first preference votes compared to Collins's 12,656 and Nugent's 6,857.[200] Similarly, in Down, de Valera was successfully elected for Sinn Féin but failed to carry his running mate, Patrick Lavery. Lynch has argued that the election highlighted the growing dominance of Sinn Féin in the six counties with republican candidates 'receiving over 20 per cent of the vote as compared to only 12 per cent for the nationalists.'[201] As Michael Laffan has observed, however, while many northern nationalists did give their first preferences to prominent republican leaders such as de Valera, Griffith and Collins they 'then deserted Sinn Féin and gave their second preferences to nationalist candidates who were local men.'[202] This was certainly the case in Armagh where Collins's second preference votes clearly went to Nugent, but this is not necessarily explained by the fact that the latter was a local figure. Aiken was, after all, also a native of Armagh. Rather, it is likely that Nugent's success reflected the residual loyalty of the majority of nationalists to the constitutionalist position at a time when it was increasingly felt that Sinn Féin could offer the greatest hope in the fight against partition.

Overall, however, the results in Northern Ireland were a disappointment for the anti-partition coalition. Sinn Féin and their nationalist allies won only six seats each. This was an exceptionally weak showing, considering the successful return of all 40 unionist candidates.[203] Republicans and nationalists were quick to contend that the result was due to unionist intimidation and gerrymandering, claims which held some truth.[204] Meanwhile, the *Frontier Sentinel*, in typical fashion, emphasised the all-Ireland result – taking into account the simultaneous elections for the new southern Irish parliament – as one repudiating partition. The 'partitionist' success in Ulster, it claimed, was 'merely an arithmetical one.'[205] Regardless of such attempts to ignore the strength of unionism in Ulster, however, there was little escaping the fact that the results were ultimately a poor argument against partition.

The remarkably low levels of local republican political activity in response to partition in late 1920 and 1921 are a reminder of the degree to which politics had been side-lined by the violence of the revolutionary campaign. Indeed, as Laffan has observed, amid the 'fear and repression' of the conflict 'there often seemed little for politicians and other civilians to do except keep their heads down and wait for the shooting to stop.'[206] By the time this finally happened, however, with the agreement of a truce on 11 July 1921, the IRA had become the dominant partner in the movement, and the situation in Armagh and south Down was no exception. This was, perhaps, best illustrated in a letter from Sean Milroy to the IRA chief-of-staff, Richard Mulcahy, in September 1921, in which he related that,

> I was informed by our organiser in Armagh that he experienced considerable difficulty in furthering the Organisation by reason of the general attitude of the Volunteers. It was not, as far as I could gather, instances of specific hostility, but rather an atmosphere of aloofness on the part of the Volunteers, and an implied attitude that the Sinn Fein clubs were not serving any useful purpose.[207]

Even in the midst of peace, Sinn Féin could not regain the initiative in the campaign for independence in Armagh and south Down.

These broad developments were reflected in Aiken's own journey during the two-and-a-half years of the war for independence. His dedication to both the political activism of Sinn Féin and the militancy of the IRA had proven unsustainable amid the escalating violence of the conflict. By December 1920, there had been little other option than to commit full-time to the armed struggle, and the personal implications of this turn of events had been considerable. Yet there is little reason to suspect that the resulting sacrifice, exhilaration and radicalisation of guerrilla life – or the hardened attitudes it evidently facilitated – had prompted in Aiken the same distaste or disrespect for political methods that was now exhibited by some of his IRA comrades. Indeed, this would ultimately be borne out by events in the two years that followed. For the moment, however, now that he was commander of the Fourth Northern Division, politics would have to remain a secondary consideration.

NOTES

1. For an account by one of those involved see, D. Breen, *My Fight for Irish Freedom* (Dublin, 1981), pp 31–53.

2. R. English, *Irish Freedom: The History of Irish Nationalism* (London, 2006), p. 285; English's term 'war *for* independence' is suggested here as a more fitting epithet for the republican campaign in 1919–21 in the six counties that became Northern Ireland.

3. See, for example, *Frontier Sentinel*, 5 Apr., 12 Apr., 17 May and 16 Aug. 1919.

4. Ibid. 15 Mar. 1919.

5. J. Augusteijn, *From Public Defiance to Guerrilla Warfare: The Experience of Ordinary Volunteers in the Irish War of Independence, 1916–1921* (Dublin, 1996), p. 89.

6. 'Chronology', *c.*1933, Irish Military Archives (hereafter, IMA), Bureau of Military History Contemporary Documents (hereafter, BMH CD) 6/36/22.

7. G. Evans, 'The Raising of the First Internal Dáil Loan and the British Response to It' (M. Litt Thesis, National University of Ireland, Maynooth, 2012), p. 154.

8. Ibid.

9. For references to Irish Volunteers performing these types of local duties see, John Grant, IMA, Bureau of Military History Witness Statement (hereafter, BMH WS) 658; Peadar Barry, ibid., 853; John McCoy, ibid., 492.

10. See M. Coleman, *County Longford and the Irish Revolution, 1910–1923* (Dublin, 2003), p. 115; Augusteijn, *From Public Defiance to Guerrilla Warfare*, p. 89.

11. C. Townshend, *Political Violence in Ireland: Government and Resistance since* 1848 (Oxford, 1983), pp 334–6.

12. M. Hopkinson, *The Irish War of Independence* (Dublin, 2002), p. 26.

13. RIC County Inspectors' reports (hereafter, CI), Armagh, June 1919, The National Archives (hereafter, TNA), Colonial Office papers (hereafter, CO) 904/109.

14. Rankin to Collins, 7 Nov. 1919, IMA, Collins papers, A/0314 VIII (I); 'Rev. Foy compensation claim', Public Record Office Northern Ireland (hereafter, PRONI), D1616/14/9.

15. CI, Armagh, Nov. 1919, TNA, CO 904/110.

16. P. Hart, *The IRA and its Enemies: Violence and Community in Cork. 1916–1923* (Oxford, 1998), p. 67; J. Borgonovo, *The Dynamics of War and Revolution: Cork City, 1916–1918* (Cork, 2013), pp 90–1, 196–7.

17. For the raid on the Orange hall see, *Irish Times*, 15 Jan. 1919. For raids on gentry homes see *Irish Times*, 5 Feb. 1919; *Irish Independent*, 12 May and 12 Aug. 1919.

18. For accounts of the Ballyedmond raid, and details of the outside assistance received see, Patrick Rankin, IMA, BMH WS 671; James McGuill, ibid., 353; Frank Thornton, ibid., 510. For the Loughgall raid see, Frank Donnelly, ibid., 941; John Cosgrove, ibid., 605.

19. Edward Fullerton, ibid., 890.

20. For Aiken's involvement in disciplinary matters see Rankin to Collins, 10 Dec. 1919, IMA, Collins papers, A/0314, VII, VIII. For continued organisational efforts see 'Chronology', c.1933, IMA, BMH CD 6/36/22; John McCoy, IMA, BMH WS 492.

21. Frank Thornton, IMA, BMH WS 510; for more on Nugent's role in the UVF in south Down see *Belfast News-Letter*, 4 Dec. 2012.

22. John Cosgrove, IMA BMH WS 605; Charles McGleenan, ibid., 829; *Irish Times*, 12 Aug. 1919.

23. E. O'Malley, *On Another Man's Wound* (Boulder, 1999), pp 121–2; Michael Doherty, IMA, BMH WS 1583. Ernie O'Malley was later sued for libel over his account of the incident, see *Irish Times*, 17 Nov. 1937; R. English, *Ernie O'Malley: IRA Intellectual* (Oxford, 1998), pp 49–50.

24. M. Valiulis, *Portrait of a Revolutionary: Richard Mulcahy and the Founding of the Irish Free State* (Dublin, 1992), pp 40–1.

25. Ibid; see also, C. Townshend, *The British Campaign in Ireland, 1919–1921: The Development of Political and Military Policies* (Oxford, 1975), pp 24–7, 30–2.

26. *Frontier Sentinel*, 9, 16 Aug. 1919.

27. Ibid., 20 Sept. 1919.

28. *Irish Independent*, 21 Nov. 1919; CI, Armagh, Nov. 1919, TNA, CO 904/110.

29. CI, Armagh, Dec. 1919, TNA, CO 904/110.

30. Ibid., Jan. 1920, TNA, CO 904/110.

31. Townshend, *Political Violence in Ireland*, p. 335.

32. Patrick Casey, IMA, BMH WS 1148; Jack McElhaw, ibid., 634; John McCoy, ibid., 492; *Armagh Guardian*, 13 Feb. 1920; *Frontier Sentinel*, 15 May 1920.

33. See, for example, *Irish Independent*, 27 Feb. 1920; CI, Down, Oct. 1920, TNA, CO 904/113.

34. C. S. Day, 'Political Violence in the Newry/Armagh Area 1912–1925' (PhD, Queen's University, Belfast, 1998), p. 131.

35. Jack McElhaw, IMA, BMH WS 634.

36. See, for example, *Frontier Sentinel*, 22 May 1920, 24 June 1920.

37. Mick Donnelly, University College Dublin Archives Department (hereafter, UCDAD), O'Malley notebooks P17b/116; John McCoy, IMA, BMH WS 492.

38. Patrick Casey, ibid., 1148.

39. *Irish Independent*, 23 Nov. 1920.

40. For details of the strike in Newry see *Frontier Sentinel*, 17 Apr. 1920, 1 May 1920.

41. See Appendix II, Table IV.

42. Ibid., Table V.

43. M. Laffan, *The Resurrection of Ireland: The Sinn Féin Party, 1916–1923* (Cambridge, 1999), p. 328.

44. See, for example, *Freeman's Journal*, 7 June 1920.

45. M. Daly, *The Buffer State: The Historical Roots of the Department of the Environment* (Dublin, 1997), p. 50, 52.

46. See p. 12.

47. Armagh County Council Minute Book, June 1920–Dec. 1921, PRONI, LA/2GA/12.

48. Sinn Féin's majority in the council was bolstered by three co-opted representatives; Newry No.2 RDC Minute Book, 15 June 1920, PRONI, LA57/2FA/10.

49. *Irish Times*, 24 June, 14 July 1920.

50. Newry No. 2 RDC Minute Book, 11 Sept. 1920, PRONI, LA57/2FA/10.

51. Laffan, *Resurrection of Ireland*, p. 330.

52. Newry No. 2 RDC Minute Book, 9 Oct. 1920, 18 Dec. 1920, 11 Aug. 1921, PRONI, LA57/2FA/10.

53. Hopkinson, *Irish War of Independence*, p. 201.

54. Jack McElhaw, IMA, BMH WS 634.

55. John McCoy, ibid., 492.

56. Edward Fullerton, ibid., 890.

57. See testimony of a member of the relief party, 'Witness A Prosecution', PRONI, J. H. Collins papers, D/921/2/2/1–57.

58. Townshend, *British Campaign in Ireland*, pp 119–23, 149–50.

59. Jack McElhaw, IMA, BMH WS 634.

60. John McCoy, ibid., 492.

61. See above, p. 68.

62. In all, 19 men were shot on Bloody Sunday, 15 of whom died; see J. Leonard, '"English dogs" or "poor devils"? The dead of Bloody Sunday morning', in D. Fitzpatrick (ed.), *Terror in Ireland, 1916–1923* (Dublin, 2012), pp 102–40. For the Kilmichael ambush see Hart, *The IRA and its Enemies*, pp 21–39.

63. John McCoy, IMA, BMH WS 492.

64. *Irish Independent*, 17, 19 Jan. 1921.

65. *Frontier Sentinel*, 8 Oct. 1921.

66. See Augusteijn, *From Public Defiance to Guerrilla Warfare*, pp 124–6.

67. John McCoy, IMA, BMH WS 492; Jack McElhaw, ibid., 634; *Frontier Sentinel*, 15 Jan. 1921.

68. John McCoy, IMA, BMH WS 492.

69. Aiken to Molly Childers, 1 Nov. 1923, Trinity College Dublin Archives (hereafter, TCDA), Childers papers, Ms 7847.

70. In Aiken's absence, the rents continued to be collected by family friend, Patrick Maginn; J. H. Collins to Aiken, 14 Nov. 1927, UCDAD, Aiken papers, P104/214.

71. See copies of *Our Homes and Garden*, Dec. 1920, and *House and Garden* Nov. 1921, Jan. 1922 and Feb. 1922, UCDAD, Aiken papers, P104/20–23.

72. See, for example, *Irish Independent*, 28 Mar. 1921; *Frontier Sentinel*, 9, 23 Apr. 1921.

73. John Grant, IMA, BMH WS 658; John (Jack) Plunkett, IMA, BMH WS 488; HQ Fourth Northern Division to Mulcahy, 24 June 1921, UCDAD, Mulcahy papers, P7/A/20; *Frontier Sentinel*, 2 July 1921; R. Lynch, *The Northern IRA and the Early Years of Partition* (Dublin, 2006), p. 79.

74. D. Fitzpatrick, 'The geography of Irish nationalism 1910–1921', in *Past and Present*, 78 (Feb., 1978), pp 117–20.

75. Lynch, *Northern IRA and the Early Years of Partition*, p. 83.

76. E. O'Halpin, 'Counting terror: Bloody Sunday and the dead of the Irish Revolution', in D. Fitzpatrick (ed.), *Terror in Ireland, 1916–1923* (Dublin, 2012), p. 153.

77. See Appendix II, Table VI.

78. *Freeman's Journal*, 14 Jan. 1921; John McCoy, IMA, BMH WS 492.

79. *Irish Times*, 6 July 1921; Teresa McAnuff file, *c.*1921, PRONI, HA/5/550.

80. Mulcahy to Aiken, 14 Apr. 1921, UCDAD, P7/A/17.

81. J. J. Murray, IMA, BMH WS 1096.

82. John Webster statement, PRONI, D1290/66; *Freeman's Journal*, 9 Nov. 1920; T. Bowman, *Carson's Army: The Ulster Volunteer Force, 1910–1922* (Manchester, 2007), pp 190–201.

83. T. K. Wilson, *Frontiers of Violence: Conflict and Identity in Ulster and Upper Silesia, 1918–1922* (Oxford, 2010), pp 17, 192–3, 196–7.

84. John McCoy statement, IMA, BMH WS 492.

85. *Irish Times*, 7 Sep. 1920; CI, Down, Oct. 1920, TNA, CO 904/113; John 'Ned' Quinn interview transcript (2/2), COFLA, O'Kane papers, LOK/IV/B.30.0003.01.

86. Contemporary press reports suspected that three were injured, one perhaps fatally so, but republican sources claim that there was only one casualty, see *Irish Times*, 10, 15 Jun. 1920; James J. Smyth, IMA, BMH WS 559.

87. CI, Down, Oct. 1920, TNA, CO 904/113.

88. For a detailed account of the Banbridge riots see P. Lawlor, *The Burnings, 1920* (Cork, 2009), pp 64–82; see also *Frontier Sentinel*, 31 July 1920.

89. John McCoy, IMA, BMH WS 492.

90. Day, 'Political violence in the Armagh/Newry region', p. 354, map 12.

91. John Grant statement, IMA, BMH WS 658.

92. *Anglo-Celt*, 21 May 1921; *Frontier Sentinel*, 8 Apr. 1922.

93. *Freeman's Journal*, 13 Apr. 1920.

94. Responsibility for this attack is unclear. For more see, James McGuill, IMA, BMH WS 353; D. Hall, 'Violence and Political Factionalism and their Effects on North Louth, 1874–1943' (PhD, National University of Ireland, Maynooth, 2009), pp 138–9.

95. John McCoy, IMA, BMH WS 492.

96. See, for example, R. Lynch, 'The people's protectors? The Irish Republican Army and the "Belfast Pogroms" 1920–1922', *Journal of British Studies*, 47: 2 (Apr., 2008), p. 381.

97. Wilson, *Frontiers of Violence*, pp 107–8.

98. For details of disciplinary action against members of the USC see, *Freeman's Journal*, 21 Jan. 1921, 15, 25 Apr. 1921; see, for example, details of the shooting of O'Reilly brothers, *Irish Times*, 11 July 1921.

99. See above, p. 74.

100. Wilson, *Frontiers of Violence*, p. 197.

101. See, for example, T. Harden, *Bandit Country: The IRA and South Armagh* (London, 1999), pp 127–8; R. Lynch, 'Explaining the Altnaveigh massacre', in *Eire/Ireland*, 45: 3 & 4 (fall/winter, 2010), p. 206.

102. Thomas McCrave, IMA, BMH WS 995; *Freeman's Journal*, 11 Apr. 1921.

103. *Freeman's Journal*, 27 Apr. 1921; Charles McGleenan, IMA, BMH WS 829; CI, Armagh, Apr. 1921, TNA, CO 904/115.

104. F. McGarry, *Eoin O'Duffy: A Self-Made Hero* (Oxford, 2007), pp 54–5.

105. Hart, *The IRA and its Enemies*, p. 97.

106. Augusteijn, *From Public Defiance to Guerrilla Warfare*, p. 247.

107. McGarry, *Eoin O'Duffy*, pp 59–61.

108. John T. Connolly, IMA, BMH WS 598.

109. *Frontier Sentinel*, 16 Apr. 1921.

110. *Irish Independent*, 7 July 1921.

111. John Grant, IMA, BMH WS 658; Grant's version of Holmes' death is supported by the testimonies of witnesses reported in the press, see *Freeman's Journal*, 11 July 1911.

112. F. Wright, *Northern Ireland: A Comparative Analysis* (Dublin, 1987), pp 11–12.

113. John Grant, IMA, BMH WS 658.

114. Jack McElhaw, ibid., 634; *Irish Independent*, 8 Sept. 1920; *Frontier Sentinel*, 11 Sept. 1920.

115. Patrick Beagan, IMA, BMH WS 612.

116. Augusteijn, *From Public Defiance to Guerrilla Warfare*, p. 290.

117. See, for example, Hart, *The IRA and its Enemies*, pp 93–6; Valiulis, *Portrait of a Revolutionary*, p. 75.

118. For more on how this was determined see Appendix I.

119. Hickey was pinned with a notice claiming his was an informer in an attempt to shift the blame for the killing to the IRA. The IRA denied this, and took the unusual step of writing to the young man's mother to make clear that they were not involved, and that he was not a member of the organisation. Given the failed abduction attempts earlier in the evening it is most likely that he was killed by the USC; *Irish Independent* 2 July 1921; *Freeman's Journal* 5 July 1921; Edward Fullerton, IMA, BMH WS 890.

120. See Appendix II, Table VI.

121. John McCoy, IMA, BMH WS 492; *Freeman's Journal*, 26 Apr. 1921.

122. CI, Armagh, June 1921, TNA, CO 904/115.

123. John Quinn interview transcript (1), Cardinal Ó Fiaich Memorial Library Armagh (hereafter, COFLA), O'Kane papers, LOK/IV/B.14.0002.10; John McCoy, IMA, BMH WS 492; *Freeman's Journal*, 8 June 1921.

124. John Quinn interview transcript (2), COFLA, O'Kane papers, LOK/IV/B.30.0003.01; *Frontier Sentinel*, 15 Jan. 1921.

125. 'General Order No.20', 20 Apr. 1921, UCDAD, Mulcahy papers, P7/A/45.

126. Hart, *The IRA and its Enemies*, pp 293–323; for more on the targeting of ex-soldiers see, J. Leonard, 'Getting them at last: The IRA and ex-servicemen', in Fitzpatrick (ed.), *Revolution? Ireland 1917–1923* (Dublin, 1999), pp 118–29.

127. J. Borgonovo, *Spies Informers and the 'Anti–Sinn Féin Society': The Intelligence War in Cork City 1920–1921* (Dublin, 2007).

128. Ibid, pp 83–91.

129. CI, Armagh and Down, Apr. 1921, TNA, CO 904/115.

130. Wilson, *Frontiers of Violence*, p. 129.

131. McGarry, *Eoin O'Duffy*, p. 67.

132. *Frontier Sentinel*, 10 Aug. 1918.

133. *Irish Times*, 17 Oct. 1918.

134. See above, p. 81.

135. John Quinn interview transcript (2), COFLA, O'Kane papers, LOK/IV/B.14.0002.10.

136. 'Divisional Order No. 4: Intelligence', 28 June 1921, PRONI, CAB 6/27/1.

137. Wilson, *Frontiers of Violence*, pp 130–1.

138. McGarry, *Eoin O'Duffy*, p. 67.

139. *Frontier Sentinel*, 18 Mar. 1922; *Irish Independent*, 15 Mar. 1922.

140. For the land dispute theory see John Quinn interview transcript (1), COFLA, O'Kane papers, LOK/IV/B.14.0002.10. For the AOH reprisal theory see Day, 'Political violence in the Newry/Armagh area', p. 196.

141. CI, Armagh, June 1921, TNA, CO 904/115; John McCoy, IMA, BMH WS 492.

142. C. Townshend, *The Republic: The Fight for Irish Independence* (London, 2013), pp 140–1.

143. E. Phoenix, *Northern Nationalism: Nationalist Politics, Partition and the Catholic Minority in Northern Ireland, 1890–1940* (Belfast, 1994), pp 72–3.

144. Laffan, *Resurrection of Ireland*, p. 230.

145. See pp 54–5.

146. *Dáil Éireann Debates (*hereafter, *DÉD)*, vol. 1 (6 Aug. 1920), cols 191–4.

147. John McCoy, IMA, BMH WS 492.

148. J. J. Murray, ibid., 1096.

149. Lynch, *The Northern IRA and the Early Years of Partition*, p. 45.

150. CI, Armagh, Dec. 1920, TNA, CO 904/113.

151. John McCoy, IMA, BMH WS 492.

152. 'The Divisional idea', *c.*Apr. 1921, UCDAD, Mulcahy papers P7/A/47.

153. Augusteijn, *From Public Defiance to Guerrilla Warfare*, p. 172.

154. Unidentified GHQ Officer to Chairman of the Pensions Board, 2 Apr. 1936, National Library Ireland, O'Connell papers, Ms 22,117.

155. Lynch, *Northern IRA and the Early Years of Partition*, p. 47.

156. Augusteijn, *From Public Defiance to Guerrilla Warfare*, pp 156–7.

157. Interview with Dr Eoin Magennis, 19 May 2010.

158. John McCoy, IMA, BMH WS 492; 'Frank Aiken', *c.*1922, TNA, War Office papers (hereafter, WO) 35/206.

159. Collins to Aiken, 4 Sept. 1919, IMA, Collins papers, A/0314, VII, I.

160. For more on Quinn and O'Hanlon see, Mick O'Hanlon, UCDAD, O'Malley notebooks, P17b/106; Michael Roger O'Hanlon, IMA, Military Service Pensions Collection (hereafter, MSPC), MSP34REF20993; Padraig Quinn memoir, Kilmainham Gaol Museum (hereafter, KGM), McCann Cell Collection, 20/M5/IP41/08.

161. Patrick Rankin, IMA, BMH WS 671.

162. See above, pp 67–8.

163. The Knocklong attack is one of the better known incidents of the war of independence. Its aim was to rescue Seán Hogan, an IRA prisoner. During the attack two RIC men were killed; D. Breen, *My Fight for Irish Freedom* (Dublin, 1981), pp 54–66.

164. *The Times*, 8 July 1920, 9 July 1920.

165. See above, p. 71.

166. M. Laffan, *Partition of Ireland, 1911–1925* (Dublin, 1983), p. 75.

167. For the ambush at Plaster see John McCoy, IMA, BMH WS 492; Patrick Casey, ibid., 1148. For progress prior to the truce see Aiken to Mulcahy, 16 June 1921, UCDAD, Mulcahy papers, P7/A/20.

168. Lynch, *Northern IRA and the Early Years of Partition*, p. 47; see above, pp 71–5.

169. 'The Fourth Northern Division', *c.*Apr. 1921, UCDAD, Mulcahy papers, P7/A/17.

170. Patrick Rankin, IMA, BMH WS 671.

171. This chronology of events is suggested by information from Military Service Pension applications lodged by Aiken and Rankin in the 1930s; Frank Aiken, IMA, MSPC, MSP34REF59339; Patrick Rankin, Ibid., MSP34REF2806.

172. Johnnie McKay [McCoy], UCDAD, O'Malley notebooks, P17b/94.

173. Patrick Casey, IMA, BMH WS 1148.

174. R. English, *Ernie O'Malley: IRA Intellectual* (Oxford, 1998), p. 76.

175. Frank Donnelly, IMA, BMH WS 941.

176. E. Magennis, 'Frank Aiken: Family, early life and the revolutionary period, 1898–1921', in Evans and Kelly (eds), *Frank Aiken: Nationalist and Internationalist* (Dublin, 2014).

177. John McCoy, IMA, BMH WS 492.

178. See, Johnnie McKay [McCoy], UCDAD, O'Malley notebooks, P17b/94; Frank Aiken, UCDAD, O'Malley notebooks, P17b/90. For arms purchases see, James McCullough, IMA, BMH WS 509; Patrick Casey, ibid., 1148. Later in the period Aiken apparently advised Mick O'Hanlon that joining the IRB 'wasn't necessary', which could be taken as an indication of declining interest in the organisation; Mick O'Hanlon, UCDAD, O'Malley notebooks, P17b/106.

179. See the accounts of John McCoy, IMA, BMH WS 492; Jack McElhaw, ibid. 634.

180. Aiken to de Valera, 1 July 1923, UCDAD, de Valera papers, P150/1752.

181. McGarry, *Eoin O'Duffy*, p. 62.

182. Harden, *Bandit Country*, p. 140.

183. P. Hart, *Mick: The Real Michael Collins* (London, 2005), pp 418–19.

184. Padraig Quinn memoir, KGM, McCann Cell Collection, 20/M5/IP41/08.

185. C. S. Andrews, *Dublin Made Me: An Autobiography* (Dublin, 1979), p. 242.

186. *DÉD*, vol. 208 (12 Mar. 1964), col. 992–3; *DÉD*, vol. 208 (9 Apr. 1964), cols 1375–6.

187. Kevin O'Shiel, IMA, BMH WS 1770.

188. Laffan, *Resurrection of Ireland*, pp 336–7.

189. *Freeman's Journal*, 10 May 1921; *Frontier Sentinel*, 21 May 1921.

190. *Irish Independent*, 10 May 1921; M. Coleman, 'Nugent, John Dillon', from *Dictionary of Irish Biography* (hereafter, *DIB*), www.dib.cambridge.org (accessed 10 Jan. 2010).

191. *Freeman's Journal*, 10 May 1921.

192. *Frontier Sentinel*, 21 May 1921.

193. *Irish Independent*, 10 May 1921.

194. *Newry Telegraph*, 26 May 1921.

195. Ibid., 17 May 1921.

196. *Irish Independent*, 13 May 1921.

197. Laffan, *Resurrection of Ireland*, p. 340.

198. *Newry Telegraph*, 26 May 1921.

199. *Armagh Guardian*, 3 June 1921.

200. B. M. Walker, *Parliamentary Election Results in Ireland: 1918–92: Irish Elections to Parliaments and Parliamentary Assemblies at Westminster, Belfast, Dublin, Strasbourg* (Dublin, 1992), p. 45.

201. Lynch, *Northern IRA and the Early Years of Partition*, p. 78.

202. Laffan, *Resurrection of Ireland*, p. 341.
203. Ibid., p. 340.
204. Ibid.
205. *Frontier Sentinel*, 4 June 1921.
206. Laffan, *Resurrection of Ireland*, p. 284.
207. Milroy to Mulcahy, 22 Sept. 1921, UCDAD, Mulcahy papers, P7/A/36.

FIVE

INTERLUDE

—

In Newry and south Armagh, an escalating cycle of reprisal and counter-reprisal came to an abrupt halt with the announcement of the truce on 11 July 1921. In Armagh, the RIC noted that 'since the advent of the truce there has been a total absence of political crime and as a consequence a genuine feeling of relief prevails amongst the people.'[1] For the local republican movement, the new conditions presented a range of challenges and opportunities. As the threat of arrest and suppression subsided, Sinn Féin once again became a visible feature of public life. Demonstrations resumed and there were determined, if belated, efforts to establish and maintain elements of the Dáil counter-administration. Men who had spent months 'on the run' returned home and, after a brief period of respite, IRA units were soon training and rearming in expectation of further hostilities. The confidence and optimism of the truce was short-lived, however. The signing of the Anglo-Irish Treaty in December 1921 created renewed uncertainty for northern nationalists and precipitated a political crisis in the south. As 1922 commenced, Aiken and his men faced renewed fighting in Northern Ireland and the disastrous consequences of the Treaty split in the nascent Irish Free State. Unsurprisingly, it was the northern agenda that came to dictate Aiken's responses to the Treaty and the emerging schism within the IRA, but despite his best efforts to remain neutral his division would not escape unscathed.

On the eve of the truce, the Fourth Northern Division was facing considerable difficulties. Arms and ammunition, the scarcity of which was a long running issue, remained in short supply and the authorities were scoring significant successes through arrests and extrajudicial killings of republican suspects. In spite of these pressures, Aiken later offered an optimistic appraisal of his division's position in July 1921; 'the morale of all ranks was good', he recalled, 'and our operations had been on the increase every month.'[2] Recorded with hindsight after the civil war, such a view was consistent with the positive assessments of those provincial IRA leaders who came to oppose the Treaty. The IRA's ability to continue a guerrilla campaign became a point of consider-able debate in the wake of the settlement, with the pessimistic outlook of the predominantly pro-Treaty GHQ differing significantly from that of provincial anti-Treaty officers.[3]

Although it is possible that the Treaty split influenced Aiken's retrospective assessment, it must also be considered within the unique context of the IRA campaign in Northern Ireland. Although it is generally argued that the conflict had reached a stalemate in July 1921 – and in hotspots such as Munster, Longford and Dublin this is certainly a convincing view – the position in six-county Ulster was complicated by the constraints under which the IRA had operated for the previous two years.[4] The development of the organisation and the escalation of its campaign had been stifled by the hostility of the local population, both unionist and constitutional nationalist. Even in the districts of Newry and south Armagh, where there was considerable republican sympathy, the Fourth Northern Division struggled to make progress. It had certainly made its presence felt, but it was unlikely to accomplish the levels of violence or operational frequency attained by IRA units in the most active areas of southern Ireland. With little prospect of achieving any substantial military success, the local IRA campaign effectively became a method of protest. As has been observed earlier, violence was increasingly viewed as a symbolic means of demonstrating opposition to British rule and partition, as well as a way of damaging claims of unionist hegemony in the province. In this context, the maintenance of the local campaign required little more than the continuance of the type of low intensity operations that had characterised the final six months of the conflict, and there was little indication of such activity abating.

For Aiken and his men, as for many of their comrades throughout the country, the announcement of the truce was a most unexpected development. As he later recalled, 'it came as a great surprise to us and we did not think it would last long.'[5] Nevertheless, it provided a welcome breathing space and an opportunity to improve the fighting capability of local units, and after a few weeks of inactivity attentions quickly turned to the tasks of training and rearming. Divisional training camps were established in south Armagh, the largest of which stood at Killeavy, in a remote and mountainous spot near Slieve Gullion.[6] At first, these camps focused on improving the quality of officer ranks. Men from across the division arrived in south Armagh to receive instruction in the use of various firearms and explosives, and to take part in tactical exercises. Aiken played an active role in delivering this programme and later boasted that these men were 'well trained in guerrilla tactics before the end of the summer.'[7] As the truce extended into the autumn months, the scope of the training regime broadened. Regular drilling was ordered at company level and work inside the camps was directed towards the development of special services, such as signalling, first aid and engineering. By this time, however, the camps were under threat. In September, a visiting officer informed GHQ that they 'will hardly be able to continue much longer [. . .] I gather that the division is now heavily in debt and ready money is very scarce.'[8] Nevertheless, the division struggled on and the Killeavy camp remained operational until at least December 1921.

Training became a particularly important aspect of the Fourth Northern Division's truce time activities. This was due, in part, to an influx of new and inexperienced recruits. Rising IRA membership was a nationwide phenomenon during this period. As Laffan has observed, membership 'on paper' rose from 30,000 to 75,000 between July and December 1921.[9] Commonly known as 'trucileers', these new recruits were often criticised for seeking the glory of the IRA's perceived victory against Britain without having contributed to the fighting.[10] In Armagh and south Down, entire companies were recruited for the first time since 1918, but existing members offered a negative assessment of their new comrades. Patrick Casey, for example, believed that 'the vast majority were simply climbing on the bandwagon [. . .] it became obvious to us that should there be a resumption of hostilities the fighting burden would fall on the same shoulders as hitherto.'[11] There were undoubtedly earnest young recruits amongst the throng, however. John 'Ned' Quinn, for example, was keen to defend the reputation of a number of youths that joined the Mullaghbawn Company at this time: 'they were all brave young fellows [. . .] they were just too young to have been in it from 1919.'[12] Indeed, one of the group was later executed during the civil war, a poignant reminder that there is good reason to question negative depictions of the 'trucileers', particularly in the context of Ulster. The future of the north was by no means secure in this period and, as Lynch observes, many of those joining IRA units in the region would face intense fighting in early 1922, active service as pro- or anti-Treaty combatants during the civil war, and the hardships of internment in both northern and southern Ireland until as late as 1925.[13]

Alongside training, the manufacture of munitions became another truce time preoccupation. This constituted the division's main effort to improve its impoverished arsenal. Although some local unionists suspected that republicans were conducting a large-scale gunrunning operation in Armagh – and duly reported these concerns to the RIC – there is little evidence to suggest that local IRA units received any significant quantities of arms or ammunition in this period.[14] Instead, as Aiken later recorded, various 'factories' were created which focused on manufacturing and stockpiling explosive devices. The Ballymacnab Company established an engineering section and began to construct concrete landmine casings.[15] The Lurgan Battalion focused on building 'shrapnel mines' that were then planted on local roadsides in anticipation of further hostilities.[16]

The creation of such devices was a convenient means of improving the division's fighting capabilities as they could be improvised using readily available materials.

The focus on homemade explosive devices reflected Aiken's proclivity for invention and engineering. This was something that remained with him throughout his life. In his later years he spent much of his free time sketching plans and creating prototypes for, among other things, an air-soled shoe, a turf burning stove and a large wind turbine that he constructed to generate electricity at his farm in Sandyford.[17] Yet the focus on explosives also owed much to Aiken's developing views on guerrilla warfare. Early in the conflict, he and his most dedicated officers – in particular John McCoy and Seán Quinn – were constantly forced to find new and innovative ways to meet the shortfall in arms and ammunition within the Newry Brigade, and later the Fourth Northern Division. They modified bullets to fit whatever guns they had to hand. Early operations also made a creative use of everyday equipment, as illustrated during the Newtownhamilton attack when a potato sprayer was used to help set the building on fire.[18] Such innovation was not uncommon within the IRA at this time, but for Aiken and his staff it led to an early realisation that, in McCoy's words, 'field engineering was as important as musketry'.[19] Along with his quartermaster, Seán Quinn, Aiken thoroughly explored the potential uses of explosives in guerrilla operations.[20] Although not a particularly notable aspect of pre-truce operations, a clever and creative use of explosives became an increasingly discernible trend thereafter. The groundwork for this innovation was laid during the truce, and by November 1921 the division had stockpiled 330 homemade devices and 102 grenades.[21]

Developments within the military sphere of the republican movement during the truce period were matched by political advancements. In some areas the influx of new IRA recruits was matched by increases in Sinn Féin membership.[22] Republican demonstrations enjoyed larger turnouts, and the crowds were representative of a much broader spectrum of nationalist opinion than in previous years. An IRA funeral in Newry in October 1921 was a striking example of this. The deceased were Peter Shields and John O'Hare, two volunteers who had been fatally wounded at the Egyptian Arch ambush in December 1920.[23] Shields died shortly after the confrontation and was buried secretly in Omeath. O'Hare lingered for many months before finally succumbing to his wounds in October 1921. When O'Hare died, it was decided to use the occasion to also reinter Shields's body. The resulting joint funeral was an impressive republican display. Press reports estimated the crowds at 'not less than twenty thousand' and observed that 'never before in the history of Newry were such manifestations of popular feeling witnessed.'[24] Significantly, all of

Catholic-nationalist Newry was represented. Alongside local republicans the cortège included clergy, pupils from the local CBS, representatives from the Catholic Workingmen's Club, the Irish National Foresters and, most astonishingly, the AOH.

Such displays of sympathy and support reflected the notion that the republican movement presented the best hope for bringing a speedy end to partition. Collins's election success in Armagh in May 1921 was an early indication of this emerging perception.[25] The announcement of the truce and the subsequent negotiations between republican leaders and the British government appear to have reinforced such a view. So too did Collins's appearance in Armagh in September 1921, his first visit to his new constituency since 1918. Addressing a large crowd, he used the occasion to state the republican case against partition and to assure local nationalists that 'no matter what the future will bring, we shall not desert them.'[26] At the same meeting, Eoin O'Duffy also appeared to advocate the pursuit of a united Ireland by force, warning local unionists that 'if necessary they [republicans] would have to use the lead on them.'[27] Amidst the uncertainty of the truce period, Collins's rhetoric undoubtedly appealed to a broad section of local nationalist opinion. O'Duffy's strong words, on the other hand, are more likely to have been aimed at placating the local IRA. Large contingents of the Fourth and Fifth Northern Divisions were present at the meeting, providing security for the nationalist crowds under Aiken's command, and this articulation of a more hard-line Ulster republican viewpoint clearly sat well with these men. Indeed, in discussing various provocative announcements made by O'Duffy in this period which 'did a lot to infuriate the Orange mob', Aiken later reflected that his attitude 'was merely representative of that of the whole army. We were great believers then in the power of the gun alone to cure all evils.'[28] Nevertheless, the day's proceedings, and perhaps O'Duffy's address, did cause tension in Armagh city. As nationalist crowds departed there was a brief affray with a hostile unionist crowd in Scotch Street. Hissing and groaning directed at passing republican cars quickly escalated to the throwing of missiles and, finally, a brief exchange of shots in which one Sinn Féin supporter was wounded. By chance, Aiken's sister Nano happened to be travelling in the same car as the victim.[29]

Increased support for the republican movement during the truce period should not be overstated. For most nationalists, supporting Sinn Féin was a pragmatic decision and did not represent a sincere ideological commitment. Indeed, tensions between republicans and constitutional nationalists remained rife. Charles McGleenan, an IRA officer from Blackwatertown, maintained that until as late as 1921 'Sinn Féin had no worse enemies than the Blackwatertown Division of the AOH.'[30] John McCoy believed that young Hibernians were trying to break up the truce by stealing IRA weapons and firing on local police patrols. Belfast IRA leader Roger McCorley expressed similar suspicions during this period, and although there is no evidence to corroborate the claims they do highlight the level of hostility and suspicion which continued to exist between the two groups.[31] Indeed, Aiken himself displayed a continued aversion to constitutional nationalism and, as late as 1922, warned Collins against any future dealings with the Belfast nationalist leader Joe Devlin: 'there can be no vigorous or harmonious policy on our part inside Ulster if his people occupy any position in our circle.'[32]

Nevertheless, the apparent growth of republican sympathy amongst nationalists in Armagh and south Down signalled an opportunity to develop elements of the Dáil counter-administration in the region. This was most visible in the emergence of Dáil courts and republican police patrols. Elsewhere in the country, such activities had emerged as early as 1919. The courts had their origins in Sinn Féin arbitration hearings that had been used to diffuse agrarian tensions in the west of Ireland in 1917 and 1918. They were subsequently placed under the control of the Dáil and became one of its greatest successes. By 1920, having expanded their remit to include the hearing of criminal cases, they effectively replaced the crown courts as the rule of law in large parts of the country. Likewise, the IRA had been performing policing duties in some districts as early as 1919. The Republican Police, sometimes also known as the Irish Republican Police (IRP), was subsequently created in 1920 to provide an alternative to the RIC and to enforce law and order in those areas where the latter force had been withdrawn.[33] Although there is limited evidence to suggest that republican police, and possibly Dáil courts, were operating in Armagh and south Down earlier in the conflict, they apparently made little impact and quickly fell dormant.[34] Locally, the republican movement simply did not command enough support to sustain such institutions. Alongside unionists, the majority of nationalists continued to look to the RIC and the crown courts for public order and legal redress. By mid-1921, however, conditions seemed much more favourable.

Although ostensibly a political initiative, the IRA was the driving force for renewed republican efforts to develop an alternative justice system in Armagh and south Down. As early as August 1921, IRA police patrols were in operation in the Newry area. The initiative emerged in response to a spate of local robberies and resulted in an early success when a thief was apprehended and turned over to a bewildered USC patrol.[35] Yet crime was becoming an ever-pressing local concern. John Cosgrove recalled that south Armagh had experienced an 'epidemic of robberies and acts of criminal violence against householders who were old or infirm', many of which were carried out 'under the name of the IRA.'[36] Although he dismissed the notion that republicans were responsible for these crimes, it is certainly possible that rogue IRA members were involved. Regardless of the identities or affiliations of the perpetrators, republican police patrols became increasingly prevalent from September onwards in an attempt to deter such crime. There were also efforts to establish Dáil courts in the region. This development appears to have been spurred on by Aiken and his staff to avoid the embarrassment of any further public co-operation with the authorities, such as that observed in Newry in August.[37] Nevertheless, a degree of collaboration on matters of local crime does appear to have been maintained with the RIC through liaison arrangements, by which nominated IRA officers could communicate directly with the county inspector, primarily as a means of resolving alleged breaches of the truce conditions.[38]

By October 1921, an alternative republican justice system was operational in Newry and south Armagh. Dáil parish courts (the equivalent of petty sessions) were conducting hearings in the area, usually regarding land and debt disputes, or minor public order offenses. These were typically conducted by Sinn Féin officials, some of whom had been prominent in 1918, but who had virtually disappeared from public life amid the violence of the preceding two years. A court in Carrickbracken, for instance, was presided over by Thomas Woods, the Bessbrook IRB figure and founding president of the Camlough Sinn Féin club.[39] In Newry, meanwhile, John Quinn, the father of Aiken's quartermaster Seán, and a local Sinn Féin councillor, was apparently appointed as a district judge, though it is unclear if Dáil district courts (the equivalent of county courts) were actually functioning in the area.[40]

The courts were supported by the IRA, who aside from their policing duties also took responsibility for enforcing its decrees, collecting fines and (on occasion) intimidating litigants into withdrawing their cases from the crown courts in favour of the republican alternative.[41] In many instances, they also appear to have reserved the right to act independently in the prosecution of more serious crimes. The Ballymacnab Company, for example, arrested, tried and carried out sentence on two alleged thieves during this period, tying the men 'to a tree opposite the chapel gate at Ballymacnab with a history of the crime each man was guilty of attached to his person.'[42] Meanwhile, one of the IRA's most significant breaches of the truce in Armagh came as the result of a similar incident when two tramps were arrested and tried by volunteers at Keady and held in a makeshift gaol. The authorities subsequently rescued them.[43]

Such activities provided idle volunteers with a purpose. This was particularly important as the truce wore on and morale and discipline declined. This was a common problem throughout the country. As Garvin has observed, 'IRA soldiers were in many areas becoming uncontrollable. Drink parties and joyriding in "commandeered" cars became major distractions.'[44] The situation within the Fourth Northern Division was not so pronounced, but Aiken certainly sensed that the prolongation of the truce 'was bad for any units which were not well disciplined and hardworking' and further observed that 'officers and men in such units were inclined to have a good time and do no work.'[45] Indeed, this inclination towards a 'good time' resulted in the dismissal of two officers for drunkenness during the autumn.[46] It was perhaps as a result of this worrying trend that republican police patrols became so prevalent from September onwards.

Republican efforts to maintain law and order also had considerable propaganda potential. The movement was determined to present its system of vigilante justice as being more effective than that of the RIC. This attitude was captured perfectly by John McCoy when recounting an argument with the RIC county inspector for Armagh in his capacity as an IRA truce liaison officer: 'I pointed out that all over the county a wave of lawlessness existed and that the Republican Police and Republican Courts in some districts were more likely to succeed in dealing with it.'[47] Other aspects of republican policing may also be viewed as an attempt to strengthen community support. The suppression of the poitín industry is a good example of this. Manufacturers of the illicit spirit became a popular target for IRA justice during the truce, facing fines and intimidation.[48] McGarry has observed that similar activities in Monaghan won support from some within the community, in particular 'wives and mothers'.[49] Indeed, the indignation that the illicit trade provoked ensured that, in tackling such a social evil, the IRA could present themselves as moral guardians; though there is little indication of the responses their mini-crusade provoked locally in Armagh and south Down. Yet the motives for such a crackdown were not entirely cynical. Like many of their IRA contemporaries, Aiken and his fellow officers conformed to the IRA's somewhat puritanical republican ethos, and displayed a genuine disdain for drinking and drunkenness. As Patrick Casey later recalled, 'anyone who drank even mildly was considered untrustworthy and of no use to any self-respecting revolutionary movement.'[50]

Dáil courts and republican police patrols continued to operate throughout the autumn and winter of 1921. Despite the apparently promising conditions in Armagh and south Down, however, they ultimately failed to attract sufficient local support. Unionists, of course, remained hostile, as did the majority of local nationalists. John McCoy also attributed some of the blame for their failure to inadequate support from GHQ.[51] When the fragile truce in Ulster began to unravel in January 1922, the position of both the courts and the republican police finally became untenable and they were quietly abandoned.

Republican efforts to build an alternative justice system constituted a breach of the truce. So too did the IRA's training camps and munitions 'factories'. Elsewhere in Northern Ireland such activities often provoked an aggressive response from the authorities. As Lynch has observed, by November 1921 raids on IRA training camps by mixed forces of RIC and USC were commonplace.[52] The Fourth Northern Division, however, faced no significant interference. Locally, the authorities were content to simply observe and record truce breaches in line with agreed liaison arrangements. The only exception was the RIC's raid on the aforementioned makeshift IRA gaol at Keady, an action presumably undertaken out of concern for the unfortunate individuals incarcerated there.

This relatively subdued approach appears to have owed much to the attitudes of individual RIC officers. John McCoy's recollections of his first meeting with the county inspector for Armagh are revealing in this respect. He found that the latter 'did not know how he and I could engage usefully in liaison work; that he would have to find out if he should recognise me officially.' Though unsure of the official position regarding truce liaison in Northern Ireland, the inspector nevertheless eventually decided to recognise McCoy's presence and apparently looked favourably on the arrangement. Indeed, for the most part their relations remained amicable until early 1922.[53] This was aided by the fact that most truce breaches were of a minor nature. Violent incidents were relatively uncommon, though IRA volunteers were responsible for numerous acts of intimidation and, possibly, the non-fatal shooting of a Hibernian near Armagh in January 1922. These incidents do not appear to have been orchestrated by the divisional leadership, however.[54] Rather, they were indicative of poor discipline within local units that became increasingly pronounced as the truce wore on. The same can be said of various breaches committed by the authorities during this period. These tended to consist of little more than drunk or ill-disciplined constables acting provocatively towards local nationalists. In August, for example, O'Duffy complained that 'lorries containing armed RIC still traverse Camlough District firing shots in the air.' McCoy, meanwhile, recounted various incidents involving drunken or disgruntled members of the USC who seemed intent on goading the IRA.[55]

In theory, liaison arrangements provided a means through which minor transgressions of this nature could be resolved. Redress was, however, rarely forthcoming for the authorities or the IRA. Complaints seldom resulted in any practical action by either side. Excuses might be offered, or investigations promised, but ultimately the aggrieved party would be left with little option but to file a report to their superiors, after which the matter would be quietly dropped.[5]

TREATY

As the truce extended into the autumn and winter of 1921, Aiken and his fellow officers became increasingly uneasy. 'It seemed to us that the truce negotiations were dragging out too long', he later recalled, 'it puzzled us greatly how our representatives could talk to the British so long without the vital points cropping up and causing a breach.' Their concerns were alleviated somewhat by reassurances from O'Duffy, now assistant chief-of-staff of the IRA, to the effect that 'GHQ had asked the President to keep the negotiations going until the winter', the most favourable season in which to resume a guerrilla campaign.[57] This belief was undoubtedly encouraged by recurring speculation of an impending breakdown of the negotiations in London, including numerous 'false alarms' during which provincial IRA units were told to prepare for an imminent return to hostilities.[58]

Aiken clearly had faith in such pronouncements. In October 1921, when GHQ officers questioned divisional leaders as to how they would respond to a settlement offering less than a republic, he failed to consider the possibility of a compromise: 'we had no suspicions of the Government and GHQ [. . .] the oath of allegiance or Partition never entered any of our heads, even after the question was put to us.'[59] This may be viewed as an indication of political naivety, but it also reflected the single-mindedness of the IRA in general. The separatist campaign had been defined by the aim of a 'republic' and few volunteers appear to have considered the possibility of settlement accepting anything less. This outlook contrasted starkly with that of many northern nationalists who, as the negotiations continued, became increasingly anxious as to what any forthcoming settlement would mean for partition.[60]

When the terms of the Anglo-Irish Treaty were announced on 6 December 1921, they came as a shock to Aiken and his division. Like units up and down the country, they learned of the settlement from the morning paper. Aiken was preparing to deliver a lecture at the divisional training camp when the news arrived. He later recalled the reactions of those gathered with him: 'none of the lads said much, they just exclaimed it's terrible or damnable. They were too crestfallen and disappointed; the thing was such a surprise, and they felt it so deeply, that they could not express their feelings coherently.'[61] The majority of Fourth Northern Division volunteers rejected the Treaty outright on the grounds of partition. Despite vague assurances of a boundary commission, which would eventually reconsider the position of the border, the settlement reinforced the existing division of Ireland. As a result, John McCoy later explained, it was the general view within the division that 'the north was let down.'[62] John Grant, a south Armagh officer, elaborated further:

As a Northerner and six-counties man I could not willingly accept partition [. . .]
I did not have to ponder over the arguments used in the heavy treaty debates in An
Dáil at the time the acceptance of the treaty was passed, to decide was the difference
between tweedledum and tweedledee. My reason for rejecting the Treaty ('partition')
was all too evident at home.[63]

Local Sinn Féin members were also quick to reject the Treaty on much the same
grounds. During the subsequent debates in the Dáil, republican members of the
Newry UDC unsuccessfully voted against a motion in favour of ratification.[64]
When the settlement was eventually ratified by Dáil Éireann, and de Valera
resigned in protest, the party's South Down constituency executive also passed
a resolution expressing their confidence in the former president.[65]

The Treaty received a more enthusiastic reception amongst the wider
nationalist community in Armagh and south Down, the majority of whom
remained largely constitutionalist in attitude. Streets in the nationalist areas of
Lurgan were decorated with flags and bunting to celebrate the event.[66] In
Armagh city, it was reported that the ratification of the settlement 'caused a
great feeling of relief and satisfaction in Nationalist circles'.[67] Like their counterparts in Tyrone and Fermanagh, the majority of nationalists in Armagh and
south Down were optimistic about the boundary clause, and were confident
that it would allow the predominantly nationalist border areas of Northern
Ireland to subsequently join the Irish Free State. As Phoenix has observed,
this created a 'border mentality' that ran against the feelings of the nationalist
community elsewhere in Northern Ireland, Belfast in particular, where there
was little hope for a speedy secession.[68] Nationalists and republicans from south
Armagh and south Down were soon organising demonstrations and sending
representatives to the capital in an effort to secure their immediate incorpor-
ation within the new Irish Free State. Padraig Quinn, then based in Dublin,
watched these men come and go, and later observed that they 'felt that the
Treaty offered them an option – certainly being solid nationalist areas they
would co-opt themselves into the South and in this they were encouraged by
Griffith and Collins.'[69]

Aiken's response to the Treaty was more complex than that of his
comrades or his fellow nationalists in Armagh and south Down. He certainly
opposed its terms, primarily with regard to partition, but also on account of
the oath of allegiance to the Free State constitution and (more crucially) the
accompanying oath of fidelity to the British monarch. This would be required
of all members of the new parliament, and quickly emerged as the focal point
for southern anti-Treaty republican ire as perhaps the most unpalatable symbol
of the settlement's compromise with regard to Irish sovereignty. Unlike many
of his northern comrades, who were preoccupied with the continuation of

partition, Aiken attributed equal importance to the two issues. Despite his clear opposition to the settlement, however, he refused to condemn it outright. In later years he even went so far as to suggest that 'I might have voted for the Treaty if I had have been a member [of Dáil Éireann].'[70] He also refused to condemn those members of the Irish delegation who signed the document. Whereas other provincial IRA leaders, such as Ernie O'Malley, had raged against the 'men who had betrayed us', Aiken believed it was 'untrue and unwise to call them traitors.' Indeed, he later stated his belief that the ratification of the Treaty owed much to the 'republican side failing to rise above the bitter "you have let us down" attitude.'[71]

Aiken's views owed much to the intervention of Collins. As a signatory of the Treaty, Collins had immediately set out to win over dubious comrades using his considerable influence within the IRA, and his position as president of the supreme council of the IRB.[72] On the issue of the oath, Aiken, like many others, was placated by his promises of an 'Irish interpretation' of the Treaty and a constitution for the new Free State which would reinstate republican values.[73] More crucially, with regards to partition, Collins demonstrated a commitment to renewed IRA violence in the north. During January 1922, he established the Ulster Council, a secretive body tasked with co-ordinating IRA operations in Northern Ireland and along the border. The council was composed of the commandants of each IRA division with an operational presence in the six counties; namely the First, Second, Third, Fourth and Fifth Northern Divisions, the First Midland Division and the Third Western Division. O'Duffy, who had recently been promoted to the position of IRA chief-of-staff, was also a member.[74] Aiken became chairman of the council, with Seán Mac Eoin, commandant of the First Midland Division, as his deputy.

Lynch has suggested that the Ulster Council can be viewed as an early attempt to secure at least nominal loyalty from Aiken and his well-equipped Fourth Northern Division.[75] There is certainly reason to suspect this. Seán Mac Eoin later suggested that Aiken's appointment as chairman of the body was due to Collins's patronage.[76] Collins and his supporters in GHQ had good reason to try to placate Aiken and his men. The Fourth Northern Division was the strongest IRA unit in Northern Ireland. In commanding a significant portion of Louth it also represented a potential security threat for the new Free State. A firm commitment to further fighting was crucial in assuring the unit's continued goodwill, and the establishment of the Ulster Council achieved this. In providing a degree of reassurance as to the emerging pro-Treaty leadership's continued opposition to partition, it ultimately succeeded in maintaining Aiken's continued allegiance to GHQ throughout the early months of 1922. Indeed, this may have been the entire point as Aiken – having been won over by Collins's reassurances – very quickly emerged as a voice of compromise and unity during GHQ's initial clashes with those officers who opposed the Treaty.

This was most strikingly illustrated by Aiken's response to the demands for an army convention which first emerged during a meeting of IRA divisional commandants in Dublin on 10 January, three days after the Dáil's ratification the Treaty. Aiken was present at the meeting, but initially offered neither support nor opposition to the proposal. Yet in the week that followed he aligned himself with other IRA officers who called for the convention to be postponed until the publication of the new constitution. Until then, it was argued, there was no definite policy to put before such a gathering.[77] Aiken's stance undoubtedly reflected his confidence in Collins's promises regarding an 'Irish interpretation' of the Treaty and a republican constitution. Though the chronology of events is somewhat elusive, it is also possible that his decision to support GHQ may have been influenced directly by Collins's Ulster Council initiative. Aiken's primary concern, however, appears to have been his firm belief that 'if a convention was held a split was inevitable'.[78] This was a particularly disconcerting prospect for northern IRA units as any wavering in southern support would prove disastrous for republican ambitions in Ulster.

The threat of an immediate army convention was averted when a compromise was reached at a meeting on 18 January. Aiken was present at the gathering, and personally forwarded a proposal that led to the postponement of the convention in anticipation of the publication of the new constitution. In the discussions that followed, it was agreed to delay any such gathering until March.[79] Demands for an immediate convention did, however, sporadically resurface in the weeks that followed during moments of tension between the emerging pro- and anti-Treaty factions. Aiken's response to the issue changed little and continued to be guided by the northern agenda and his hopes for an 'Irish interpretation' of the Treaty. He persevered in voicing his opposition to the convention within IRA circles and, in his own words, 'tried to keep down bitterness and to keep the army together in order to force the pro-Treatyites to produce the promised Republican Constitution.'[80] Aiken was in a relatively good position to attempt this. He was well-known amongst the IRA elite in Dublin. During the truce his visits to the capital had become more regular, and he could frequently be found socialising with GHQ officers at Vaughan's Hotel.[81] As chairman of the Ulster Council, moreover, he was in a strong position to push for army unity on the basis that it was necessary for continued action in the north. Consequently, as the divisions within the IRA gradually deepened during February and March, he made every effort to use these circumstances to informally lobby for compromise and moderation.

Although the Ulster Council proved useful as a means of keeping Aiken on side amid the developing schism within the IRA, this was not necessarily

Collins's only aim in pursuing the initiative. Indeed, to some extent, it also represented a more general effort to guarantee some form of influence over the organisation's discontented northern units. The latter were anticipating further hostilities in Northern Ireland, regardless of the Treaty and its consequences in the south. Aiken certainly expected as much. Shortly after learning of the settlement's terms in December, for instance, he had told his men that 'whatever the outcome of the treaty in the south, whether there would be peace or war in the twenty-six counties, there was bound to be fighting in the North; and that it was our duty to be prepared for it.'[82] Renewed IRA violence in Northern Ireland was a mixed prospect for the pro-Treaty leadership in the south. On the one hand it held the potential to jeopardise the entire Treaty settlement, particularly if the new provisional government was found to be complicit. On the other hand – and as later events would demonstrate – if used in the right way it could have a strategic value during continued negotiations with the northern government. Either way, control of the situation was clearly desirable. And with this in mind it seems likely that the creation of the Ulster Council ultimately served a dual purpose; conciliating Aiken and his fellow northern divisional commandants, while pre-emptively ensuring a degree of influence over their future actions.

The renewal of hostilities in Northern Ireland was certainly a likely prospect in January 1921. The announcement of the Treaty had immediate repercussions for the fragile truce in the region. Almost immediately, fresh orders were issued to the RIC and the USC stating that 'in future the ordinary law will be enforced, and that any previous instructions restricting their action in enforcing ordinary law are hereby cancelled.' This was further elaborated later that month with an instruction that 'the liaison arrangements hitherto in force with the Sinn Féin authorities in Northern Ireland are no longer necessary and are to cease forthwith.'[83] As January opened the new crackdown commenced. As John Grant later recalled, 'armed patrols in motor tenders in some instances accompanied by armoured cars started to patrol the roads in our area [. . .] the B Specials commenced to patrol their areas and whilst armed to act in a provocative and aggressive manner'.[84] In south Down, meanwhile, aggressive patrolling was accompanied by arrests, and eight members of a republican police patrol were subsequently tried for unlawful assembly for searching a house at Warrenpoint.[85]

The first Craig-Collins Pact, agreed later that month, briefly interrupted the renewed activities of the authorities. Announced on 21 January, this agreement was an attempt to improve relations between the Northern Ireland government, represented by James Craig, and the new provisional government of the Irish Free State, represented by Collins. Its terms primarily concerned the removal of British involvement in an eventual boundary commission, the discontinuation of the Belfast boycott and assurances from Craig that he would do his utmost to ensure the return of expelled Catholic shipyard workers in Belfast. The deal floundered within weeks, however, when it became clear that the British government had given each side very different impressions as to the amount of territory likely to be exchanged when the border was revised. Republicans were led to believe that they would make large territorial gains, leaving Northern Ireland an unviable entity and hastening the demise of partition. Unionists, however, were informed that any adjustments would be minor, though they remained vehemently opposed to even the slightest change to the existing boundary.[86] Already under considerable strain, the pact finally collapsed in early February amidst renewed IRA activity on the border.

The spark for the renewed republican aggression in Northern Ireland was the arrest of the 'Monaghan footballers' on 14 January 1922. The men were officers of the Fifth Northern Division who had been travelling with the Monaghan GAA team to an Ulster final match in Derry. The trip was being used as cover for a reconnaissance mission aimed at eventually rescuing three IRA prisoners who were awaiting execution in Derry gaol. In response to the arrests, the Ulster Council planned a series of retaliatory raids aimed at kidnapping prominent unionists in Fermanagh and Tyrone. The operations commenced on 7 February and resulted in the abduction of around 40 people, among them both civilians and members of the USC, who were subsequently held hostage across the border in Clones.

The kidnappings caused uproar in Northern Ireland, and provoked a stern response from the authorities. There was a sudden intensification of security measures all along the border, and it was reported that 'about 5000 fully armed "Special" police are engaged in patrols.'[87] Four days later, the already tense atmosphere was exacerbated by a bloody, and unplanned, confrontation between the IRA and the USC at Clones railway station. A party of USC constables was passing through the station on their way to Enniskillen, a poorly chosen route considering the events of the preceding week. As their train was about to depart, they were confronted by the IRA. Although it remains unclear who fired first, a fierce gun battle ensued leaving four USC constables and one IRA officer dead, and many others wounded.[88]

In Armagh and south Down, the renewed vigour of the USC led to further arrests. On 10 February, five volunteers were detained at Hilltown for their role as the firing party at a republican funeral a month earlier. This was followed on 14 February with the arrests of three IRA officers near Kilkeel, one of whom was mistakenly identified as commandant of the Fourth Northern Division.[89] The increased hostility of the authorities also led to the final collapse of the truce liaison arrangements in Ulster. IRA liaison officers, who had continued in their role throughout January, became an easy target for the authorities. In Armagh, shortly after John McCoy relinquished the position to return to his role with the divisional staff, his successor was arrested. Similar incidents occurred elsewhere in Northern Ireland and, as a result, the IRA finally abandoned the liaison arrangements in March.[90]

Aiken's role in the renewed IRA activity of February 1922 is unclear. Although he was chairman of the Ulster Council, he appears to have played a peripheral role in the kidnapping raids. O'Duffy originally proposed the operations. This is not surprising given that the 'Monaghan footballers' were officers from his former division and included his close comrade and successor Dan Hogan. At a subsequent meeting of the Ulster Council, detailed arrangements were put in place. Collins and Mulcahy – the latter now minister for defence in the provisional government – then sanctioned the final plans.[91] Indeed, Collins's complicity was such that the raids were briefly postponed while he waited to see if the pact negotiations with Craig could achieve significant results. There is also little evidence of Aiken's role at an operational level, although there are indications that units from his division were involved on the night.[92] The raids may have been carried out under the aegis of the Ulster Council, but they were clearly orchestrated by figures higher in the chain of command. This lends credence to Padraig Quinn's recollection that, as chairman of the body, Aiken had 'no authority whatever', only 'a certain amount of prestige.'[93]

The Ulster Council's activities in early 1922 are typically viewed as the militant component of a broader northern policy directed by Collins.[94] Alongside renewed IRA operations in Ulster, this consisted of encouraging northern nationalists to refuse to recognise the northern government – most strikingly illustrated by the provisional government's decision to pay the wages of Catholic school teachers in Northern Ireland – and continued negotiations with James Craig.[95] Evidently, the main purpose of the non-recognition policy was to destabilise the northern state. It is also likely that – alongside the activities of the Ulster Council – it served as a further means of placating northern IRA units, and perhaps as part of a more general attempt to foster unity within the organisation in the south through the common cause of opposition to partition. The negotiations with Craig, meanwhile, were primarily an attempt to secure some kind of safeguards for the beleaguered nationalist minority in the north, as well as the release of republican prisoners.

Not all historians are convinced by this broad interpretation of events, however. Indeed, Hart, in his refreshingly iconoclastic biography of Collins, has questioned the extent to which Collins even had a northern policy. The political strategies adopted towards Northern Ireland, he argues, were those of the entire provisional government of the Irish Free State, of which Collins was now chairman, and were based upon policies formulated by the Dáil prior to the truce. Hart also completely dismisses the suggestion that Collins was in a position to influence IRA activity in the north:

> He had no military strategy or even the ability to direct one [. . .] what the northern situation demonstrates is the same ambivalence and lack of control over 'his' men as was the case in the south. Here again, O'Duffy, MacEoin and other IRA leaders on the border had their own ideas.[96]

By this logic, Aiken can presumably be counted alongside O'Duffy and Mac Eoin as just another uncontrollable border leader.

Although it is reasonable to question the degree of Collins's personal responsibility for a northern policy in early 1922 – and there is certainly some validity in Hart's assertions regarding political initiatives towards the north – the suggestion that renewed IRA violence in Ulster was due to the actions of rogue provincial leaders is unconvincing. Figures such as O'Duffy, Mac Eoin and Aiken could certainly be considered as a radicalising influence on Collins in this period, but it is also clear that Collins was capable of exerting a considerable degree of control over their militant urges.[97] Indeed, events in Armagh and south Down between January and April 1922 are a striking example of this, and demonstrate that far from being uncontrollable, the renewed activity of Aiken and his Fourth Northern Division was strongly influenced by the broader strategies pursued in the north by Collins and his colleagues.

Throughout the truce period, the Fourth Northern Division had been preoccupied with the task of preparing for a renewal of hostilities. When the authorities in Northern Ireland unilaterally ended the truce over the course of January and February 1922, however, the division's initial response was subdued. As John McCoy later recalled,

> We decided to meet the Government's intensification of military and psycho-logical measures by a campaign of preparation for warfare; the provision of arms and munitions; safety measures to safeguard against arrests and imprisonment of officers [. . .] Our idea in the military side of things was to let the government take the initiative in any extreme measures; that the IRA should carry on their activities in organisation in a fairly open manner which would give the government forces the idea that their 'cold warfare' had not its desired psychological effect.[98]

At first this attitude may seem rather difficult to explain, yet it soon makes sense when viewed in the broader political and military context of January and February 1922, when aggressive IRA activity was precluded by both the first Craig-Collins pact and the tense situation resulting from the continued incarceration of the 'Monaghan footballers'. In late January, Collins was clearly eager to see if his agreement with Craig could deliver significant results. Consequently, renewed IRA activity in Northern Ireland was stifled. The postponement of the Ulster Council's planned kidnapping raids in Fermanagh and Tyrone are a telling indication of this. In early February, when it became clear that the pact had failed, and the kidnapping operations did finally occur, it may still have been desirable to avoid widespread IRA violence in the region. The raids were aimed at exerting pressure on the northern administration and providing the provisional government with leverage in the negotiations for the release of the 'Monaghan footballers'. Generalised IRA violence in Northern Ireland would have proven counter-productive to this strategy, and this may account for the absence of any significant escalation in the Fourth Northern Division's activities throughout February.

By the beginning of March 1922, the first Craig-Collins pact was no longer an issue. The 'Monaghan footballers', and the three IRA prisoners awaiting execution in Derry gaol, were also now free. There was, therefore, no impediment to renewed IRA hostilities in Northern Ireland. The Ulster Council subsequently commenced a general scheme of offensive operations in the region, the most notable of which involved a series of barracks raids in Fermanagh, Tyrone and Derry.[99] In the Fourth Northern Division, this return to violence was marked by a series of attacks. The first incident occurred near Blackwatertown when a USC patrol shot and seriously wounded John Garvey, a local republican, after he allegedly refused to halt.[100] The local IRA company responded by shooting two constables believed to have been part of the patrol. One was killed, and the other seriously wounded. The second – remarkably similar – incident occurred near Keady. On 17 March an elderly farmer named James McGleenan was shot dead by B Specials, also after allegedly refusing to halt. The event provoked outrage amongst local nationalists because of the victim's age and the fact that he was known to be hard of hearing.[101] As a reprisal William Fleming, a local Protestant farmer, was shot dead outside his home. His brother had been a member of the patrol that shot McGleenan and his death was evidently a case of mistaken identity.[102] These shootings, which emerged in response to local events, were accompanied by co-ordinated attacks on the authorities closer to the border. The first was an ambush at Cullaville on 29 March that resulted in the deaths of two USC constables and the wounding of two others. Aiken planned the operation alongside Dan Hogan, commandant of the Fifth Northern Division, under the aegis of the Ulster Council.[103] This was followed two days later with an ambush on a USC patrol in Newry, which left one constable dead and another wounded.[104]

This surge of violence within the Fourth Northern Division came to an abrupt halt, however, with the announcement of the second Craig-Collins pact on 30 March. Considerably more detailed than its predecessor, this new agreement covered a wide range of issues aimed at improving north-south relations, and attempted to bring some relief to the beleaguered northern nationalist minority, particularly in Belfast. Among the provisions were clauses proposing the recruitment of Catholics to the USC to ensure mixed patrols for areas of mixed allegiance, the intervention of both administrations to ensure the safe return to their homes and jobs of those expelled during the recent trouble, and the creation of a conciliation committee which would investigate allegations of intimidation. Efforts were also made to lay the foundations for an agreement on the issue of prisoner releases, and to lay plans for future negotiations on the issue of the border and Irish unity. More importantly, however, the pact called for a cessation of IRA activity in Northern Ireland; an objective that was incentivised with a provision that, once this was achieved, the above mentioned reforms to the USC would be rolled out beyond Belfast.[105]

The announcement of the second Craig–Collins pact did much to quell IRA activity in Armagh and south Down during April. There were violent incidents during the month, but these tended to be of lower intensity or spontaneous in nature. At Charlemont, for example, two USC constables were wounded during a brief shoot-out with a group of men whom they had called upon to halt. A republican account of the incident suggests that the IRA party had returned to attack the constables after they were held up and ill-treated earlier in the day. Either way, it was clearly an unsanctioned and reactionary operation.[106] There were also a few incidences of sniping at patrols and intimidation.[107] A significant increase in activity relating to the Belfast boycott was visible in Dundalk during the month, but this appears to have been the work of local anti-Treaty units in the aftermath of the IRA split on 26 March.[108] Indeed, the most shocking violence to occur in Armagh and south Down after the announcement of the pact was the work of local loyalists (most likely the USC). As a reprisal for the ambush in Newry on 31 March, Joseph Garvey, a local Catholic with no obvious political connections, was shot and dumped on the roadside outside the town.[109] Later that month, a youth named John Kelly was abducted and shot by two uniformed men after his car was stopped near Keady. He managed to find help and survived the attack.[110] Two nationalist halls were also burned in the Camlough area.[111]

Events in Armagh and south Down thus suggest a strong correlation between local IRA activity and the political initiatives of Collins and the provisional government in early 1922. It is likely that this was facilitated by Aiken's dual role as chairman of the Ulster Council and commandant of the Fourth Northern Division. The Ulster Council's military strategy was evidently influenced by the political aims and objectives of Collins and the pro-Treaty leadership, and Aiken accordingly ensured that the activities of his own division did not deviate. It is likely, moreover, that Collins's personal influence was pivotal in making sure that Aiken toed the line. Despite his misgivings about the treaty, he clearly still had confidence in Collins. As April 1922 opened, however, and the crisis within the IRA deepened, it became increasingly uncertain how much longer this might last.

SPLIT

As renewed violence gathered pace in Northern Ireland during March 1922, the already tense situation in southern Ireland took a turn for the worse. In accordance with the compromise arrangement reached on 18 January, an IRA army convention had been scheduled for 26 March. In the intervening months, however, the depth of anti-Treaty sentiment within the organisation had become clear, and it seemed almost certain that the event would result in a declaration of army independence which would remove the IRA from the control of Dáil Éireann. Fearing the consequences of such a move, the provisional government issued an order on 16 March, banning the convention, and describing its intentions as illegal. But neither the ban, nor Mulcahy's subsequent threats that those attending the convention would receive no further support from GHQ, had much effect on the anti-Treaty faction's emergent leaders, who were clearly intent on pressing ahead.[112]

Aiken remained consistent in his opposition to the army convention, which he believed would inevitably lead to a split. In responding to events in March, therefore, he once again tried to use his familiarity with IRA figures in Dublin to privately agitate for compromise. He focused his attentions on Rory O'Connor, the former GHQ director for engineering, and now an increasingly prominent figure within the IRA's anti-Treaty faction. Travelling to Dublin, Aiken met O'Connor at Vaughan's Hotel, and after a long discussion apparently agreed to submit his views on the convention to the latter in writing. Although neither the details of the discussion, nor the contents of the letter, are known, Aiken evidently urged O'Connor to further postpone the convention until the publication of the new Free State constitution, which was still in the process of being drafted by a provisional government committee. In the event that he failed to do this, Aiken also made clear that neither he, nor any members of his division, would attend the meeting.[113]

The majority of the Fourth Northern Division's members supported Aiken's stance. Despite the disappointment and disillusionment with which his men had greeted the Treaty, there was little outward sign of dissent or disunion in the immediate aftermath of its ratification in January 1922. Following

Aiken's lead, the majority were content to remain aligned with the pro-Treatyite GHQ so long as there was the prospect of further fighting in the north. When the convention finally took place, however, the first signs of disunion became apparent. Despite Aiken's stated intention that no representatives would attend, two delegates were sent to Dublin on behalf of the First Brigade. Aiken later claimed that he had given permission for these men to attend the convention, but there is no evidence to corroborate this, and it seems rather unlikely given the broader scheme of events.[114] When, as a result of the convention, the IRA formally split, the First Brigade staff and two of its four battalions transferred their allegiance to the new anti-Treaty IRA executive.[115]

The most striking feature of the split within the Fourth Northern Division was its geographic dimension. The First Brigade was based primarily in north Louth and was under the command of Patrick McKenna, a native of Monaghan who had been sent to Dundalk by GHQ in 1920 to act as the local IRA commandant. It was McKenna's staff, and the brigade's two Louth-based battalions that aligned with the executive forces after the convention. Meanwhile, the brigade's two Armagh-based battalions remained loyal to Aiken and the divisional staff.[116] This highlights an important point regarding the Fourth Northern Division. In covering a large area and transcending county boundaries, it was not a homogeneous entity. Prior to the Treaty, however, there was no evidence of local tensions. In a sense, the situation within the division was similar to that observed within the republican movement more generally during the revolutionary period. The separatist struggle had unified various sections – regional, social and political – in a common aim, concealing their inherent differences. With the Treaty, however, these differences became increasingly visible and divisive. This is a theme most often referenced with regards to the republican political elite in this period, where the alliance of moderate nationalist and republican blocs had resulted in the most visible emergence of previously dormant internal divisions.[117] Broadly speaking, the emerging fault lines within the Fourth Northern Division were regional, with units in north Louth, and later south Down, asserting their own stance with regards to the split and in opposition to the views of the more dominant Armagh contingent.[118]

There were, of course, a variety of factors that influenced the north Louth units' decision to oppose Aiken and adopt the anti-Treaty position, although purely ideological reasons can be ruled out. Generally speaking, the Fourth Northern Division was united in its opposition to the Treaty's terms. For the majority of volunteers this was due to its recognition of partition. For others, including Aiken, there was also concern over constitutional issues. The difference of opinion between the north Louth units and the divisional staff was one of policy. Aiken and the majority of his men were willing to remain under the authority of GHQ and, until the publication of the constitution at least, to adopt a neutral stance in the emerging split. McKenna and his units in north Louth were not. Regional differences were crucial in this respect. North Louth's inclusion in the Free State was assured. IRA units in that region were, therefore, less concerned about partition and the continuation of a campaign in the north than their counterparts in Armagh and south Down. Accordingly, they were less inclined to pursue the course adopted by Aiken and his staff in restraining their criticism of the settlement and attempting to maintain unity for the sake of republican ambitions in the north.

It is also significant that the north Louth units were a relatively late addition to Aiken's command. As a consequence, they were not as well integrated into the division as their counterparts in Armagh and south Down which had constituted the original Newry Brigade. They were viewed as outsiders, to an extent, and some members of the division regarded them with contempt due to their relative inactivity prior to the truce.[119] Their lack of integration was further reflected by the fact that by January 1922 only one of seven officers on the divisional staff was from north Louth.[120] This lack of integration ensured that Aiken was unable to exert the same influence over the north Louth units as he could over those from Armagh and south Down. This was strikingly illustrated shortly after the army convention when he arranged for Mulcahy and O'Duffy to attend a divisional meeting in Dundalk. Officers from the newly independent First Brigade were present, but walked out once Mulcahy and O'Duffy entered the room. Mick Donnelly, a member of the First Brigade staff, later observed that 'Aiken was very bitter about that. I suppose Mulcahy and O'Duffy came there to talk us over.'[121] Aiken's lack of influence over the north Louth units is revealing, given that the responses of provincial units to the Treaty and the split were very often determined by the stance of local leaders.[122]

A further factor that may have influenced the First Brigade's anti-Treaty position was its poor relationship with GHQ. The low levels of activity in the region prior to the truce had caused friction between local officers and the Dublin leadership.[123] This was most evident during an inspection of the Fourth Northern Division in the summer of 1921 when Mulcahy, then still chief-of-staff, berated two north Louth officers for the inactivity in their area throughout the conflict.[124] Hopkinson has observed that similar negative experiences with GHQ are likely to have influenced the Sligo Brigade to adopt the anti-Treaty position in these months.[125] It is possible, therefore, that the First Brigade's difficult relationship with GHQ sparked a similar reaction amongst its officers.

In the aftermath of the army convention and the resulting split there was a determination within the Fourth Northern Division to avoid any conflict or tension between the local pro- and anti-Treaty factions. To this end, a liaison was established between the divisional staff and the anti-Treatyite First Brigade and provisions made to allow any local unit so inclined to change allegiance without fear of repercussions.[126] Only the Crossmaglen Company appears to have made use of this option, becoming the only Armagh-based unit to join the executive forces during these months.[127] Aiken also issued a circular to all officers and men outlining the official stance of the divisional staff with regards to the changed military situation. The division was to remain under the authority of the department of defence until the publication of the new Free State constitution, which Collins, in attempting to maintain unity, had assured Aiken (amongst others) would reflect republican values. It was re-iterated that, for the Fourth Northern Division, the immediate task at hand was 'to get Ulster to recognise the principle of a United Ireland.' The tone of the document was, however, also calculated to retain the good will of the anti-Treaty faction. Its rhetoric ensured that the division could by no means be considered unreservedly pro-Treaty: 'our objective is a Republic for an undivided Ireland [. . .] if we cannot honourably work the constitution as the quickest way to that end, the constitution must go.' Furthermore, it was made clear that the division would withdraw its allegiance from GHQ if it was 'asked to do something which is dishonourable'; the clear implication being that it would refuse any orders to attack anti-Treaty forces.[128]

Attempts to maintain harmony within the Fourth Northern Division were particularly important in the weeks that followed the army convention as the evacuation of British troops and the RIC commenced in Dundalk. In many parts of the country, the withdrawal of these forces led to confrontations between pro- and anti-Treaty IRA units as they rushed to occupy vacated barracks and police stations. In Dundalk, there were three potential flash points, two RIC stations in Ann Street and Bridge Street, and a much larger British military barracks at Point Road. The military barracks was the most impressive of the three installations, but held a lesser strategic value than the two RIC stations. Although these were little more than converted three storey houses, they commanded the northern and southern entrances to the town.[129] When they were vacated by the RIC on 29 March they were handed over to Mick Donnelly who, despite being a member of the anti-Treaty First Brigade, had remained the truce liaison officer for Louth. Executive forces subsequently occupied both.[130]

The evacuation of the British military barracks was a more complicated affair, however. This was the only military installation within the Fourth Northern Division which was due to be vacated under the terms of the Treaty, and from early March 1922 Aiken had been seeking definite information as to when it would be handed over.[131] With the situation intensifying north of the border, he was keen to take possession of the barracks and to establish it as a new divisional headquarters. At this time, his staff was operating out of a boarding house in Newry and concerns were growing as to the security of this arrangement.[132] Having remained under the authority of GHQ and the department of defence, Aiken was ostensibly the pro-Treaty commander for the region and fully expected to take possession of the military barracks on behalf of the provisional government. When a date for the evacuation was finally set, however, Aiken was not informed. Members of his divisional staff, who were actively searching for a suitable property to occupy in the Dundalk area, learned of the impending British withdrawal through local rumours. Much to Aiken's dismay, it was discovered that arrangements were in place for the barracks to be handed over to J. J. O'Connell, the assistant chief-of-staff, and placed in the possession of a garrison of provisional government troops from Dublin.[133]

GHQ had attempted this tactic before, most notably in Limerick where it almost sparked a confrontation with local anti-Treaty units, and the intention behind it was clear.[134] Aiken's position of neutrality, and his conditional allegiance to GHQ, had earned him the distrust of the pro-Treaty leadership. He could not be relied upon in any future confrontation with the anti-Treaty faction and, as a result, GHQ was keen to ensure he did not occupy a military barracks. As Padraig Quinn recalled, Aiken and his staff viewed this as 'an intolerable position' and felt that they had been 'double crossed by GHQ.'[135] Aiken immediately went to Dublin and challenged Mulcahy over the decision. At first, Mulcahy was defiant and was forthright in his admission that the provisional government did not trust the Fourth Northern Division. Nevertheless, a compromise was soon brokered. A GHQ officer would sign for control of the barracks and the Fourth Northern Division would then occupy it. Aiken also gave Mulcahy his word that he would immediately hand the barracks back to GHQ if, or when, they required it; though this promise was unknown to other members of the divisional staff.[136]

Aiken's faith in GHQ was severely shaken by this confrontation. For the first time, he expressed his doubts about the true motives of the pro-Treaty leadership. As Padraig Quinn later recalled, whilst recounting the stress and apprehension of the night before the barracks transfer:

> We talked through the night and I remember clearly and distinctly a question from Frank towards daylight – 'did I think that Michael Collins could be wrong' – 'Could he be arming and fixing the Free State army for a trial of strength and surely Dick [Mulcahy] and the whole General Headquarters Staff could not be going that way.' I said I thought so. There was no audible response.[137]

Aiken's concerns appear to have been assuaged by GHQ's failure to send a representative to Dundalk the following day. The Fourth Northern Division was permitted to take possession of the barracks unchallenged and the transfer occurred with little fuss or fanfare.[138] The divisional staff established the base as their new headquarters and by mid-April the majority of active units in Armagh and south Down had also completed the move south of the border, establishing make-shift camps at Dungooley, Ravensdale and Bridge-a-Crin, in Louth, and Castleblaney and Castleshane in Monaghan.[139] Nevertheless, the episode had revealed emerging tensions between Aiken and GHQ and marked a turning point in his relationship with the pro-Treaty triumvirate of Collins, O'Duffy and Mulcahy.

Despite this, however, the Fourth Northern Division was in a relatively secure position. It may not have escaped the ill effects of the IRA split, but Aiken's emerging policy of neutrality had survived a critical test. Though there had been tensions, for the moment he had succeeded in maintaining cordial relations with both GHQ and the anti-Treaty First Brigade in Dundalk; ensuring, within his own unit at least, that delicate balance of unity which he believed so crucial for continuing action in Northern Ireland. Indeed, amid all his interventions and politicking in Dublin, this remained his primary concern.

NOTES

1.   RIC County Inspectors' Reports (hereafter, CI), Armagh, July 1921, The National Archives (hereafter, TNA), Colonial Office (hereafter, CO), 904/116.

2.   Untitled statement by Frank Aiken, c.1925, Irish Military Archives (hereafter, IMA), Bureau of Military History Contemporary Documents (hereafter, BMH CD) 6/36/23.

3.   M. Valiulis, *Portrait of a Revolutionary: General Richard Mulcahy and the Founding of the Irish Free State* (Dublin, 1992), p. 81.

4.   For stalemate argument see, M. Coleman, *County Longford and the Irish Revolution, 1910–1923* (Dublin, 2003), p. 133; D. Fitzpatrick, *Politics and Irish life, 1913–1921: Provincial Experience of War and Revolution* (Dublin, 1977), p. 230; P. Hart, *The IRA and its Enemies: Violence and Community in Cork, 1916–1923* (Oxford, 1997), pp 104–8.

5.   Untitled statement by Frank Aiken, c.1925, IMA, BMH CD 6/36/2.

6.   Reports of IRA Truce Breaches, July–Dec. 1921, TNA, CO 904/151.

7.   Edward Fullerton, IMA, BMH WS890; Untitled statement by Frank Aiken, c.1925, IMA, BMH CD 6/36/23.

8.   Reports of IRA Truce Breaches, July–Dec. 1921, TNA, CO 904/151; Fourth Northern Division Correspondence, c.1921, IMA, Collins papers, A/0666; Report on Fourth Northern Division Training Camp, 12 Sept. 1921, University College Dublin Archives Department (hereafter, UCDAD), Mulcahy papers, P7/A/25.

9.   M. Laffan, *The Resurrection of Ireland: The Sinn Féin Party, 1916–1923* (Cambridge, 1999), p. 302.

10. M. Hopkinson, *Green Against Green: The Irish Civil War* (Dublin, 1988), p. 16.

11. Patrick Casey, IMA, BMH WS 1148.

12. John Quinn interview transcript (1/2), 8 May 1966, Cardinal Ó Fiaich Library Armagh (hereafter, COFLA), O'Kane papers, LOK/IV/B.14.0002.10.

13. R. Lynch, *The Northern IRA and the Early Years of Partition* (Dublin, 2006), p. 81.

14. Reports of IRA Truce Breaches, Armagh, TNA, CO 904/151.

15. John Cosgrove, IMA, BMH WS 605.

16. J. J. Murray, ibid., 1096.

17. 'Aiken: Gunman and Statesman' (Mint Productions, 2006); Interview with Dr Eoin Magennis, 19 May 2010.

18. John McCoy, IMA, BMH WS 492.

19. See, for example, Coleman, *County Longford and the Irish Revolution*, pp 136–8; Augusteijn, *From Public Defiance to Guerrilla Warfare: The Experience of Ordinary Volunteers in the Irish War of Independence* (Dublin, 1996), pp 149–50; John McCoy, IMA, BMH WS 492.

20. Padraig Quinn memoir, Kilmainham Gaol Museum (hereafter, KGM), McCann Cell Collection 20/M5/IP41/08.

21. Fourth Northern Division Inventory, *c*.Nov. 1921, UCDAD, Mulcahy papers, P7/A/28.

22. Charles McGleenan, IMA, BMH WS829.

23. *Frontier Sentinel*, 15 Oct. 1921; Patrick Casey, IMA, BMH WS 1148.

24. *Frontier Sentinel*, 15 Oct. 1921.

25. See above, pp 94–5.

26. *Frontier Sentinel*, 10 Sept. 1921.

27. As quoted in F. McGarry, *Eoin O'Duffy: A Self-Made Hero* (Oxford, 2005), p. 80.

28. Aiken to Molly Childers, 18 Apr. 1924, Trinity College Dublin Archives (hereafter, TCD), Childers papers, Ms 7,847.

29. CI, Armagh, Sept. 1921, TNA, CO 904/116; L. Skinner, *Politicians by Accident* (Dublin, 1947), p. 169.

30. Charles McGleenan, IMA, BMH WS 829.

31. John McCoy, ibid., 492; A. C. Hepburn, *Catholic Belfast and Nationalist Ireland in the Era of Joe Devlin, 1871–1934* (Oxford, 2008), p. 220.

32. As quoted in Hepburn, *Catholic Belfast and Nationalist Ireland in the Era of Joe Devlin*, p. 235.

33. For more on republican policing see J. Augusteijn, *From Public Defiance to Guerrilla Warfare*, pp 285–9; Valiulis, *Portrait of a Revolutionary*, pp 60–1.

34. John Grant, IMA, BMH WS 658; significantly, RIC reports make no mention of Dáil courts or IRA policing prior to the truce.

35. *Irish Independent*, 18 Aug. 1921.

36. John Cosgrove, IMA, BMH WS 605.

37. Aiken to Mulcahy, 19 Oct. 1921, UCDAD, Mulcahy papers, P7/A/34.

38. John McCoy, IMA, BMH WS 492.

39. Reports of IRA Truce Breaches, 8 Sept. 1921, TNA, CO 904/151.

40. Padraig Quinn memoir, KGM, McCann Cell Collection, 20/M5/IP41/08.

41. Reports of IRA Truce Breaches, July–Dec. 1921, TNA, CO 904/151; John Quinn interview transcript (1/2), COFLA, O'Kane papers, LOK/IV/B.14.0002.10; see also Laffan, *Resurrection of Ireland*, pp 310–18; M. Kotsonouris, 'The courts of Dáil Éireann' in Farrell (ed.), *The Creation of the Dáil* (Dublin, 1994), pp 91–105; John Grant, IMA, BMH WS 658.

42. John Cosgrove, ibid., 605.

43. *The Times*, 15 Nov. 1921.

44. T. Garvin, *1922: The Birth of Irish Democracy* (Dublin, 2005), p. 50.

45. Untitled statement by Frank Aiken, *c*.1925, UCDAD, P104/1308.

46. Ibid.

47. John McCoy, IMA, BMH WS 492.

48. See, for example, Edward Boyle, ibid., 647; John Grant, ibid., 658; *Irish Times,* 27 Oct. 1921; CI, Armagh, Oct. 1921, TNA, CO904/116.

49. McGarry, *Eoin O'Duffy*, p. 52.

50. Untitled statement by Frank Aiken, *c*.1925, IMA, BMH CD 6/36/23; Patrick Casey, IMA, BMH WS 1148.

51. John McCoy, IMA, BMH WS 492.

52. Lynch, *Northern IRA and the Early Years of Partition*, p. 81.

53. John McCoy, IMA, BMH WS 492; see also see McCoy to Dalton, 15 Nov. 1921, IMA, Truce Liaison and Evacuation papers, LE 4–16b.

54. CI, Armagh, Oct. 1921, TNA, CO904/116; Reports of IRA Truce Breaches, July–Dec. 1921, TNA, CO 904/151; 'Reports of breaches of the truce, for the week ending 28/1/22', IMA, Truce Liaison and Evacuation papers, LE 4–16b.

55. *Frontier Sentinel*, 13 Aug. 1921; McCoy to Dalton, 16 Nov. 1921, IMA, Truce Liaison and Evacuation papers, LE 4–16b; John McCoy, IMA, BMH WS 492.

56. For an indication of the outcomes regarding individual incidents see McCoy's reports and correspondence to the IRA's chief liaison officer; Truce Liaison and Evacuation papers, IMA, LE/4/16A.

57. Untitled statement by Frank Aiken, *c*.1925, IMA, BMH CD 6/36/23.

58. Valiulis, *Portrait of a Revolutionary*, p. 86.

59. Untitled statement by Frank Aiken, *c*.1925, IMA, BMH CD 6/36/23.

60. E. Staunton, *The Nationalists of Northern Ireland, 1918–1973* (Dublin, 2001), p. 46.

61. Untitled statement by Frank Aiken, *c*.1925, IMA, BMH CD 6/36/23.

62. Johnnie McKay [McCoy], UCDAD, O'Malley notebooks, P17b/90.

63. John Grant, IMA, BMH WS 658.

64. *Irish Independent*, 3 Jan. 1922.

65. Ibid., 10 Jan. 1922.

66. J. J. Murray, IMA, BMH WS1096.

67. *Freeman's Journal*, 10 Jan. 1922.

68. E. Phoenix, *Northern Nationalism: Nationalist Politics, Partition and the Catholic Minority in Northern Ireland* (Belfast, 1994) p. 115.

69. *Irish Independent*, 30 Jan. 1922; *Frontier Journal*, 1 Feb. 1922; Padraig Quinn memoir, KGM, McCann Cell Collection, 20/M5/IP41/08.

70. Untitled statement by Frank Aiken, *c*.1925, IMA, BMH CD 6/36/23.

71. E. O'Malley, *The Singing Flame* (Dublin, 1978), p. 42; Untitled statement by Frank Aiken, *c*.1925, UCDAD, P104/1308.

72. P. Hart, *Mick: The Real Michael Collins* (London, 2005), p. 363.

73. Untitled statement by Frank Aiken, *c*.1925, IMA, BMH CD 6/36/23; Hart, *Mick*, p. 363.

74. Confidential Department of Defence Memo, *c*.1926, UCDAD, FitzGerald papers, P80/457.

75. Lynch, *Northern IRA and the Early Years of Partition*, p. 100.

76. *Dail Éireann Debates* (hereafter, *DÉD*), vol. 208 (12 Mar. 1964), cols 992–3; *DÉD*, vol. 208 (9 Apr. 1964), cols 1375–6.

77. Untitled statement by Frank Aiken, *c*.1925, IMA, BMH CD 6/36/23; Valiulis, *Portrait of a Revolutionary*, pp 125–26; Hopkinson, *Green Against Green*, p. 59.

78. 'Position of the Fourth Northern Division, Jan. 1922–17th July 1922', *c*.July 1922, National Library of Ireland (hereafter, NLI), Johnson papers, Ms 17,143.

79. Valiulis, *Portrait of a Revolutionary*, pp 125–6; 'Position of the Fourth Northern Division, Jan. 1922–17th July 1922', *c*.July 1922, NLI, Johnson papers, Ms 17,143.

80. 'Chronology', *c*.1933, IMA, BMH, CD 6/36/22.

81. Padraig Quinn memoir, KGM, McCann Cell Collection, 20/M5/IP41/08.

82. Untitled statement by Frank Aiken, *c*.1925, IMA, BMH CD 6/36/23.

83. Watt to Wickham, 12 Jan. 1922, Public Records Office, Northern Ireland (hereafter, PRONI), HA/32/1/4; Watt to Wickham, 22 Dec. 1921, PRONI, HA/32/1/4.

84. John Grant, IMA, BMH WS 658.

85. 'Bi-monthly report on the state of affairs in Northern Ireland for the period up to the 15th Jan.', PRONI, HA/5/152.

86. For more on the boundary commission and the opposing objectives of republicans and unionists, see M. Laffan, *The Partition of Ireland, 1911–1925* (Dublin, 1983), pp 91–105.

87. *Frontier Sentinel*, 11 Feb. 1922.

88. For a detailed account of both the kidnapping raids and the incident at Clones, see Lynch, *Northern IRA and the Early Years of Partition*, pp 101–15.

89. *Freemans Journal*, 16 Feb. 1922; 'Bi monthly Report for the latter half of Feb., 1922', PRONI, HA/5/152; Ibid. *Frontier Sentinel*, 14 Jan. 1922; *Freemans Journal*, 18 Feb. 1922; Collins to Churchill (telegram), undated, National Archives of Ireland (hereafter, NAI), Department of Taoiseach (hereafter, TSCH), /3/S5462.

90. Dalton to Mulcahy, 27 Mar. 1922, IMA, Liaison and Evacuation papers, LE/4/16A; John McCoy, IMA, BMH WS 492.

91. McGarry, *Eoin O'Duffy*, p. 99; Confidential Department of Defence Memo, *c*.1926, UCDAD, FitzGerald papers, P80/457.

92. Lynch, *Northern IRA and the Early Years of Partition*, p. 101.

93. Padraig Quinn memoir notes, KGM, McCann Cell Collection (unsorted material).

94. See for example, Lynch, *Northern IRA and the Early Years of Partition*, p. 135; Staunton, *Nationalists of Northern Ireland*, pp 52–3; J. McDermott, *Northern Divisions: The Old IRA and the Belfast Pogroms* (Belfast, 2001), p. 161.

95. Lynch, *Northern IRA and the Early Years of Partition*, p. 99.

96. Hart, *Mick*, p. 380.

97. McGarry has argued that O'Duffy's role in the Fermanagh and Tyrone kidnapping raids demonstrates his role as a radicalising influence on Collins. This is also true of other militants in the Ulster Council, such as Aiken, who were clearly keen to resume hostilities in the region; see McGarry, *Eoin O'Duffy*, p. 100.

98. John McCoy, IMA, BMH WS 492.

99. Lynch, *Northern IRA and the Early Years of Partition*, pp 117–19; Confidential Department of Defence Memo, *c*.1926, UCDAD, FitzGerald papers, P80/457.

100. *Irish Times*, 17 Mar. 1922.

101. Ibid., 29 Mar. 1922; *Freemans Journal*, 21 Mar. 1922.

102. *Freeman Journal*, 29 Mar. 1922; Patrick Beagan, IMA, BMH, WS 612.

103. McGarry, *Eoin O'Duffy*, p. 100; *Irish Times*, 30 Mar. 1922.

104. *Irish Independent*, 1 Apr. 1922.

105. M. Hopkinson, 'The Craig-Collins pacts of 1922: Two attempted reforms of the Northern Ireland government', in *Irish Historical Studies*, 17: 106 (Nov. 1990), p.151.

106. *Irish Times*, 10 Apr. 1922; Charles McGleenan, IMA, BMH WS 829.

107. 'Bi-monthly report of the Divisional Commissioner for first half of Apr., 1922', 18 Apr. 1922, PRONI, HA/5/152; 'Bi-monthly report of the Divisional Commissioner for the latter half of Apr. 1922', 1 May 1922, PRONI, HA/5/152.

108. See, for examples, *Irish Times*, 4, 5, 7, 11, 26 Apr. 1922.

109. *Irish Independent*, 3 Apr. 1922.

110. *Frontier Sentinel*, 15 Apr. 1922.

111. 'Bi-monthly report of the Divisional Commissioner for the latter half of Apr. 1922', 1 May 1922, PRONI, HA/5/152.

112. Hopkinson, *Green Against Green*, pp 66–7.

113. Padraig Quinn memoir, KGM, McCann Cell Collection, 20/M5/IP41/08.

114. 'Notes of interview with Frank Aiken in Leinster House', 18 June 1952, NLI, O'Donoghue papers, Ms 31,421; 'Position of the Fourth Northern Division, Jan. 1922–17th July 1922', c.July 1922, NLI, Johnson papers, Ms 17,143.

115. John McCoy, IMA, BMH WS 492.

116. Ibid.

117. Laffan, *Resurrection of Ireland*, p. 353.

118. See below, pp 177–8.

119. See, for example, Patrick Casey, IMA, BMH WS 1148.

120. 'Divisional Staff at Various Dates', UCDAD, Aiken papers, P104/1310.

121. Mick Donnelly, UCDAD, O'Malley notebooks, P17b/116; Padraig Quinn memoir, KGM, McCann Cell Collection, 20/M5/IP41/08; there is some uncertainty as to whether this incident occurred before or after the army convention. Details in Donnelly's testimony suggest it occurred afterwards.

122. Coleman, *County Longford and the Irish Revolution*, p. 144; Hart, *The IRA and Its Enemies*, p. 263.

123. See D. Hall, 'Violence, political factionalism and their effects on North Louth' (PhD, National University of Ireland Maynooth, 2009), pp 130–52; P. Hart, *The IRA at War* (Oxford, 2003), pp 38–9, Maps 3 and 4.

124. Patrick Casey, IMA, BMH WS 1148.

125. Hopkinson, *Green Against Green*, p. 41.

126. John McCoy, IMA, BMH WS 492.

127. Thomas Luckie, ibid., 672.

128. Fourth Northern Division Circular, 18 Apr. 1922, UCDAD, Aiken papers, P104/1237.

129. Hall, 'Violence, political factionalism and their effects on North Louth', pp 159–60.

130. *Dundalk Examiner*, 1 Apr. 1922.

131. Aiken to Dalton, 8 Mar. 1922, IMA, Liaison and Evacuation correspondence, LE/4/16A.

132. John McCoy, IMA, BMH WS 492.

133. Padraig Quinn memoir, KGM, McCann Collection, 20/M5/IP41/08.

134. O'Malley, *The Singing Flame*, pp 55–62.

135. Padraig Quinn memoir, KGM, McCann Cell Collection, 20/M5/IP41/08.

136. Ibid.

137. Ibid.

138. *Dundalk Examiner*, 15 Apr. 1922; *Frontier Sentinel*, 15 Apr. 1922.

139. John Grant, IMA, BMH WS 658.

SIX

OFFENSIVE

—

Throughout April 1922, IRA activity in Northern Ireland declined in accordance with the terms of the second Craig-Collins pact.[1] In Armagh and south Down the Fourth Northern Division effectively ceased its operations and used the enforced hiatus to move its headquarters, and the majority of its active units, to north Louth and the safety of Free State territory. Yet this lull in activity did not last long. As April drew to a close, the pact collapsed with neither the northern nor southern administrations proving capable of fulfilling their obligations. The demise of the agreement precipitated renewed IRA violence in Northern Ireland, but there was no return to the intermittent activity of previous months. Instead, plans were laid for a large-scale offensive in the region with the backing of both pro- and anti-Treaty factions in southern Ireland. As chairman of the Ulster Council, Aiken became a key figure in the preparations for this joint-IRA offensive. His conduct when the attacks commenced, however, earned him the opprobrium of his northern IRA comrades. The Fourth Northern Division's pursuit of reprisal violence in south Armagh in the aftermath of the doomed offensive has also led some present-day northern unionists to brand Aiken as a perpetrator of ethnic cleansing and genocide.[2] Indeed, the events of May and June 1922, which witnessed two of the greatest controversies in Aiken's career, have been of critical importance in determining his legacy and perceptions of his revolutionary past.

The concept of a large-scale offensive in Northern Ireland had been circulating within the IRA as early as spring 1921. In March that year, amid the process of divisionalisation, strategy documents created by GHQ had stressed the growing importance of Ulster, describing the province as 'a bridge-head that the English cannot afford to lose and must spend lavishly to defend.'[6] A bespoke strategy document created for the Fourth Northern Division the following month included specific references to a 'general offensive' in the region, in which the Fourth Northern Division was 'to be regarded as the spear point [. . .] for which the driving power would be supplied from the South.'[4] In the final months of the war for independence, these grandiose notions were far beyond the IRA's actual capabilities. In the changed political and military circumstances of spring 1922, however, the conditions emerged in which an offensive of this nature was not only seriously considered, but actively attempted.

Determined plans for a joint-IRA offensive appear to have first emerged in March 1922. Florence O'Donoghue, a Cork IRA officer close to the anti-Treaty leader Liam Lynch, recalled that even before that month's army convention, pro- and anti-Treaty officers were co-operating in support of further action in the north amidst various meetings aimed at averting a split. The outcome of the convention did not affect this emerging joint-IRA policy. If anything, it served to intensify efforts to reach an agreement on the issue as negotiations aimed at reunification commenced.[5] It would be wrong to suggest, however, that the joint-IRA policy was an entirely cynical exercise driven by southern Irish political concerns. Northern opinion was well represented in both factions. The majority of the IRA's divisions in Ulster had remained loyal to GHQ in spite of their continued opposition to the Treaty and partition. Pro-Treaty leaders such as Collins, O'Duffy and Mulcahy had displayed a sincere concern for the plight of the northern nationalist minority.[6] A number of northern officers had also joined the anti-Treaty ranks. The most notable was Joe McKelvey, former commandant of the Third Northern Division, who was elected to the newly formed anti-Treaty IRA executive.[7] Alongside southern political concerns there was, therefore, a genuine desire on both sides of the split to take further action in Northern Ireland in the hopes of bringing a speedy end to partition.

The second Craig-Collins pact appears to have delayed any further discussion of the offensive until 21 April 1922, when representatives from GHQ announced the plan at a meeting of the Ulster Council at Clones. This appears to have been the first time that Aiken – or his fellow northern divisional commandants – had been made aware of the plans and his immediate reaction was one of caution. In the course of the meeting, he was offered the command of the operation but refused. That evening he explained his reasons to Padraig Quinn, the Fourth Northern Division's quartermaster: 'if I became general officer commanding these divisions – responsible for the whole northern campaign they [GHQ] would be able to blame me for failure – alternately if they failed in their commitments in their supplies to us.'[8] Aiken's distrust of GHQ reflected his broader reservations regarding the motives of the pro-Treaty leadership. His confrontation with Mulcahy regarding the occupation of Dundalk Barracks had occurred only weeks earlier.[9] Although he viewed the proposal with caution, he did agree to take charge of an important preparatory task, the smuggling of weapons into Northern Ireland for use in the offensive.[10]

During the Clones meeting GHQ representatives had asked the commandants of the IRA's five northern divisions to provide details of the arms and equipment they would require for the proposed offensive. A start date of 2 May was also set for the attack, allowing two weeks to transfer the necessary material into Northern Ireland. The bulk of this military hardware was to be provided by GHQ using the steady supply of arms and equipment it was receiving from the British government for the new Free State army. It is frequently observed that in order to disguise the provisional government's complicity in supplying northern units these newly acquired British arms were swapped with those of southern anti-Treaty units. These anti-Treaty arms were then sent to the IRA in the north.[11] This 'swap' arrangement is one of the few commonly known aspects of the offensive, yet it may not have been as significant as is sometimes assumed within the historiography. As quarter-master of the Fourth Northern Division, Padraig Quinn worked closely with Aiken in his gunrunning efforts prior to the offensive. He later recorded that, in the beginning, it was understood that GHQ would supply the arms for the offensive using the material supplied by Britain. It was only when the effort was well underway that GHQ realised that the arms and equipment it was providing could be traced through their serial numbers. Supplies to northern units were suddenly suspended. As Quinn observed, 'there was no downright refusal of arms, it was just put off which meant postponing or deferring our operation.' Amidst this uncertainty Aiken and Quinn approached Liam Lynch to seek help from the anti-Treaty IRA. After various discussions between Aiken, Mulcahy and Lynch, the swap arrangement was brokered. The actual quantity of weapons supplied was miniscule, however; a 'token transfer' of around 100 rifles. Although more material was apparently exchanged between pro- and anti-Treaty units in the weeks that followed, most of the arms sent north through Dundalk continued to be supplied directly by GHQ with IRA units being instructed to file off the serial numbers to prevent their identification.[12]

Aiken was responsible for supplying the Second and Third Northern Divisions, as well as his own units throughout Armagh, south Down and north Louth. During these weeks he became a frequent visitor to Beggars Bush Barracks and personally transported much of the material provided between Dublin and Dundalk.[13] From there, it was distributed to units throughout Northern Ireland by various means. Many consignments were smuggled by road, hidden in oil tankers.[14] Some IRA men recalled that fishing boats were used to drop arms and equipment at pre-designated spots on the coast.[15] There is also evidence to suggest that Aiken had utilised IRB networks to assist in the task.[16]

There is no definite record of the quantities of arms that were provided to northern units. Quinn suggested that each division had requested around 500 rifles, 250-300 revolvers and large quantities of ammunition. The one exception was the Third Northern Division. Given that its main strength was in Belfast, it was to receive 500 revolvers and 300 rifles (revolvers being considered more useful for urban fighting).[17] Writing in 1924, Aiken claimed that the Third Northern Division had received its requested number of rifles and twice the number of revolvers recorded by Quinn. His own division, meanwhile, had received 400 rifles, 500 revolvers and 'a few Thompsons [sub machine guns]'.[18]

This influx of arms was a significant boon for the Fourth Northern Division, and at a local level the arms consignments dramatically increased the military potential of its chronically underequipped companies. John Cosgrove recalled that the Ballymacnab Company's consignment provided 'sufficient arms to equip all our trained and active men with a rifle and a revolver each.'[19] Nevertheless, he also noted, 'I don't know if our expectations as to the quantities of arms intended for us was unduly optimistic, but when the arms arrived we felt somewhat disappointed.'[20] At first, such sentiments are difficult to explain, but it seems likely that they arose from the company's understanding of what was envisioned in the coming offensive.

The joint-IRA offensive's plan of attack has long been a source of speculation. In later years various contemporaries gave differing impressions of what was envisioned. Some spoke of it in terms of a large-scale conventional attack. Others described it as a mere extension of the IRA's existing guerrilla operations in the region.[21] Drawing on testimonies submitted to the Bureau of Military History, Lynch has concluded that 'on paper at least the offensive involved a virtual full-scale invasion of Northern Ireland.'[22] This was certainly how members of the Fourth Northern Division perceived it. Cosgrove, for example, described his company's planned operations as follows:

> The Ballymacnab Company were first to take over a newly erected house – a residence for the local clergyman – as a hospital. We were then to join up with the Lislea section of the Armagh Company and the Markethill outpost of the Ballymacnab Company and to deal with any local opposition from the Lisnadill B/Specials and from the B/Specials in Markethill and Red Rock areas. After dealing with any local opposition we were ordered to move in the direction of Armagh city where we should join up with all the other battalion units from Armagh, and when the local military garrison was subdued we were all to move in the direction of Lough Neagh from where the 3rd Brigade would launch an attack on the town of Portadown which we understood was a key point in the British defences.[23]

In south Down, Hugh Gribben recalled plans for an attack on Newry while Patrick Casey, vice-commandant of the Second Brigade, spoke ambitiously of applying 'a general scorched earth policy in the entire area.'[24]

Padraig Quinn later recorded the most remarkable description of what was envisioned in the offensive, as northern units understood it. Included amongst unsorted and previously unpublished notes, his recollections provide a rare glimpse of the IRA's overall plan of attack in Northern Ireland. The First Northern Division, based in Donegal, was 'to take all posts in [a] general sweep from Donegal concentrating on Derry [city].' In Tyrone and Derry, the Second Northern Division was 'to occupy all posts in area attempting no mass movements of troops but more or less preparing the ground for occupancy by 1, 5, 4 [Northern] Divisions.' The Third Northern Division's operations were divided up amongst its various component areas. In Antrim, 'movement of troops [was] to be on a moderately large scale [with] attempts to be made to capture one or two key positions'. Belfast was 'to be held up' with republican troops occupying positions in sufficient strength so as to hold the city. Units in north Down, meanwhile, were 'to devote attention to harassing and annoying concentrations of English forces' at Newtownards and Ballykinlar. Various towns were to be 'occupied' and a junction effected with the Fourth Northern Division for an advance towards Belfast. As indicated in Cosgrove's statement, the Fourth Northern Division was to launch an assault on Armagh Military Barracks and 'advance on Portadown.' Banbridge was to be occupied and the advance continued towards Belfast with troops from Down. All RIC and USC 'posts and personnel' were to be wiped out in all areas and 'all effectives in every division' were to be mobilised for the attacks.

Certain details are absent from Quinn's account. There is, for example, no indication of the operations to be carried out by the Fourth Northern Division in south Down, although veiled references are made to an attack on Newry elsewhere in his notes. There is also confusion regarding the intended role of the Fifth Northern Division and the First Midland Division. Both units were represented on the Ulster Council and it is generally believed that they were to participate in the offensive. Quinn only makes reference to the Fifth Northern Division, claiming that it was 'to attempt to occupy all posts within [its divisional] area, paying special attention to Enniskillen' and then to join up with the Fourth Northern Division above Armagh. Enniskillen, however, was part of the First Midland Division's command area. It is possible that Quinn simply confused the divisions or, perhaps, failed to distinguish between them in describing their intended movements. Nevertheless, his testimony provides a compelling sketch of what was envisioned and highlights the extent to which the Fourth Northern Division was to be a key player.[25]

It is uncertain who authored these plans. Their ambitious visions of conventional warfare suggest the influence of GHQ, as similar ideas and rhetoric were expressed in its earlier strategy documents.[26] The more detailed plans for local operations were presumably left to the various northern divisional commandants. As chairman of the Ulster Council Aiken is likely to have been involved in overseeing these preparations, but there is little evidence of his specific role. Regardless of who created the plans, they were extremely unrealistic. Northern IRA units were not capable of undertaking such an ambitious attack. Generous estimates place the organisation's membership in Ulster at 8,500 men in early 1922.[27] More conservative estimates suggest a figure of 4,000.[28] These figures, moreover, only represented its membership 'on paper'. In each case, the number of active members is considered to have been significantly lower than the total.[29] The Northern Ireland government, on the other hand, had at its disposal an estimated 27,563 USC constables (full-time, part-time and emergency reservists).[30] This was further supplemented by the remnants of the RIC in the province, the growing number of new recruits for its replacement, the Royal Ulster Constabulary (RUC), and approximately 5,000 British troops.[31] Even with the support of the First and Fifth Northern Divisions, and the First Midland Division, the prospects for the offensive were extremely unfavourable and any meaningful success was highly unlikely.

This begs the question, was any significant military success seriously expected? The ultimate aim of the offensive has proven an even greater source of speculation than its proposed plan of attack. Hopkinson has observed that various contemporaries appeared to disagree over what the offensive was intended to achieve. Northern IRA officers, such as Aiken and his divisional staff, clearly envisioned it as an attempt to bring down the fledgling Northern Ireland government and smash partition, regardless of the consequences for the Treaty. At least one anti-Treaty IRA officer, meanwhile, believed that the operations were intended simply to provoke a political or diplomatic incident.[32]

The pro-Treaty faction's objectives in supporting the offensive are particularly difficult to ascertain. Historians such as John Regan and Fearghal McGarry have suggested that GHQ's involvement may have been a ploy geared towards maintaining the loyalty of northern IRA units in the period leading up to the civil war. Leaders such as Collins and O'Duffy, it is argued, never intended a serious attack on partition but may have misled northern officers as to the nature of the offensive and the degree of support they could expect from pro-Treaty divisions across the border.[33] Regan has also observed, however, that there is evidence to suggest that the initiative for the attack came from within northern IRA units. 'In such circumstances', he argues, 'Collins had little choice but to go along with the plan and let the northerners burn themselves out.'[34]

Although there is certainly evidence that suggests that the initiative for the offensive came from within the Ulster Council, there is equally valid evidence to suggest the opposite. Lynch's groundbreaking research indicates that the decision to renew IRA activity in the north after the second Craig-Collins pact emanated from pro-Treaty leaders, Collins in particular.[35] This was certainly the impression of Fourth Northern Division officers such as Quinn, who later noted, 'I understood from F. [Aiken] that Michael Collins was the inspiration for this general offensive.'[36] It is, of course, possible that the decision for renewed IRA activity in Northern Ireland was that of GHQ, but that the Ulster Council was responsible for its overambitious scale.

Fourth Northern Division officers such as John McCoy and Padraig Quinn believed that the support of pro-Treaty leaders was genuine at first, but that their enthusiasm cooled once the full implications of the attack became apparent. McCoy recalled that 'the pro-Treaty party seemed to suddenly realise that operations in the north might, and possibly would, cause a complete smash up of all the treaty plans with the British.'[37] Quinn similarly sensed a changed attitude amongst pro-Treaty leaders after a car provided to the Fourth Northern Division by GHQ was captured near Banbridge and found to contain ammunition. According to Quinn, the serial number of the vehicle was soon traced back to Beggars Bush and Collins was summoned to London. The affair was also alleged to have created tension between Collins and other members of the provisional government, especially Griffith. As Quinn recalled, 'all kinds of rumours were current about what happened between them [...] we have no knowledge except that things were changed.'[38] The recollections of Quinn and McCoy appear to support Kevin O'Shiel's view that the offensive, and its ultimate collapse, were due to Collins's tendency to come to 'quick decisions without consulting many'.[39] Nevertheless, even if the pro-Treaty faction's support was genuine at the outset, once the full implications of the offensive became clear, they began to mislead northern units. This lends credence to Regan's belief that O'Duffy and Collins eventually manipulated the situation to produce a 'tactical advantage' in the period leading up to the civil war.[40]

The confusion surrounding the offensive's aims was exacerbated by the complicated means through which it was planned, prepared and co-ordinated. There were essentially three separate entities involved; the northern IRA, as represented by the Ulster Council, the pro-Treaty GHQ, and the anti-Treaty IRA executive. In discussing their respective duties, Lynch has observed that, 'while the pro-Treaty side would be largely responsible for supplying the arms and equipment, the anti-Treaty IRA would provide the leadership. It would be left to the Northern IRA to supply the majority of the actual manpower.'[41] Responsibility for the co-ordination of the attacks apparently lay with GHQ. Some contemporaries disputed this, however, claiming that Aiken was to take overall command of the offensive.[42] Aiken's position as chairman of the Ulster Council was undoubtedly the source of these claims, but in reality he held no responsibility for the co-ordination of the offensive. As has already been observed, he refused the command when it was first offered to him during the meeting at Clones on 21 April. A second offer was made shortly before the attacks were to commence, but he again refused. Aiken later recalled, 'Mulcahy asked me if I would take command of all the divisions in the north for the purposes of carrying on whatever activities were agreed upon there. I asked if I took responsibility would I be given authority and a free hand. He said no and I did not accept.'[43] Once the offensive began, the responsibility for its co-ordination ultimately fell to GHQ and O'Duffy as chief-of-staff. This was most clearly illustrated by events once the offensive commenced.

COLLAPSE

The offensive was scheduled to begin on 2 May 1922, but it soon became clear that the two-week period allocated for the transfer of arms and material to northern units was insufficient. Consignments were delayed, possibly as a result of GHQ's unease regarding serial numbers.[44] Consequently, Seamus Woods, commandant of the Third Northern Division, approached O'Duffy to request more time to prepare. O'Duffy agreed, but permitted the Second Northern Division to commence as planned on 2 May. With the other divisions having postponed their operations, the Second Northern Division was quickly overwhelmed. Despite a promising start, with co-ordinated strikes on three police barracks and a wave of arson attacks and shootings, the division soon faced intense pressure from the USC. Its campaign effectively collapsed before any other division had mobilised.[45]

On 5 May, O'Duffy presided over a meeting of northern officers at Clones and granted a further two weeks for the other divisions to complete their preparatory work. The offensive was now scheduled to begin on 19 May, and it was to be signalled by an audacious raid on Musgrave Street RIC Barracks in Belfast by members of the Third Northern Division. The aim of the operation was to capture arms and a number of armoured cars for use in the offensive. It was planned for the early hours of 18 May, and Woods received assurances from O'Duffy that all divisions would be ordered out the next day (19 May).[46]

The Musgrave Street Barracks raid took place, as planned, but ultimately failed in its objective. The presence of the raiding party was discovered and it was forced to withdraw empty handed. Despite this setback, the Third Northern Division began its offensive the following day, yet found itself acting alone. All other divisions, including the Fourth Northern Division, failed to commence their operations. On 24 May, under intense pressure from the authorities, the Third Northern Division made a desperate plea to O'Duffy to order Aiken's men out immediately.[47] It was hoped that a second front would stretch the authorities' resources and relieve IRA units in Belfast and north Down. Although O'Duffy promised he would do so, there is no evidence that an order was issued, and Aiken's division remained inactive. With relative peace on the border, USC constables in south Down were sent further north to help quell the violence. In an attempt to preserve its forces, the Third Northern Division wound down its operations. Woods later reported that the whole episode had so demoralised his men that 'the Military Organisation is almost destroyed.'[48]

The events surrounding the setting of the dates for the offensive, and the fact that the Third Northern Division approached the chief-of-staff, rather than Aiken himself, to order out the Fourth Northern Division, indicates that GHQ was responsible for the co-ordination of the offensive. A department of defence memo further suggests this, noting that 'detailed reports of the actual operations were furnished to the Chief of Staff, GHQ'.[49] The misapprehension that Aiken was in overall command of the offensive has greatly influenced the perception of his division's inaction. It lends a particular sense of treachery to the episode, as well as the implication that the decision to withdraw from the attack was his alone. This was not necessarily the case, but why did the Fourth Northern Division ultimately fail to commence its attacks?

The testimonies of Fourth Northern Division members indicate that the division was due to start its offensive operations on 22 May, not 19 May as suggested elsewhere.[50] This inconsistency may have been due to confusion resulting from the Third Northern Division's failed raid on Musgrave Street Barracks. It was intended that the armoured cars captured in the operation would be brought to Dundalk. According to Quinn, the Fourth Northern Division duly received word that the raid was to take place and mobilised its units in south Armagh and south Down 'to facilitate and cover the passage of the armoured cars through their commands.' When the operation failed, and the armoured cars did not arrive, these forces 'were withdrawn having been on duty from midnight to 6-7 in the morning.'[51] In the resulting confusion, divisional officers may have believed that the offensive was to once again be postponed and, therefore, did not commence their operations as planned on 19 May. Indeed, Belfast IRA officer, Roger McCorley, later indicated that a second postponement did occur which pushed the date of the operations back to 22 May. Yet this contradicts the narrative suggested by the bulk of the available evidence.[52]

The revised start-date may also have been due to Aiken's absence from the division. On 16 May he had led a delegation of local republicans to Dublin to lobby for unity during the negotiations for the Collins-de Valera pact, an agreement aimed at maintaining political unity in the upcoming southern elections.[53] Aiken was present for the announcement of the resulting agreement in Dáil Éireann on 20 May.[54] He subsequently returned to Dundalk, where his division was presumably preparing for its scheduled attacks on 22 May. Yet the evening before the attack was due to commence, with units mobilised and positioned throughout Armagh and south Down, he issued a cancellation order. As Patrick Casey recalled, 'I asked what the position was and he [Aiken] replied that our division was taking no part in the rising, but that there was no cancellation so far as the remainder of the northern counties was [sic] concerned.'[55] Some local units did not receive the orders until the following day. Meanwhile, in response to the disorder elsewhere in Northern Ireland, internment was introduced on 22 May. In the absence of IRA activity in Armagh and south Down, the USC raids were unchallenged and around 36 republicans were taken prisoner.[56]

The reasons for the Fourth Northern Division's withdrawal from the offensive have been a source of speculation for historians. Did Aiken issue the cancellation order himself, or did it originate with GHQ? Patrick Casey seems to have believed that it was Aiken's decision, recalling that he 'gave as his reason the fact that the Armagh Brigade was not fully equipped.' He continued, however, 'I could never understand Aiken's real motive in not fighting his division on this important occasion'.[57] Concerns over the Armagh Brigade's equipment levels certainly seem an odd rationale for such a late decision, although Aiken's reservations may have been justified. The brigade had an ambitious plan of attack, which included an assault on Armagh Military Barracks and an advance on Portadown. As has already been observed, some members of the units were concerned about the quantities of arms they had received to undertake such a mission.[58] Their reservations are further qualified by the testimony of Seán McConville, who recalled that the Lurgan Battalion received only 60 rifles, a Thompson machine gun, 60 grenades and 'some revolvers' in preparation for the offensive.[59] For a battalion with approximately 220 members ('on paper' at least) these quantities were certainly low, and wholly inadequate for the operations anticipated.[60]

Aiken's concerns about the Armagh Brigade's equipment levels may have been a manifestation of a more general unease regarding his division's prospects. It is telling that during this period he had made efforts to acquire a further 500 rifles from GHQ.[61] This suggests that his reservations about equipment levels were not necessarily confined to one brigade area. His judgement must also have been affected by events elsewhere. The fate of the Second Northern Division in the preceding two weeks could not have escaped his attention. The initial reports of the Third Northern Division's operations may also have influenced his outlook. As Lynch has observed, having commenced its operations on 19 May, this division's offensive lasted only a week 'with virtually all the violence confined to the first two days.'[62] In these first 48 hours, three barracks attacks failed. The burning of property and various shootings in Belfast had proven a greater success, but hardly lived up to expectations of what had originally been envisioned. In this context, the cancellation order may have resulted from a simple, and very understandable, loss of nerve. To push ahead with the planned operations, with the Second Northern Division effectively defeated and the Third Northern Division in serious difficulty, would have been futile and would have needlessly weakened, if not destroyed, the division.

John McCoy's testimony, although vague, appears to suggest that the cancellation order issued by Aiken originated from GHQ:

> Orders to the effect came to us with only sufficient time to enable the operations to be called off. In some other areas, notably Tyrone, Derry and Belfast, Co. Antrim and East Down the cancellation did not reach the men in time and the operations commenced. I am not in position to define exactly how this muddle of the orders cancelling the rising occurred. I believe that in the case of the Third Northern Division the fault lay with the pro-Treaty headquarters in not providing an alternative means of notification which would ensure the order arriving by at least one route. [63]

There is nothing in Patrick Casey's testimony that rules out this possibility, although he certainly appeared convinced that the order originated with Aiken. Yet McCoy's testimony contradicts Casey in one important respect. Casey claimed that, on notifying him of the division's withdrawal from the offensive, Aiken made clear that the cancellation did not apply to other northern divisions. Both testimonies are problematic, however, as the Second and Third Northern Divisions had already commenced their operations ahead of the Fourth Northern Division's start-date of 22 May. It could be assumed, therefore, that any cancellation order handed down to Aiken applied to his division only.

It is certainly plausible that a cancellation order from GHQ arrived in Dundalk on the eve of the attacks. Communication links with Dublin were good as a result of the direct rail link. It is also possible that Aiken received the order while in Dublin that weekend. If it did originate with GHQ, however, why was it issued? A defence department memo from 1926 indicated that a decision was taken 'that there would be no fighting on the border or around it – which decision meant [sic] that there were no "offensive" operations carried out by the 1 Northern, or 1st Midland or 5th Northern Divisions.'[64] This most likely reflected GHQ's desire to hide its involvement in IRA activity in

Northern Ireland. It also explains the inaction of the other units on the border. Logically, this decision should have applied to the Fourth Northern Division and it may account for the cancellation of its operations. The division was based in Free State territory and occupied a military base on behalf of the provisional government. Its participation in the offensive would have constituted fighting on or around the border and would have made clear the pro-Treaty leadership's complicity in the violence. If the cancellation order did originate with GHQ, this was the most probable cause. Indeed, it is intriguing that the only two divisions that were allowed to proceed with their operations unhindered, the Second and Third Northern Divisions, were those with command areas based entirely within Northern Ireland.

This scenario has lent further credence by the fact that Aiken and his staff continued to believe that an offensive was in the offing even after the collapse of the May operations. In late June, only two days before provisional government forces attacked anti-Treaty positions in Dublin, Aiken recalled getting into an argument with O'Duffy while pressing for more rifles for the offensive.[65] Quinn also recalled approaching Mulcahy on 16 June, the day of the southern elections, to ask for more material for the initiative. Mulcahy, he alleged, advised burning when he could not give me [the] requisite rifles. [He] advised burning Banbridge, Lawrencetown [. . .] as a matter of fact I was ordered to burn half of Newry.'[66] Not only did the officers of the Fourth Northern Division believe that an offensive was still to come, they were encouraged in these beliefs by pro-Treaty leaders.

It is tempting to speculate further as to the reasons for the Fourth Northern Division's withdrawal from the offensive, but the scenarios outlined above are the only suggestions that are supported by the available evidence. McCoy and Casey were well placed within the Fourth Northern Division (as divisional adjutant and vice-commandant of the Newry and South Down Brigade respectively) and their testimonies provide the only first-hand account of Aiken's actions. Their varying interpretations of the episode and the differing emphasis as to who was responsible for the division's withdrawal may be explained by subsequent events. Casey was one of the few officers in the division to support the pro-Treaty position during the civil war and became a member of the Free State Army. McCoy stayed loyal to Aiken as a member of the anti-Treaty faction and remained close to him in later years. These civil war loyalties may account for the inconsistencies in their testimonies. In the absence of further evidence, however, the extent of Aiken's culpability for his division's withdrawal remains unclear.

Though Aiken and his fellow officers may not have realised it, the collapse of the planned attacks in May ended any hope of a large scale IRA offensive in Northern Ireland. It did not, however, spell the end of the Fourth Northern

Division's activities there. In Armagh and south Down, the month that followed was the most violent of the revolutionary period. In May 1922 there had only been five conflict-related deaths in the division. In June, the figure rose sharply to seventeen, most of which occurred in Newry and the adjacent districts of south Armagh.[67] While some historians have viewed this upsurge as a late attempt by the Fourth Northern Division to pursue a 'limited offensive' in the area, it did not form part of the IRA's broader schemes in Northern Ireland.[68] On the contrary, it was notable for its reactionary nature and apparent lack of forward planning.

Throughout May 1922, the Fourth Northern Division's attentions had been firmly focused on the preparations for the offensive. Nevertheless, IRA activity had resumed in Armagh and south Down and a few noteworthy operations did occur. At Derrymacash, outside Lurgan, a USC patrol was ambushed.[69] In Camlough an attempt was also made to capture the local police barracks by ruse. The operation was attempted on a Sunday morning. In preparation, the raiding party held up Canon Quin, and fifteen of his congregation, at the nearby Irish National Foresters hall. Various complications ultimately resulted in the raid being called off, but the treatment of Canon Quin and his parishioners received considerable attention in the national press.[70]

A significant escalation in IRA activity did not occur until later in the month, after the cancellation of the Fourth Northern Division's offensive operations and the introduction of internment. In the course of one week, Newry and south Armagh experienced more IRA activity than would usually have occurred in a month. It began on 28 May with a prolonged skirmish between the IRA and the USC on the Armagh-Louth border. The incident was sparked when USC constables from Jonesborough looted a public house situated on the Free State side of the border.[71] IRA officers, encamped in the ruins of Ravensdale Castle, surprised the looters and opened fire on them. The shots alerted the nearby USC garrison and a firefight ensued. As Jack McElhaw later recalled, 'the IRA camp and the Specials barracks at Jonesboro [sic] are on elevations facing each other and very soon rifles and machine guns were working full blast from both positions.'[72] Both sides were quickly joined by reinforcements, including British military from Newry, and it was not long before the line of fire had extended along the border from 'the Dundalk main road to beyond the village of Jonesborough.'[73] The skirmish was ended through negotiations between Aiken and the USC. During the confrontation a group of four uniformed members of Cumann na mBan had been arrested while carrying explosives and field dressings to the IRA positions from dumps in south Armagh. Aiken consented to a truce in return for their release. The skirmish lasted approximately 30 hours and resulted in the wounding of five USC constables and two civilians.[74]

This spontaneous confrontation was followed on 31 May by a series of abductions throughout the Fourth Northern Division area. Aiken had ordered the kidnapping of prominent unionists and members of the USC in the area.[75] Six abductions were reported in Armagh. Meanwhile, in Rathfriland, a failed attempt was made to seize a local doctor.[76] In the days that followed further 'hostages' were seized. A USC officer named Captain McMorran was accidently captured by a party of IRA men commandeering cars near Newtownhamilton.[77] Alongside those individuals forcibly abducted in Northern Ireland, a number of men were taken prisoner while in Louth. These included three fishermen (two of whom were B Specials) from Kilkeel, who were seized at Greenore while trying to dispatch their produce to England.[78] In all, around ten hostages were taken and detained at Dundalk Barracks, where they remained until July 1922 when they were finally released by provisional government troops.[79]

Members of the Fourth Northern Division frequently attributed Aiken's decision to take hostages to a desire to protect the nationalist community in Armagh and south Down. John McCoy later claimed that the decision was motivated by loyalist reprisals in south Armagh, and stated that,

> The form that we decided to employ as countermeasures to the shooting of our people was the capture of hostages who were men of influence and undoubted imperialistic outlook who would be held as guarantors for the good conduct of the Unionist elements in their respective districts.[80]

These sentiments were echoed by John Grant, captain of the Mullaghbawn Company, who recalled that those abducted were 'informed that they were being held as hostages for the good conduct of the other unionists in their district.'[81]

This image of the IRA as a defender of the wider nationalist community is integral to the northern republican narrative of the revolutionary period. Lynch has challenged this view, however. Focusing on events in Belfast, he has argued that republican violence usually 'had more to do with seeking revenge against those responsible for killing IRA comrades than with a general wish to avenge the activities of murder gangs who threatened the wider Catholic community.'[82] This was certainly true of the Fourth Northern Division's decision to take hostages. The shootings that McCoy claimed had provoked the operations did not occur until two weeks after the abductions had taken place. Indeed, no reprisal shootings of nationalists had occurred in the divisional area in the weeks previous.[83] Far from being motivated by reprisal killings, the kidnappings were actually an attempt to secure the release of republican prisoners.

The real motives for the operations are all too clear from the letters that various hostages at Dundalk Barracks were compelled to write to loved ones. Harry Macintosh, for example, wrote to his mother:

> I was talking to the O/C this evening and he says the minute the three men that were arrested at Lisnacree, Murney, Monaghan and Murray, are released we three will get free and a guarantee to get home boat and all so will you let Col. Warren and the B men know, so get to work as soon as possible.[84]

The O/C, to whom he referred, was Seán Quinn who was filling in for a week in Aiken's absence.[85] Another hostage, Jim Murdock, wrote to a local unionist solicitor:

> I was told today if I wrote to you [and] got you to go to the Specials [and] got them to release a man named Ben McArdle of Mullaghbawn which lives in our house for the last 10 years [sic], he is a prisoner at Forkhill House at present, that they would exchange me for him hoping you will see to have this done [sic].[86]

Although the men referenced in Macintosh's letter had been arrested earlier in the year, the renewed efforts to secure the release of republican prisoners were most likely motivated by the introduction of internment on 22 May.

The prisoner issue also motivated the Fourth Northern Division's targeting of Newry's Resident Magistrate, James Woulfe Flanagan, on 3 June. In light of his position, Woulfe Flanagan had long been an enemy of the republican movement. Indeed, it was he who had presided over Aiken's trial for illegal drilling in 1918. Yet it was likely that his more recent actions had led to his being singled out by the IRA. In late May 1922, he had been involved in a number of trials involving republicans. Among them was the case of Michael Fearon, a long-standing and active member of the local IRA. Fearon was stationed at Dundalk Barracks, but was picked up by police in south Armagh and charged with the possession of a single round of ammunition.[87] The party involved in Woulfe Flanagan's killing were instructed to 'arrest or shoot' him, and apparently resorted to the latter option when 'we found we were not able to force him to come with us'.[88] Neither the hostage policy, nor Woulfe Flanagan's assassination, was motivated by concern for the nationalist population, and ultimately these events did nothing to improve the minority's plight. If anything they merely served to heighten tension in the region and further provoke the USC.

Shortly after the initial kidnapping operations, on 1 June, another less intense confrontation erupted on the border close to the Fourth Northern Division's camp at Dungooley. The *Irish Times* reported that the firing had originated from the Free State side of the border and was directed at a USC patrol that had been involved in a road accident.[89] McElhaw, however, claimed that the USC were attacked after they were spotted stealthily approaching the frontier. Given the hostage takings of the previous days, it is possible that the patrol was attempting to attack or reconnoitre the division's camp at Dungooley. This second round of border fighting was again sustained by reinforcements, including British military from Newry. The shooting lasted into the early hours of the following morning with the line of fire extending for over a mile. As with the previous outbreak, the incident was eventually defused through negotiation and an agreed ceasefire.[90]

Amidst the kidnappings and skirmishes, the Fourth Northern Division also renewed its guerrilla operations in south Armagh. After the second round of border fighting at Dungooley, it was decided to avoid any further prolonged confrontations on the frontier. To maintain the momentum of IRA activity in south Armagh, however, it was decided to form a new column drawing on the experienced members of the Camlough and Mullaghbawn companies at Dungooley camp. From early June this unit began to cross into south Armagh to attempt ambushes. Despite its best efforts, however, it consistently failed to engage with its chosen targets, the mixed parties of USC and British military that frequently patrolled the area. Despite setting up at least nine ambushes, only one resulted in an actual engagement. Some members interpreted this lack of success as an indication that the authorities were deliberately avoiding confrontations with the IRA.[91] Whatever the reasons for the column's difficulties, the return to guerrilla warfare certainly had a minimal impact on the escalating violence in the region. Of the 17 conflict-related deaths in Armagh and south Down in June 1922, only five were members of the state forces. The remaining 12 victims were civilians, with the possible exception of three individuals who may have been members of the IRA.[92] The Fourth Northern Division's attacks on the authorities were of little direct influence on that month's high casualty rate. Rather, the increase was determined by a horrific sequence of reprisal and counter-reprisal perpetrated by the Fourth Northern Division and the local USC.

The IRA's activities in late May and early June had undoubtedly raised tensions in the Newry and south Armagh area, but the USC were slow to respond with reprisal attacks like those witnessed in July 1921. Two business premises in Newry had been burned in an apparent reprisal shortly after the assassination of Woulfe Flanagan, but it was another week before there were any renewed killings.[93] In that time, continuing IRA column activity served to exacerbate the already tense local situation. It also served as a pretext for the USC's actions when it finally responded on the night of 13–14 June with two incidents that would have dire repercussions in the days that followed.

The first incident occurred at Lislea, near Camlough, when Patrick Creggan and Thomas Crawley were abducted from their respective homes in the Derrymore and Whitecross districts, shot dead and dumped on the road. Their bodies were deliberately placed over two holes where landmines had been laid by the Fourth Northern Division column during an ambush attempt sometime previously.[94] Despite the fact that numerous witnesses had seen the victims being driven through the district in a motor tender by men in police uniform, an official inquiry into the deaths found that there had been no involvement by the RUC or the USC. Instead it was concluded that persons disguised as policemen had killed Creggan and Crawley. It was further implied that the actual culprits were the IRA, and that the men were shot for informing on the location of the mine holes at Lislea.[95] These claims had little substance, however, and although neither victim appears to have been personally involved in the republican movement, Creggan's brother (Michael) was an active member of the IRA.[96]

The second incident occurred at Dromintee at a public house owned by James McGuill, a prominent Sinn Féin councillor. A long-standing target of raids by police, military and the USC, McGuill had been staying in Free State territory for his own safety, leaving his family behind to take care of the business. In the early hours a group of armed men, believed by the IRA to be disguised USC constables from Forkhill Barracks, forced their way into the house. They claimed to be looking for McGuill in connection with the shooting of a USC constable on the Armagh-Monaghan border near Caledon, some 30 miles away.[97] What followed was described in a Fourth Northern Division report:

> After breaking into the shop they helped themselves to drink and any cash they could find but were unable to open the safe. They searched the house for men, but the only occupants were four women, McGuill's wife, mother in law, two women servants, and two children under three. Finding no men they commenced torturing the women for the keys of the safe. Mrs McGuill who is about to be confined [in late stages of pregnancy] was caught by two of them, thrown on the bed, abused, and night clothes torn in an attempt to get the keys. In the excitement to escape from the brutes with blackened faces she tried to throw herself through the window but was dragged back by one of the other women. Three of the Specials caught a young female servant, kicked her, threw her on the bed, and attempted to outrage her. They failed owing to her struggle and the help of the others.[98]

The language used to describe the assaults committed against Mrs McGuill and her maid clearly indicates sexual violence, although it leaves a degree of ambiguity as to its nature. Aiken, during a speech in the Dáil in 1929, described the incident as an 'attempted rape.'[99] In conjunction with other reports, most of which broadly conform to the above text, it is clear that at the very least both Mrs McGuill and her maid were victims of a violent sexual assault. Other reports, despite the ambiguous language used to discuss such matters, very plausibly suggest that Mrs McGuill had been raped.[100]

The two attacks provoked much outrage amongst the local nationalist community. In delivering the oration at the funeral of Thomas Crawley a local priest used the occasion to denounce 'those wretched scoundrels in uniform supported and paid by the British Government.'[101] The attack on the McGuill household had further reverberations. Collins informed Churchill of the incident. Churchill, in turn, demanded an explanation from the Northern Ireland government.[102] The northern authorities dismissed the reports of the raid as nothing more than a false allegation concocted for propaganda and a compensation claim.[103] Intriguingly, despite this stance, they did eventually pay Mrs McGuill £100 compensation for personal injury in relation to the incident; an act which could be viewed as a belated admission of wrong-doing.[104] Perhaps the most important outcome of the attacks, however, was that they provided the immediate provocation for the Fourth Northern Division's infamous reprisal attacks at Altnaveigh and Lisdrumliska.

OUTRAGE

In the early hours of 17 June the Fourth Northern Division carried out a series of reprisal attacks in south Armagh. The operations began at Dromintee at approximately 1 a.m. when an IRA column ambushed a USC patrol outside McGuill's Pub. One constable was killed and another wounded before the attacking party withdrew.[105] The violence continued at approximately 2.40 a.m. when the home of Mary Thompson, a Protestant widow, was fired upon by a separate group of armed men as they moved through the townland of Ballymacdermott. Around 40 minutes later this reprisal party of approximately 20 men arrived in the townlands of Altnaveigh and Lisdrumliska. It divided into sections and launched simultaneous attacks on a number of Protestant households. Four families bore the brunt of the attacks, having their homes burned and selected family members shot dead or seriously wounded. A further four properties were attacked with gunfire and incendiaries with no resulting casualties. Having completed their operations the reprisal party departed, with part of the group leaving by car to round off the night's activities with further incendiary attacks at Derrymore and Cloughreagh, including a failed attempt to burn down Derrymore House, a target that was possibly selected for its symbolism as the site where the Act of Union was drafted in 1800.[106]

Although not the only reprisal operations that night, the attacks at Altnaveigh and Lisdrumliska proved the most shocking and brutal. In 1922, the townlands formed a small rural community on the outskirts of Newry, straddling the Belfast to Dublin railway line. Census returns from 1911 suggest that 68 per cent of the area's inhabitants were Protestants, in contrast to south Armagh as a whole, where they accounted for around 30 per cent of the population. The area was considered to be predominantly unionist, the townland of Altnaveigh particularly so. During the home rule crisis just over half of that district's eligible Protestant population (around 54.8 per cent) had signed the Ulster Covenant or the accompanying women's pledge. At least 25 of the district's menfolk had also joined the UVF in the same period.[107] In the days that followed the attacks, the *Frontier Sentinel* described the area as a 'stronghold of unionism from which many members of the B Specials have been recruited'.[108] This claim was integral to the Fourth Northern Division's supposed rationale in carrying out the attacks, though none of the victims was a member of the USC.[109]

The details of the individual killings make for harrowing reading. Amongst the victims were Thomas and Eliza Crozier, a couple who were gunned down on their doorstop after recognising their attackers. At another household, James Heaslip and his teenage son Robert were killed attempting to flee. Joseph Gray was dragged from his bed and shot, dying the next day from his wounds. His father John was also seriously wounded while desperately trying to stop the gunmen. In similar circumstances, James Lockhart was shot dead whilst attempting to comfort his mother as she pleaded with the gunmen for his life.[110] Indeed, the majority of the victims were killed in front of family members amidst desperate pleas for mercy.

The operations were well planned and were executed with speed and efficiency. Various reports estimated that the attacks lasted somewhere between 30 minutes and one hour.[111] To ensure no police or military interference, landmines were detonated on the Dublin road, the main thoroughfare off which the district was located.[112] The raiders were also alleged to have worn police style caps and bandoliers in an effort to disguise themselves as a USC patrol. The attire was later judged to be items of prison warder uniform from Dundalk gaol, which was at that time under IRA control.[113] It is likely that the party's 'disguises' were actually little more than the usual mixed batch of military-style clothing worn by Fourth Northern Division members in lieu of an actual uniform. Indeed, the division's ambush parties had been mistaken as USC patrols before, particularly as the force's B Special class did not at first wear a full uniform.[114] Press reports were keen to emphasise the high level of local knowledge exhibited in the attacks, observing that the townlands were positioned 'off the main road a distance of about half a mile, and it would be utterly impossible for strangers to locate them without local assistance as the roads leading to them form a perfect net of bye-roads.'[115] Local knowledge was also demonstrated in the party's flawless targeting of only Protestant households, as well as the fact that Thomas and Eliza Crozier apparently recognised their killers.[116]

Given his later prominence in Irish politics, Aiken's role in the Altnaveigh massacre has become a focal point for discussion. In southern Ireland, where he continues to be respected for his role in international affairs in the 1950s and 1960s, the reprisal is viewed as a 'foul stain' on an otherwise noble political career.[117] In Northern Ireland individuals in both communities have used his complicity in the attacks as a means of attacking the southern state. South Armagh unionists look upon Aiken as a symbol of the Irish government's longstanding complicity in republican terrorism in Ulster.[118] In the early 1980s, meanwhile, the republican movement seized upon his pursuit of such violence as evidence of the southern administration's hypocrisy in condemning the activities of the Provisional IRA.[119]

There can be little doubt that Aiken ordered the reprisals. This was acknowledged by Casey who recalled his shock at learning that 'Frank Aiken had planned and authorised' the attack.[120] Aiken himself made veiled references to the operations in later years. In a handwritten chronology of his IRA activities composed in the early 1930s, he stated that he had 'directed operations which cured the Specials of a tendency to carry out the Belfast pogrom tactics in Armagh & Down.'[121] In a 1924 letter he also boasted that the USC had 'never hit a Nationalist but we hit back twice as hard and we had them cowed in our own area.'[122] Aside from the kidnapping raids a few weeks earlier, the only operations that fit such descriptions are the reprisals at Altnaveigh and Lisdrumliska. Further anecdotal evidence also suggests that he admitted his role in the reprisals to a family member in later life.[123] The often referenced notion that Aiken had given a general order for reprisals of '6 to 1' for attacks on nationalists in the Fourth Northern Divisional area, however, is false. This order was actually issued by the Second Northern Division and has since been misattributed to Aiken, though it is unlikely that he would have disagreed with its logic.[124]

Perhaps more noteworthy is the evidence to suggest that GHQ, and O'Duffy in particular, was well aware of the Fourth Northern Division's activities and took no action, even after the fact. Aiken later recalled that during this period he was 'almost daily in touch' with O'Duffy and expressed the belief that his division's activities were meeting with 'O'Duffy's whole hearted approval'.[125] More damning, however, are the observations of a 1926 department of defence memo which stated that Fourth Northern Division reports for June 1922 'were received [by GHQ] and copies of some of them are still extant. They are of a very controversial nature and are available for inspection.' By 1926 the originals bearing Aiken's signature had been destroyed. The same fate has apparently since befallen the copies.[126]

Although it is likely that Aiken ordered the reprisals, he did not take part in the actual attacks at Altnaveigh and Lisdrumliska. Instead, he had led the ambush party at Dromintee.[127] This operation was quite typical of Aiken's past reprisal attacks. It targeted the USC patrol believed to have been responsible for the raid at McGuill's pub. It took place at the pub itself so as to leave no doubt for the reasons behind the attack. In this respect it bore more than a passing resemblance to a similar reprisal ambush Aiken had carried out at Carrickbracken in January 1921 after his home was burned by the USC.[128] The attack at Dromintee, however, did not go according to plan. The ambush party was surprised by a USC foot patrol that was noticed 'advancing stealthily along each side of the road'.[129] After a brief skirmish, the column withdrew and returned to Dundalk Barracks. Casey, a participant in the ambush, observed that a second party carried out the attacks at Altnaveigh and Lisdrumliska, and that this group of men had left Dundalk Barracks shortly after Aiken and his column had departed for McGuill's pub.[130]

Aiken's presence at Dromintee, rather than Altnaveigh, reflected his motivations for ordering the reprisals. For him, it was the attack on Mrs McGuill, not the shootings of the men at Lislea, which provided the emotional impetus for the violence that night. The McGuills were close friends. James, as a Sinn Féin councillor, had been a colleague on both Newry No.2 RDC and Armagh County Council. Aiken had often stayed with the family after the destruction of his own home. Indeed, his first Christmas on the run was spent with the McGuill family.[131] Speaking in the Dáil in 1927 he recalled his rage upon seeing Mrs McGuill after her ordeal at the hands of the USC: 'I saw her the next day in the most frightful state, and I swore that if I could take it out of the skins of the men who did it I would do it.'[132] Aiken's anger and desire for revenge provides some explanation for his uncharacteristic lack of restraint in authorising the reprisals in south Armagh that evening. Indeed, it was in these terms that he later described the incident to a relative; feelings were running high, orders were given, things happened which should not have.[133] John McCoy provides a telling indication of his state of mind on the evening of the attacks. Recalling the Dromintee ambush, he observed that a few untested members of Aiken's column panicked when the fighting began, throwing down their weapons and running away. 'Aiken was going to shoot some of these men', McCoy recalled, and although he did eventually show leniency it is telling that this was the first instance where he had even so much as threatened the death penalty for a matter of internal discipline.[134]

Wilson has argued that the sexual assaults at McGuill's pub explain the exceptional nature of the violence at Altnaveigh and Lisdrumliska. 'This linkage', he suggests, 'makes sense of the Altnaveigh killings which otherwise defy comprehension'.[135] Alongside Aiken's desire for vengeance, the sexual nature of the assaults at Dromintee may help explain the ferocity of his division's response. Sexual violence was not particularly common during the Irish revolution, even if allowances are made for the fact that such incidents were likely underreported. Indeed, the attack on Mrs McGuill and her maid is the only verifiable instance of such violence in Armagh and south Down during this period.[136] As Sarah Benton has observed, the scant evidence for rapes and other assaults reflects the fact that such violence did not become a 'weapon of war' in the conflict and was never used to produce a mass intimidatory effect.[137] Louise Ryan has disputed this view, however, arguing that 'rape can also be a weapon of war even if it is carried out inside private homes and it is not widely publicised outside the local communities where it occurs.'[138] The nature and impact of the attack at Dromintee would certainly support this hypothesis. Whether intended or not, the incident had an intimidatory effect locally. It was reported in detail in the local nationalist press.[139] Even without such publicity, however, it is likely that the details of the attack would have soon spread throughout the nationalist population of south Armagh due to James McGuill's prominence as a local politician and businessman.

More importantly, given subsequent events, such violence was certainly capable of producing an intimidatory effect amongst the men of the Fourth Northern Division. Like James McGuill, many of those who had relocated to north Louth had left female relatives at home. For some, fears of such attacks had been present before the incident at Dromintee. Charles McGleenan recalled,

> I had only two sisters at home at this time and my father worried over what they might be subjected to. I had to go on the run, but I slept not more than 200 yards from our house [...] if anything happened to our house or any of its inmates my intentions were to pay back in triple measure.[140]

For Aiken the incident must also have prompted anxiety regarding his own sister, Nano, who was staying at the homes of various friends and relatives following the destruction of the family home at Carrickbracken.[141] Indeed, much of the ferocity of the Fourth Northern Division's attacks on 17 June may be attributable to the strong sense of fear and outrage that sexual violence could provoke. Alongside the shootings of Creggan and Crawley it also played into the worst fears of Aiken and other local republicans, expressed only a month earlier, that the USC were 'thirsting to proceed with the extermination of the Nationalist and Catholic population.'[142]

The killings of Creggan and Crawley at Lislea should not, however, be discounted as a contributing motivational factor for the reprisal. Just as the assaults at Dromintee provided the main emotional impetus for Aiken, the Lislea killings had their own resonance with those directly involved in the operations. The available evidence suggests that members of the Camlough and Corrinshego companies carried out the attacks at Altnaveigh and Lisdrumliska. The authorities subsequently identified four suspects, all of whom were certainly plausible. The Croziers reportedly identified two of their assailants – Michael Creggan and Willie McQuaid – before their deaths. Jack McElhaw, captain of the Camlough Company, was to face an identity parade while interned in Northern Ireland after the civil war. Having learned of this, however, he managed to get word to friends in south Armagh who intimidated the witness into withdrawing his co-operation with the authorities. Bernard Kelly, meanwhile, was noticed to have gone 'on the run' after the attacks and was eventually apprehended in 1923 bringing provisions across the border to Ravensdale, where Creggan and others were believed to be hiding. He was interned for a period, before being permitted to emigrate.[143]

Michael Creggan was the brother of the Lislea victim Patrick Creggan. This fraternal link to the IRA undoubtedly provided a further emotional impetus for the reprisals in south Armagh that evening. It also played a considerable role in determining the selection of Altnaveigh and Lisdrumliska as targets. McElhaw later explained that the shooting of Patrick Creggan 'pinpointed attention' to Altnaveigh as his brother had been arrested in September 1920 for involvement in an IRA arms raid in the district.[144] This linkage of Altnaveigh to the Lislea killings was tenuous, but the Fourth Northern Division held a longer-standing grudge against the unionist population of the district that undoubtedly exerted a further influence on the decision.

The townlands of Altnaveigh and Lisdrumliska fell within the Corrinshego Company's area of operations. In July 1921, four of the unit's members were rounded up in the districts by the USC in late night raids, shot dead and dumped at the roadside. In response, a reprisal was attempted against a group of 'off duty B Specials' from Altnaveigh. Ultimately the operation failed and one civilian from the district, Draper Holmes, was killed. Although not a member of the USC, Holmes was later described by one of his killers in terms that made clear the IRA's attitude towards the unionists of the district: '[Holmes] had such an intense hatred for everything republican that he would go to extreme limits to destroy the movement. In this the man was no different from his other unionist neighbours in his local village.'[145] The memory of the previous year's events would still have been fresh in the minds of many within the division, particularly as the compensation cases for the victims occurred only months earlier in March and April 1922.[146] For some within the division, the failure of the original reprisal may have added a particular sense of unfinished business to the night's attacks. This was particularly true for members of the Corrinshego Company. Indeed, it is notable that one of the four IRA victims in July 1921 had been seized at the home of Willie McQuaid's sister, a fact which further illustrates the complicated mixture of personal motives which may have influenced the night's proceedings.

Personal vendettas, complex emotional responses, and long standing antagonisms go some way to explaining the attacks at Altnaveigh and Lisdrumliska, as well as their uncharacteristic aggression. It is their sectarian aspect, however, which has attracted the most attention. All the victims were Protestants. All of the properties attacked that evening were Protestant owned and occupied. Specific details of the attack further hint at its sectarian dimensions. When one victim pleaded for mercy, for example, her attacker was said to have replied that 'Belfast Catholics got no mercy' before firing further shots into the bodies of her already wounded husband and son.[147]

Yet the popular notion that the reprisal was nothing more than an expression of irrational and indiscriminate religious bigotry – fuelled by petty hatreds and antipathies – is ultimately flawed. There were undoubtedly emotive motivational forces at play in the event, but the underlying logic was essentially political. The victims at Altnaveigh and Lisdrumliska were not killed because they were Protestants, but rather because they were perceived (correctly or incorrectly) as northern unionists. This is not a particularly novel observation in itself. As Donald Bloxham and Robert Gerwarth have argued, with regard to political violence in twentieth-century Europe more generally, religion 'did not play a major role as a motivational force [. . .] increasingly more important than belief itself was the role of religious adherence as an indicator of national identity or membership of a "civilised" community.'[148] In the context of revolutionary Ireland – Ulster in particular – this distinction, though not necessarily unrecognised, is too often lost in the understandable rush to condemn such atrocities and to reinforce both their illegitimacy and moral abhorrence. Nevertheless, its importance is strikingly illustrated by the fact that within a week of the reprisals Aiken's men were patrolling the streets of Dundalk – less than 15 miles away – in order to prevent attacks on local Protestants.[149]

Sectarian tensions had been on the rise in Dundalk since March 1922 when notices appeared in the town threatening reprisals for attacks on Catholics in Belfast. Later that same month, a group of Fianna Éireann members were also tried by a Dáil court for carrying out unsanctioned and intimidatory raids on Protestant homes in the area.[150] In late June 1922, however, intimidation turned to violence. In the early hours of 22 June 'a band of men armed with rifles' opened fire on the homes of five Protestant railway workers at Demesne Terrace in the town. The attack may have been informed by a longer running dispute concerning the dismissal and eviction of a previous employee for his involvement in the 1920 Irish railway strike, during which sympathetic workers had refused to transport British troops or munitions.[151] This was followed by a further incident in which a Catholic home was 'fired into by mistake for a protestant one' on the evening of 24–5 June.[152] Rogue members of the anti-Treatyite First Brigade were responsible for the attacks. They were acting independently, without the authority of their officers, and a number were quickly rounded up and tried by court martial. In response to the attack both the Fourth Northern Division and the First Brigade agreed to co-operate for the purpose of maintaining order in Dundalk and initiated a system of joint-patrols.[153] Aiken, meanwhile, issued a confrontational circular to 'all officers and men in the southern part of the division' to clarify the position on such attacks. It provides a rare, contemporary, insight into his views on the issue, and is worth quoting at length:

> Acts of aggression by protestants in the North against catholics do not give anyone the right to interfere with protestants in the South. Any such acts are morally wrong and are damnable wrong to the good name of the country, and the men who fought a clean, honourable fight. The men who say driving protestants out of the South is good tactics to stop protestants [sic, Catholics] being driven out of the North, if he is not mad certainly does not understand the Ulster situation [. . .] If any man or body of men wants to consolidate the Ulster Parliament for England, the best tactics he can adopt are to evict protestants from the South. The North-East Ulster protestants are quite right to have a parliament of their own if protestants in the rest of Ireland are not protected. Our duty is clear. There are only a few at this work, and it must be stopped. We men of the IRA must stop it by shooting if necessary the men who are simply making a gift of Ulster to England, and bring dishonour to the good name of our country.[154]

In addition to these measures, a number of Protestant families preparing to flee the town were prevailed upon to stay.[155]

This seemingly contradictory series of events reinforces the view that for Aiken and his divisional staff, at least, the use of violence against members of the Protestant community was ultimately guided by a political logic. South of the border, where Protestants were now a politically impotent minority in the new Irish Free State, they were not viewed as legitimate or justifiable targets. As Aiken's circular indicates, this was informed by a complex mixture of moral and political considerations, as well as the self-attributed notions of honour that he and his peers attached to the republican movement and the Irish nation in general. Violence and intimidation still occurred in north Louth, and at times IRA volunteers were certainly involved, but it was not orchestrated or condoned by the divisional leadership in the way that it was in Northern Ireland.

In stark contrast, north of the border, an incremental process of radical-isation within the local IRA, which had first become visible in late 1920 and early 1921, had reached the point where any Protestant – as a real or perceived member of the dominant unionist community – was liable to be viewed as a legitimate target for reprisal. As John Grant later put it,

> By sending our columns into certain areas we would improve the morale of our own civilians and make the unionist civilians (if any unionists could then be classed as civilians) realise that even in their own districts they were not immune from punishment for the misdeeds of their relatives serving in the B Specials.[156]

In practice the violence retained a sense of selectivity; though it may have become increasingly indiscriminate had the conflict continued to escalate beyond June 1922. As has already been shown, there were specific reasons why Altnaveigh and Lisdrumliska had been selected above any other unionist district in the area. Nevertheless, the reprisal ultimately rested on the same crude system of religious and social profiling inferred by Grant. The victims were Protestants and thus assumed to be unionists. As unionists, they were further assumed to be fervent, if not fanatical, supporters of the northern government and the activities of the USC. The menfolk, meanwhile, being of appropriate age, and (for the most part) members of the Orange Order, may also have been assumed to be members of the USC'.[157]

Such assumptions reflected the collective ignorance of the local IRA when it came to their Protestant neighbours, and were not necessarily the result of the individual pathologies of its members. There is little to suggest, for instance, that Aiken was exceptionally prejudiced or sectarian in his attitudes towards the Protestant community. Though in later life some of his colleagues apparently considered him a bigot, they based this judgement on little more than the fact that he was 'of north of Ireland stock'; an observation which says rather more about their own prejudices.[158] Yet Aiken was undoubtedly ignorant of the views and attitudes of the northern Protestant community. Growing up in Carrickbracken, he had virtually no close Protestant neighbours.[159] His schooling had been decidedly Catholic, and from an early age his social scene had revolved around nationalist pursuits in which he mixed almost exclusively with his fellow co-religionists. Furthermore, any dealings he did have with local Protestants – commercial or agricultural, for instance – are unlikely to have been particularly enlightening, given the longstanding social convention in Ulster by which the discussion of controversial topics such as religion and politics is generally avoided in 'mixed company'.[160] In this he was not alone. His comrades in the Fourth Northern Division were ultimately products of the same milieu. Indeed, that is perhaps why – with the possible exception of Patrick Casey – the events at Altnaveigh and Lisdrumliska drew so few negative reactions from within the unit itself.

In later years, some members of the Fourth Northern Division portrayed the reprisals at Altnaveigh and Lisdrumliska as a means of defending the wider nationalist community in south Armagh. Like the kidnapping raids in late May, however, it can be seen that the reprisals had more to do with avenging wrongs committed against fellow republicans and their loved ones. Furthermore, although Aiken and McElhaw later trumpeted events at Altnaveigh as a success in keeping USC aggression in check, the attacks were actually counter-productive. Loyalist reprisals followed within days. Peter Murray, a Catholic railway worker, was shot dead in Newry. A Catholic farmer was found shot to death at his home in the mainly Protestant district of Cloughenramer. In Rathfriland, meanwhile, two young nationalists were killed by the USC in circumstances that remain unclear. It is difficult to be certain about the motives behind these killings but it seems likely that they were a response to events in Altnaveigh, and they were certainly viewed as such locally. This interpretation is made all the more plausible by the fact that a group of men, some uniformed, had aggressively raided houses in the surrounding districts in the immediate aftermath of the operations in the search for republican suspects.[161] The nation-alist community ultimately remained a target for violence and intimidation well into July 1922, with the burning of a number of nationalist halls and the post-ing of intimidating notices. That month was also notable for an incident at Jonesborough when the British military shot dead two young girls and seriously wounded another during the search of a house close to the border. It appears, however, that the incident was a tragic error rather than a malicious or pre-meditated attack.[162]A noticeable decline in such attacks did not occur until later that month, and this can be attributed to the easing of tensions in the area as a result of the cessation of IRA operations following the outbreak of the civil war in the south. The only tangible effect of the Altnaveigh reprisal, therefore, was that it struck terror into both the unionist and nationalist communities in Newry and south Armagh. In McElhaw's words, 'the fear inspired by Altnaveigh and what had gone before was not confined to any one community. All were afraid of what was to come next.'[163]

For local unionists, the terror inspired by the events was further heightened in the weeks that followed with the abduction, murder and secret burial of William Frazer, a Protestant publican from Newtownhamilton. The IRA seized Frazer as he drove to Newry to collect supplies for his pub. The party ordered his daughter and another child out of the lorry in which they were travelling before compelling him to drive to north Louth where, republican sources claim, he was executed and buried close to the Dungooley camp.[164] It is unclear if Frazer was intentionally targeted or if the party of men that seized him had merely been interested in taking his lorry for use in the Fourth Northern Division's camps in north Louth. John 'Ned' Quinn, one of those involved in his abduction, claimed that Frazer was killed because he had fired upon the IRA during a raid on Newtownhamilton Barracks in 1920.[165] IRA descriptions of the Newtownhamilton attack make no references to such an event, however, and the story cannot be corroborated in contemporary news reports.

Although there is little to suggest his involvement in the incident, Aiken became central to the speculation surrounding Frazer's abduction in the months that followed when there was still no certainty if he was alive or dead. In October 1922, Frazer's daughter wrote of rumours that,

> My father was in a hut in Dundalk and was released and that the Irregulars recaptured him along with two other prisoners that were with him. He was brought before Frank Aiken and he said that the other two go away [sic] but to keep Frazer.[166]

It was only in January 1923 that the RUC received intelligence to confirm that Frazer had been killed.[167] The retrieval of a body from a bog in the Ballard Mountains near Camlough in July 1924 apparently confirmed this, although republicans remained adamant that Frazer's body was buried near Dungooley. This sparked macabre rumours – eagerly retold by John 'Ned' Quinn – that local loyalists had a Catholic body 'taken out of the grave and left in the Slieve Gullion area' so that Frazer's wife could claim compensation for his death.[168]

The details surrounding the murder of William Frazer, combined with the Altnaveigh massacre and the IRA kidnapping raids in May, did much to shape local perceptions of Aiken amongst the unionist community. During the elections of May 1921 he was a figure of ridicule in unionist speeches, but by July 1922 he had become a 'bogeyman'. In February 1923, the authorities reported that 'rumours are frequently current that Aiken has been seen in certain places [...] police heard that he was recently seen in Armagh city disguised as an old beggar man.'[169] The frequent 'sightings' and rumours as to his whereabouts provide an indication of the place he had come to occupy in the unionist psyche, in effect providing the personification of that community's worst fears regarding militant republican violence.

For modern-day unionists, Aiken's complicity in the killings of south Armagh Protestants is viewed in terms of genocide and ethnic cleansing.[170]

Such views are undoubtedly influenced by the republican violence of the more recent troubles, which has been described in similar terms.[171] They may also have been encouraged by the debate regarding sectarianism as an aspect of IRA violence in southern Ireland during the revolutionary period. The work of Hart, in particular, has popularised the 'ethnic cleansing' interpretation of IRA violence. Focusing on events outside Ulster, Hart argued that the IRA pursued a campaign of sectarian violence and intimidation against Irish Protestants resulting in a 34 per cent decline in that population between 1911 and 1926.[172] In discussing this phenomenon he went so far as to suggest that in some areas of the country, such as Cork, Tipperary and Louth, this sectarian campaign 'might be termed "ethnic cleansing"'.[173] His evidence for west Cork is compelling and does illustrate that the primary decline of the Protestant population in that region occurred in the turbulent period between 1920 and 1924.[174] Nevertheless, his findings have proven controversial. County studies of the Irish revolution suggest that sectarianism as an aspect of IRA violence during the conflict could vary greatly between regions. Although Hart observed considerable sectarian violence in Cork, for example, very little was discernible in other extremely active IRA areas such as Longford.[175] There is, therefore, some validity to the claims of critics that his work has led some historians and commentators (particularly those outside of academia) to overstate these themes in relation to incidents elsewhere in the country.[176]

Claims of genocide in south Armagh in this period are absurd, although their emotional impetus is understandable. There was no systematic attempt by the IRA to kill large sections of the Protestant population, and there is no reason to suggest that such violence was ever even considered. The same applies with regard to alleged ethnic cleansing, which was neither attempted, nor inadvertently achieved as a result of IRA violence and intimidation. Though there is anecdotal evidence that suggests that episodes such as the Altnaveigh massacre caused some Protestant residents to leave south Armagh, an analysis of local population figures indicate that IRA violence had little significant effect on local demographics.[177] Between 1911 and 1926 Armagh's Protestant population declined by approximately 11 per cent. In the same period the Catholic population declined by 8 per cent. This decline in both the Catholic and Protestant populations is in keeping with pre-existing trends in the county. Between 1901 and 1911, the Protestant and Catholic populations in Armagh had declined by 5 per cent and 4 per cent respectively.[178] The inter-communal violence of this period appears to have had a minimal influence on demographic change in the county, and any effect it did exert was clearly felt amongst both communities.

The violence experienced in south Armagh between 1920 and 1922, whether perpetrated by republicans or loyalists, is not suggestive of ethnic cleansing or genocide. Even exceptional events like Altnaveigh were not indicative of an attempt at extermination. Indeed, as Wilson has demonstrated, the violence witnessed in Ulster during these years was less frequent and intense than that experienced in Upper Silesia, a comparable and contemporary European conflict.[179] Despite inadvertently popularising the concept of 'ethnic cleansing' as an aspect of revolutionary violence, even Hart ultimately concluded that in both northern and southern Ireland the conflict lacked 'the vital ingredients of ethnic cleansing.' Indeed his reflections on the nature of northern loyalist violence in these years can be applied to the experience of the conflict in Armagh and south Down more generally. For both sides, 'this was a limited war for territorial security and political mastery, not an absolute war of extermination or elimination.'[180]

By mid-June 1922, the IRA campaign in Armagh and south Down had reached its zenith. So too had the steadily escalating cycle of inter-communal conflict in the region. Violence by no means ceased locally during 1922, but it did become increasingly sporadic and less reciprocal as republican activity in the region waned. This was largely the result of developments within the Irish Free State. Although Aiken and his men maintained their hopes for further offensive action in Northern Ireland, any such initiative was ultimately reliant on southern republican unity, and in this respect the drift of events did not look promising. Aiken, moreover, knew this all too well, for although the fighting in the north had remained his primary focus throughout the preceding months, he had increasingly found his gaze turning to the new conflict that was looming in the south.

NOTES

1. M. Hopkinson, *Green Against Green: The Irish Civil War* (Dublin, 1988), p. 83.

2. See, for example, www.victims.org.uk/altnaveigh.html (accessed 26 May 2010).

3. 'The war as a whole', 24 Mar. 1921, University College Dublin Archives Department (hereafter, UCDAD), Mulcahy papers, P7a/17.

4. 'The Fourth Northern Division', 26 Apr. 1921, UCDAD, Mulcahy papers, P7a/17.

5. F. O'Donoghue, *No Other Law* (Dublin, 1954), pp 249–51; see also R. Lynch, *Northern IRA and the Early Years of Partition* (Dublin, 2006), p. 136.

6. P. Hart, *Mick: The Real Michael Collins* (London, 2005), p. 380; F. McGarry, *Eoin O'Duffy: A Self-Made hero* (Oxford, 2005), pp 103–4; M. Valiulis, *Portrait of a Revolutionary: General Richard Mulcahy and the Founding of the Irish Free State* (Dublin, 1992), p. 141.

7. Lynch, *Northern IRA and the Early Years of Partition*, pp 131–2.

8. Padraig Quinn memoir, Kilmainham Gaol Museum (hereafter, KGM), McCann Cell Collection 20/M5/IP41/08.

9. See above, pp 126–8.

10. 'Chronology', *c.*1933, Irish Military Archives (hereafter, IMA), Bureau of Military History Contemporary Documents (BMH CD) 6/36/22.

11. See, for example, Hopkinson, *Green Against Green*, pp 83–4; Valiulis, *Portrait of a Revolutionary*, p. 141.

12. Padraig Quinn memoir, KGM, McCann cell collection 20/M5/IP41/08; Lynch, *Northern IRA and the Early Years of Partition*, p. 139.

13. 'William Nelson's Story', National Library of Ireland (hereafter, NLI), Ms 41,722.

14. Frank Aiken, UCDAD, O'Malley notebooks, P17b/90.

15. Hugh Gribben, IMA, Bureau of Military History Witness Statement (hereafter, BMH WS) 640; John McCoy, ibid., 492; R. Lynch, 'Donegal and the joint-IRA offensive', in *Irish Historical Studies*, 35: 138 (Nov. 2006), p. 190.

16. James McCullough, IMA, BMH WS 529.

17. Padraig Quinn memoir, KGM, McCann cell collection, 20/M5/IP41/08.

18. Aiken to Molly Childers, 18 Apr. 1924, Trinity College Dublin Archives (hereafter, TCD), Childers papers, Ms 7,847.

19. John Cosgrove, IMA, BMH WS 605.

20. Ibid.

21. Hopkinson, *Green Against Green*, p. 85.

22. Lynch, *Northern IRA and the Early Years of Partition*, p. 140.

23. John Cosgrove, IMA, BMH WS 605.

24. Hugh Gribben, ibid., 640; Patrick Casey, ibid., 1148.

25. Padraig Quinn memoir notes, KGM, McCann Cell Collection (unsorted material); Lynch, *Northern IRA and the Early Years of Partition*, p. 141; McGarry, *Eoin O'Duffy*, p. 103.

26. 'The Fourth Northern Division', 26 Apr. 1921, UCDAD, P7a/17.

27. E. Phoenix, *Northern Nationalism: Nationalism, Politics, Partition and the Catholic Minority in Northern Ireland, 1890–1940* (Belfast, 1994), p. 217.

28. Lynch, *Northern IRA and the Early Years of Partition*, p. 81.

29. J. McDermott, *Northern Divisions: The Old IRA and the Belfast Pogroms* (Belfast, 2001), p. 215.

30. J. M. Regan, *The Irish Counter-Revolution, 1921–1936: Treatyite Politics and Settlement in Ireland* (Dublin, 1999), p. 64.

31. C. Ryder, *The Fateful Split: Catholics and the Royal Ulster Constabulary* (London, 2004), pp 38–9.

32. Hopkinson, *Green Against Green*, pp 84–5.

33. Regan, *Irish Counter-Revolution*, p. 65; McGarry, *Eoin O'Duffy*, pp 102–3.

34. Regan, *Irish Counter-Revolution*, p. 65.

35. Lynch, *Northern IRA and the Early Years of Partition*, p. 135.

36. Padraig Quinn memoir, KGM, McCann Cell Collection, 20/M5/IP41/08. Quinn's recollections regarding the incident with the car are corroborated in contemporary documents; Officer I/C Evacuation Correspondence, Apr.–May 1922, IMA, Truce Liaison and Evacuation papers, LE/11/7.

37. John McCoy, IMA, BMH WS 492.

38. Padraig Quinn memoir, KGM, McCann Cell Collection, 20/M5/IP41/08.

39. Kevin O'Shiel as quoted in Hopkinson, *Green Against Green*, p. 85.

40. Regan, *Irish Counter-Revolution*, p. 65.

41. Lynch, *Northern IRA and the Early Years of Partition*, p. 136.

42. See, for example, Patrick Casey, IMA, BMH WS 1148; C. S. Andrews, *Dublin Made Me: An Autobiography* (Dublin, 1979), p. 222; Sean Lehane, as quoted in Lynch, *Northern IRA and the Early Years of Partition*, p. 136.

43. 'Notes of an interview with Frank Aiken', 18 June 1952, NLI, O'Donoghue papers, Ms 31,421.

44. See above, p. 136.

45. Lynch, *Northern IRA and the Early Years of Partition*, p. 143.

46. McGarry, *Eoin O'Duffy*, p. 102; Lynch, *Northern IRA and the Early Years of Partition*, pp 139–41; McDermott, *Northern Divisions*, p. 215.

47. Lynch, *Northern IRA and the Early Years of Partition*, p. 145.

48. Seamus Woods as quoted in ibid., p. 150.

49. Confidential Department of Defence memo, *c.*1926, UCDAD, FitzGerald papers, P80/457.

50. John Cosgrove, IMA, BMH WS 605; Patrick Casey, ibid., 1148.

51. Padraig Quinn memoir, KGM, McCann cell collection, 20/M5/IP41/08.

52. Roger McCorley, IMA, BMH WS 389.

53. Aiken to O'Donoghue, 9 Mar. 1953, NLI, O'Donoghue papers, Ms 31,421; for more on Collins-de Valera pact see pp 171–3.

54. *Dáil Éireann Debates* (hereafter, *DÉD*), vol. 2 (20 May 1922), cols 479–80; Frank Aiken, UCDAD, O'Malley notebooks, P17b/90.

55. Patrick Casey, IMA, BMH WS 1148.

56. John Cosgrove, ibid., 605; *Irish Times*, 24 May 1922.

57. Patrick Casey, IMA, BMH WS 1148.

58. John Cosgrove, ibid., 605.

59. Sean McConville, ibid., 495.

60. List of Fourth Northern Division Officers, Cardinal Ó Fiaich Library Armagh (hereafter, COFLA), O'Kane papers, LOK/I.E.240001.06.

61. Aiken to Molly Childers, 18 Apr. 1924, TCD, Childers papers, Ms 7,847.

62. Lynch, *Northern IRA and the Early Years of Partition*, p. 151.

63. John McCoy, IMA, BMH WS 492.

64. Confidential Department of Defence Memo, *c.*1926, UCDAD, FitzGerald papers, P80/457.

65. Aiken to Molly Childers, 18 Apr. 1924, TCD, Childers papers, Ms 7,847.

66. Padraig Quinn memoir notes, KGM, McCann Cell Collection (unsorted material).

67. Appendix II, Table VII.

68. Lynch, *Northern IRA and the Early Years of Partition*, p. 146; McDermott, *Northern Divisions*, p. 259.

69. *Irish Times*, 15 May 1922.

70. Jack McElhaw, IMA, BMH WS 634; *Irish Times*, 8 May 1922.

71. *Frontier Sentinel*, 3 June 1922.

72. Jack McElhaw, IMA, BMH WS 634; the exact number of Cumann na mBan arrested is unclear, with different reports suggesting anywhere from three to six. The figure presented here is that suggested in McElhaw's statement.

73.   *Irish Times*, 29 May 1922.

74.   *Frontier Sentinel*, 3 June 1922; *Irish Times*, 29 May 1922.

75.   Johnnie McKay [McCoy], UCDAD, O'Malley notebooks, P17b/90.

76.   'Report for the period 16/5/22 to 15/6/22', Public Record Office of Northern Ireland (hereafter, PRONI), HA/5/152.

77.   John Quinn interview transcript (1/2), 8 May 1966, COFLA, O'Kane papers, LOK/IV/B.14.0002.10.

78.   'Arrest of three Protestants at Greenore', 30 May 1922, PRONI, HA/5/228.

79.   *Irish Times*, 19 July 1922.

80.   John McCoy, IMA, BMH WS 492.

81.   John Grant, ibid., 658.

82.   R. Lynch, 'The people's protectors? The Irish Republican Army and the "Belfast Pogroms" 1920–1922', *Journal of British Studies*, 47: 2 (Apr. 2008), p. 387.

83.   Johnnie McKay [McCoy], UCDAD, O'Malley notebooks, P17b/90; McCoy claimed the kidnappings were a response to the shootings of two nationalists outside Camlough. These incidents actually occurred on 13–14 June, see below.

84.   Macintosh to his mother, 6 June 1922, PRONI, HA/5/228.

85.   Harry Macintosh statement, undated, ibid.

86.   Murdock to Fisher, 5 June 1922, PRONI, HA/5/236.

87.   *Frontier Sentinel*, 20 May 1922.

88.   Edward Fullerton, IMA, BMH WS 890; *Irish Independent*, 4 June 1922.

89.   *Irish Times*, 3 June 1922.

90.   Jack McElhaw, IMA, BMH WS 634.

91.   For details of the column and its various ambush attempts see, John McCoy, IMA, BMH WS 492; John Grant, ibid., 658.

92.   See Appendix II, Table VII.

93.   *Frontier Sentinel*, 10 June 1922.

94.   John Grant, IMA, BMH WS 658; John McCoy, ibid., 492.

95.   'Murders of Creggan and Crawley', PRONI, HA/5/239; *Frontier Sentinel*, 24 June 1922.

96.   Jack McElhaw, IMA, BMH WS 634.

97.   R. Lynch, 'Explaining the Altnaveigh massacre', in *Eire/Ireland*, 45: 3 & 4 (fall/winter, 2010), p. 197; for details of the attack near Caledon, see *Frontier Sentinel*, 10 June 1922.

98.   Aiken to O'Duffy, 15 June 1922, NAI, Department of Taoiseach (hereafter, TSCH) 3/S5462.

99.   *DÉD*, vol. 32 (23 Oct. 1929), col. 147.

100. 'File relating to alleged raid on house of James McGill/McGuill, Dromintee, Co. Armagh', PRONI, HA/5/249; 'McGuill – grant from the Dáil Special Fund', NAI, TSCH 3/S5462.

101. *Frontier Sentinel*, 24 June 1922.

102. Collins to Churchill, 20 June 1922, NAI, TSCH 3/S5462; Colonial Office to Spender, 22 June 1922, PRONI, HA/5/249.

103. Armagh County Inspector to Divisional Commissioner, 20 June 1922, PRONI, HA/5/249.

104. 'McGuill – grant from the Dáil Special Fund', NAI, TSCH 3/S8451; see Lynch 'Explaining the Altnaveigh Massacre', p. 199.

105. *Irish Times*, 19 June 1922.

106. *Armagh Guardian*, 23 June 1922.

107. Figures regarding signatories to the Ulster Covenant are derived from information from the 1911 census and the Public Record Office of Northern Ireland's Ulster Covenant database; Census of Ireland 1901/1911, www.census.nationalarchives.ie/ (accessed 30 Jan. 2014); Ulster Covenant 1912, www.applications.proni.gov.uk/UlsterCovenant/Search.aspx (accessed 30 Jan. 2014). For Altnaveigh recruits to the UVF see, Joseph Orr to Capt. Hall, 20 Jan. 1913, PRONI, Hall papers, D1540/3/5.

108. *Frontier Sentinel*, 24 June 1922.

109. *Newry Telegraph*, 20 June 1922.

110. Lynch, *Northern IRA and the Early Years of Partition*, pp 147–8; *Newry Telegraph*, 20 June 1920.

111. Head Constable Duffy to Armagh County Inspector, 21 June 1922, PRONI, HA/5/925; *Irish Independent*, 18 June 1922.

112. *Irish Times*, 19 June 1922.

113. Armagh County Inspector to District Commissioner, 20 June 1922, PRONI, HA/5/249.

114. See, for example, Patrick Casey, IMA, BMH WS 1148; Sir A. Hezlet, *The B Specials: A History of the Ulster Special Constabulary* (London, 1972), p. 22.

115. *Armagh Guardian*, 23 June 1922.

116. Head Constable Duffy to Armagh County Inspector, 21 June 1922, PRONI, HA/5/925.

117. *Sunday Independent*, 17 Dec. 2006.

118. See, for example, www.victims.org.uk/altnaveigh.html (accessed 26 May 2010).

119. R. P. Watson, *Cath Saoirse an Iúir: Newry's struggle* (Newry, 1986), p. 3; this pamphlet makes a similar argument to that in the better known Sinn Féin Publicity Department pamphlet, *The Good Old IRA: Tan War Operations* (Dublin, 1985). For more on the latter see, B. Hanley, 'Terror in twentieth century Ireland' in Fitzpatrick (ed.), *Terror in Ireland, 1916–1923* (Dublin, 2012), pp 14–15.

120. Patrick Casey, IMA, BMH WS 1148.

121. 'Chronology', *c.*1933, IMA, BMH CD6/36/22.

122. Aiken to Molly Childers, 18 Apr. 1924, TCD, Childers papers, Ms 7,847.

123. Interview with Dr Eoin Magennis, 19 May 2010.

124. This error was first published in Watson's *Cath Saoirse an Iúir: Newry's Struggle*, and has subsequently been reproduced in numerous historical works; see, for example, Lynch, 'Explaining the Altnaveigh massacre', p 207; T. P. Coogan, *Michael Collins: A Biography* (London, 1990), p. 377. For a copy of the order see, 'Divisional Commissioner's report for the latter half of Mar. 1922', 31 Mar., 1922, PRONI, HA/5/152.

125. Aiken to Molly Childers, 18 Apr. 1924, TCD, Childers papers, Ms 7,847.

126. Confidential department of defence memo, *c.*1926, UCDAD, FitzGerald papers, P80/457.

127. Patrick Casey, IMA, BMH WS 1148; *DÉD*, vol. 32 (23 Oct. 1929), col. 147.

128. See above, p. 74.

129. Patrick Casey, IMA, BMH WS 1148.

130. Ibid.

131. John McCoy, ibid., 492.

132. *DÉD*, vol. 32 (23 Oct. 1929), col. 147.

133. Interview with Dr Eoin Magennis, 19 May 2010.

134. Johnnie McKay [McCoy], UCDAD, O'Malley notebooks, P17b/90.

135. T. W. Wilson, *Frontiers of Violence: Conflict and Identity in Ulster and Upper Silesia 1918–1922* (Oxford, 2010), p. 170.

136. Lynch's suggestion that there had been previous attempts to rape Mrs McGuill is based on an ambiguous, and ultimately inconclusive, comment by James McGuill when summarising multiple raids on his home (including the incident when the sexual assaults occurred); Lynch, 'Explaining the Altnaveigh massacre', p. 201; McGuill to unknown [Kevin O'Shiel?], 12 July 1925, NAI, TSCH 3/S5462. Likewise, suggestions that sexual abuse may have occurred in the aforementioned case of the Cumann na mBan girls arrested during border fighting at Jonesborough is purely speculative. There is no evidence that the girls were mistreated in any way during their captivity, let alone sexually assaulted; see above, p. 146. Wilson, *Frontiers of Violence*, p. 77, fn. 6; Lynch 'Explaining the Altnaveigh massacre', p. 201.

137. S. Benton, 'Women disarmed: The militarization of politics in Ireland 1913–1923', in *Feminist Review*, no. 50 (summer, 1995), p. 165.

138. L. Ryan, 'Drunken tans: representations of sex and violence in the Anglo–Irish War (1919–1921)', in *Feminist Review*, no. 66 (autumn, 2000), p. 90.

139. *Frontier Sentinel*, 24 June 1922.

140. Charles McGleenan, IMA, BMH WS 829.

141. Interview with Dr Eoin Magennis, 19 May 2010.

142. 'Six County Position in the present crisis', May 1922, UCDAD, Mulcahy papers, P7a/145.

143. Jack McElhaw, IMA, BMH WS 634; Head Constable Duffy to Armagh County Inspector, 21 June 1922, PRONI, HA/5/925; Bi-monthly intelligence summary, 30 June 1923, PRONI, HA/32/1/212; Camlough and Corrinshego company roles in 11 July 1921, c.1936, UCDAD, P104/1298; Bernard Kelly file, c.1923, PRONI, HA/5/2426.

144. Jack McElhaw, IMA, BMH WS634; Mick Creggan's arrest is corroborated in press reports, *Irish Independent*, 20 Sept. 1920.

145. John Grant, IMA, BMH WS 658.

146. *Frontier Sentinel*, 18 Mar. 1922, 1 Apr. 1922.

147. *Newry Telegraph*, 20 June 1922.

148. D. Bloxham and R. Gerwarth (eds), *Political Violence in Twentieth Century Europe* (Cambridge, 2011), p. 2.

149. *Irish Times*, 22 June 1922; *Dundalk Examiner*, 1 July 1922; D. Hall, 'Violence, political factionalism and their effects on North Louth' (PhD, National University of Ireland Maynooth, 2010), p. 157.

150. Hall, 'Violence, political factionalism and their effects on North Louth', p. 157; *Freeman's Journal*, 28 Mar. 1922; *Frontier Sentinel*, 15 Apr. 1922.

151. *Irish Times*, 22 June 1922. For references to this dispute see, Brigade O/C to Chief of Police, 7 Feb. 1922, NAI, Department of Justice, H5/235. For more on the strike see C. Townshend, 'The Irish railway strike of 1920: Industrial action and civil resistance in the struggle for independence', in *Irish Historical Studies*, 22: 83 (Mar. 1979), pp 265–82.

152. Fourth Northern Division Report, 26 June 1922, NAI, North Eastern Boundary Bureau (hereafter, NEBB) 1/1/7.

153. Ibid; *Dundalk Examiner*, 1 July 1922; see also Hall, 'Violence, political factionalism and their effects on North Louth', p. 157.

154. 'To all officers and men in the southern part of the division', c.25 June 1922, NAI, NEBB 1/1/7.

155. Fourth Northern Division Report, 26 June 1922, NAI, NEBB 1/1/7.

156. John Grant, IMA, BMH WS 658.

157. Four of the five male victims were members of the Orange Order; see W. Frazer, 'The Altnaveigh Massacre: A Case Study in Genocide', www.victims.org.uk/so8zhk/pdfs/Deal_Past/Altnaveigh%20Massacre.pdf (accessed 20 May, 2014).

158. M. Manning, *James Dillon: A Biography* (Dublin, 1999), p.160. Henry Patterson has used these accusations as the basis for his assertion on Aiken's supposed bigotry; H. Patterson, *Ireland since 1939* (Oxford, 2002), p. 62.

159. In 1901 the townland was exclusively Catholic, and by 1911 there was only one Protestant family living in the area; see individual census returns for Carrickbracken in 1901 and 1911, www.census.nationalarchives.ie/ (accessed, 20 Jan. 2014).

160. R. Harris, *Prejudice and Tolerance in Ulster: A Study of Neighbours and 'Strangers' in a Border Community* (Manchester, 1969), pp 146–8.

161. *Frontier Sentinel*, 24 June 1922; *Irish Independent*, 21 June 1922.

162. *Frontier Sentinel*, 15 July 1922; *Irish Times*, 25 July 1922.

163. Jack McElhaw, IMA, BMH WS 634.

164. John Quinn interview transcript (1/2), 8 May 1966, COFLA, O'Kane papers, LOK/IV/B.14.0002.10; Burns to Hungerford, 24 Aug. 1922, PRONI, HA/5/253.

165. John Quinn interview transcript (1/2), 8 May 1966, COFLA, LOK/IV/B.14.0002.10.

166. As quoted in, Thompson to McBride, 11 Oct. 1922, PRONI, HA/5/253.

167. DI McFarland to Armagh County Inspector, 19 Jan. 1923, PRONI, HA/5/253.

168. John Quinn interview transcript (1/2), 8 May 1966, COFLA, O'Kane papers, LOK/IV/B.14.0002.10.

169. Inspector General's Office to Secretary of Home Affairs, 19 Feb. 1923, PRONI, HA/32/1/281.

170. See, for example, www.victims.org.uk/altnaveigh.html (accessed 26 May 2010); Drew Nelson speaking in 'Aiken: Gunman and Statesman' (Mint Productions, 2006).

171. See, for example, A. Foster, 'How will the law define sectarianism?', in *Fortnight*, no. 419 (Nov. 2003), p. 8; H. Patterson, 'Sectarianism revisited: the Provisional IRA campaign in a border region of Northern Ireland', in *Terrorism and Political Violence*, 22: 3 (Dec. 2010), pp 337–56; H. Patterson, *Ireland's Violent Frontier: The Border and Anglo-Irish Relations During the Troubles* (Basingstoke, 2013).

172. P. Hart, *The IRA at War* (Oxford, 2003), pp 223–40.

173. Ibid., p. 237.

174. Ibid., pp 225–6.

175. M. Coleman, *County Longford and the Irish Revolution, 1910–1923* (Dublin, 2001), pp 156–7.

176. See B. P. Murphy, 'Poisoning the well or publishing the truth? From Peter Hart's The IRA and its enemies to RTÉ's Hidden History film Coolacrease', in *Troubled History: A 10th Anniversary Critique of Peter Hart's The IRA and its Enemies* (Aubane, 2008), pp 37–40; Hart's analysis of a key incident in Cork, the killings of ten Protestants at Dunmanway, has also been vigorously challenged, see J. Regan, 'The "Bandon valley massacre" as a historical problem', in *History*, 97: 1 (Jan. 2012), pp 70–98.

177. Drew Nelson speaking in 'Aiken: Gunman and Statesman' (Mint Productions, 2006).

178. See Appendix II, Table VIII (A) and (B). A narrower consideration of population change in south Armagh has not been possible due to differences in the presentation of data regarding the religious professions of the county's inhabitants in the relevant census reports for 1911 and 1926; for information on how these figures were compiled see Appendix I.

179. Wilson, *Frontiers of Violence*, pp 166–7.

180. Hart, *IRA at War*, p. 251.

SEVEN

CIVIL WAR

Whilst Aiken and his Fourth Northern Division were preoccupied with the fighting in Northern Ireland in the spring and early summer of 1922, events in southern Ireland revolved around the search for republican unity. The months that followed the army convention were characterised by a seemingly endless series of negotiations and short-lived initiatives as pro- and anti-Treaty leaders frantically sought to avoid civil war without compromising their respective principles on the issue of the Treaty. Aiken never fully lost sight of this steadily deteriorating political situation, though as ever his responses to it were determined by his decidedly northern agenda. In striving to maintain cross-factional support for the IRA campaign in Ulster, he continued to exploit his familiarity with leaders on both sides of the Treaty divide to appeal for compromise and moderation. Yet whereas in earlier months Aiken had confined his efforts to the military sphere, in May 1922, as the joint-IRA offensive approached, he made his first foray in the politics of the split, making a brief yet significant contribution to the negotiation of the Collins-de Valera election pact.

The political split over the Treaty was a more complicated and protracted affair than that which occurred within the IRA. After the ratification of the agreement, various compromises negotiated between pro- and anti-Treaty leaders prevented a decisive split within Sinn Féin, and led to a system of dual-government in the south. Although a provisional government was formed in January 1922 to oversee the creation of the Irish Free State, Dáil Éireann continued to function, and from late February the cabinets of both entities began to meet in joint session. In May, this fragile arrangement was threatened by the prospect of a general election. During April, the provisional government had made clear its desire to hold a plebiscite on the Treaty within one month. This was opposed by the anti-Treaty faction, and in the weeks that followed, negotiations commenced to explore a possible compromise. The talks centred on a scheme through which an agreed election would give rise to coalition government with a pro-Treaty majority. This plan arose from a series of proposals forwarded by senior IRA figures aimed at providing a basis for the reunification of the army. The talks stumbled, however, on the issue of the number of seats that would be pre-assigned to each faction.[1]

It was in response to this impasse, on 16 May, that Aiken took it upon himself to intervene in the negotiations. His decision was most likely driven by a fear that any wavering in southern unity might prove disastrous for the imminent joint-IRA offensive, which was scheduled to begin on 19 May. He arrived in Dublin at the head of a delegation from Newry and south Armagh, and used his familiarity with both factions to convene a meeting in the Oak Room at the Mansion House. All of the key pro- and anti-Treaty leaders were in attendance, including Michael Collins, Eamon de Valera, Arthur Griffith, Richard Mulcahy, Eoin O'Duffy, Cathal Brugha, Liam Lynch and Rory O'Connor.

The delegation presented a familiar argument that emphasised the importance of southern unity in view of the situation in Ulster. It stressed the detrimental effect that disunity was having on the republican cause in the north, and the morale of northern IRA units in particular. Continuing loyalist violence against the nationalist minority in the province was also highlighted, and the delegation made clear its belief that 'the climax has not yet been reached [. . .] we know that these fanatics will outdo the efforts of the Black and Tans'.[2] As the meeting progressed, the discussion moved to the conditions of any agreement. It was in this respect that Aiken made, perhaps, his most valuable contribution to the proceedings. As he explained in later years,

> Collins had been insisting on the pro-Treaty section having a working majority in the new Dáil. When he mentioned this in the meeting I put it to him strongly that he wouldn't allow the attempt for unity to break down for such a small point.[3]

The intervention of the delegation certainly appears to have had an effect. As Hopkinson has observed, the day after the meeting, 'Collins pointed out the consequences of disunity in the south for their northern policy and triggered off new hopes of an agreement by a conciliatory tone in the Dáil.' An agreement was finally reached on 20 May. Sinn Féin would field a national coalition panel composed of pro- and anti-Treaty candidates, the selection of which would be based on the relative strength of each faction in the current Dáil. The only issue on which Collins had refused to compromise was that non-Sinn Féin candidates would be allowed to stand on equal terms in the election.[4]

Aiken's role in the negotiation of the Collins-de Valera pact should not be overstated. His delegation may have put pressure on leading figures, such as Collins, but it had no substantial involvement in the protracted discussions over the terms of the agreement. This episode was, however, one of the few of the civil war period that Aiken took pride in relating in later years.[5] His intervention was also of sufficient significance to convince Mulcahy to ask him to stay in Dublin for a few days, in case there were further problems and his presence might again prove useful.[6] What is most noteworthy about the incident, however, is that Aiken could exert any influence on the negotiations whatsoever. He was not an elected representative at this time. His status in the movement derived entirely from his position within the IRA. That he could intervene in the negotiations, in spite of his low political profile and lack of public prominence, was a reflection of how central the military wing of the movement had become to national events in early 1922.

The Collins-de Valera pact ultimately failed in its aim of securing unity through the formation of a coalition government. It was the intention of the pact that the election would not be fought on the issue of the Treaty, but this was immediately undermined by the decision to use proportional representation. As Hopkinson observes, this 'ensured that voters were able to express their pro- and anti-Treaty preferences.'[7] In addition, both factions frequently violated the spirit of the agreement while campaigning.[8] The provisional government was also accused of subverting the pact through its late publication of the new constitution. It had been agreed that this would be made available to the public before election day (16 June), but in the event it was only published that morning as voters went to the polls.[9] It did not help matters that the document failed to live up to Collins's assurances that it would reflect republican values. British pressure had ultimately ensured that the new constitution conformed strictly to the terms of the Treaty, and thus retained its most unpopular elements, the much despised oath to the British monarch in particular.[10]

The election results were an overwhelming endorsement of the Treaty. Pro-Treaty candidates won 128 of the 164 seats. Anti-Treaty candidates secured only thirty-six.[11] In terms of votes cast, anti-Treaty panel candidates won only 133,864 of a total 620,283, in comparison to 239,193 for pro-Treaty panel candidates and 247,276 for pro-Treaty non-panel candidates. The result in the Louth-Meath constituency, which included Aiken's north Louth command area, reflected this nationwide trend. Cathal O'Shannon, the pro-Treaty Labour Party candidate, topped the poll with 13,994 votes, while the remaining four seats went to panel candidates; three pro-Treaty and one anti-Treaty. O'Shannon's first preference vote far exceeded that of any other candidate in the constituency and he attributed this to the electorate's desire to register a protest against the panel system agreed in the pact.[12] In the aftermath of the election, the anti-Treaty faction seized upon the pro-Treatyites' alleged violations of the agreement as an explanation for their poor performance. The consensus amongst historians, however, has been that these 'subversions' of the pact were of little real significance in the outcome of the election.[13]

The failure of the pact, and the perception that the provisional government had violated its provisions, had important repercussions for Aiken's previously close relationship with Collins. He had already begun to question the latter's motives after the events surrounding the Fourth Northern Division's occupation of Dundalk Barracks in April 1922.[14] The failure of the pact added further tension. He shared the anti-Treatyite analysis of the election, and believed that Collins and the provisional government had failed to uphold the terms of the pact. In the weeks that followed he complained bitterly to Mulcahy that Collins 'has broken the pact made with E. de Valera to such an extent that [those forces] at present under G.H.Q. Beggars Bush are only an army of a political section instead of an Army of the Dáil.'[15] He expressed his newfound antipathy to Collins by shunning him, particularly after the outbreak of the fighting in Dublin on 28 June. Although Aiken remained in close contact with Mulcahy he had no further communication with Collins. In recalling a visit to Beggars Bush in this period, for example, John McCoy observed that 'F/A [Aiken] & Collins weren't speaking at this time. Collins was in the barracks that day, he seen us but he didn't come near us.'[16] This rather odd outcome might suggest both a degree of political naivety on Aiken's part, and a certain amount of stubborn immaturity on behalf of both men.

Aiken's relationship with O'Duffy also soured at this time. This was partly the result of longer-term tensions resulting from a simple personality clash. In later years, Aiken complained that O'Duffy was 'bitter', observing that he 'never mentioned the name of any of his opponents without calling them names & imputing dishonourable motives.'[17] He also claimed to have sparked a number of rows with O'Duffy by contradicting him in front of others.[18] In the more immediate term, Aiken and his staff suspected that O'Duffy was most responsible for the attempt to deprive the Fourth Northern Division of Dundalk Barracks.[19] As a result, Mulcahy became the only figure within the pro-Treaty elite with whom Aiken continued to have any significant contact. His continued esteem for Mulcahy most likely derived from the latter's seemingly greater willingness to entertain both the Fourth Northern Division's neutrality and Aiken's efforts to promote unity. Accordingly, Mulcahy was the first figure that Aiken approached after the outbreak of the fighting in Dublin in an attempt to broker a truce.

It is unclear what drove Aiken to undertake his peace mission. As was the case with his intervention in the Collins-de Valera pact negotiations, it is likely that it was his desire to see the joint-IRA offensive through to fruition. Given his seemingly successful intervention in the pact negotiations, he may also have been confident that he could again be of use as a mediator. Indeed, it could be argued that Aiken's efforts reflected an overestimation of his own influence, something which Collins and Mulcahy had partly enabled through their past willingness to entertain his initiatives for unity. Significantly, however, it is clear that Aiken held no illusions as to his prospects for success. In setting off for Dublin he brought two companions, Mick O'Hanlon and Tom Rogers. As O'Hanlon later recalled,

> Frank thought Mulcahy would arrest him so he gave me a copy of the stuff he had with him in case he was arrested. I was to get through to the south to see Lynch; and Rogers, if Frank was arrested, was to go to Liverpool and then back to our area to inform our men.[20]

Aiken met Mulcahy on 7 July. He had sent his proposals in writing the previous day, and pleaded with Mulcahy, as a provisional government minister, to 'call a truce immediately in order to first get an army convention summoned of all sections of the IRA to elect an Army Council and secondly to get the Third Dáil to frame a constitution.'[21] These suggestions were not particularly innovative, and represented an amalgamation of various initiatives that had been proposed or attempted in the preceding months.[22] They were further weakened by the fact that Aiken ultimately spoke for nobody but himself.

Mulcahy was in a difficult position at this time. Elements within the provisional government were opposed to his and Collins's conciliatory initiatives towards the anti-Treaty IRA.[23] Consequently, his response was disappointing. As Aiken recalled, Mulcahy 'said he could not see his way to advise the government to do so.' In reply, Aiken reiterated his division's position of neutrality. He warned that if ordered to attack anti-Treaty positions it would refuse and withdraw its allegiance from GHQ. In this event, however, he pledged that it would not take up arms against the provisional government. Before leaving, he also made clear his intention to go south to Liam Lynch to make further efforts to negotiate a truce.[24] Mulcahy apparently gave his tacit consent for this course of action, providing military passes for Aiken and his companions to allow their safe passage through the army cordons en route to Limerick.[25]

Aiken arrived in Limerick the following day amidst a tense and uncertain situation. The fight for the city had not yet begun. Anti-Treaty forces had a considerable military advantage. They occupied the city's main military barracks (known as the New Barracks), had greater numbers, and were also better equipped than their pro-Treaty opponents. As a result, the commanders of the provisional government forces in the city, Michael Brennan and Donnchadh O'Hannigan, had accepted a truce negotiated by a local priest. This was agreed the day before Aiken's arrival and it was against this backdrop that he approached Liam Lynch at the New Barracks.[26] Aiken recorded what transpired a few weeks later:

I saw him [Lynch] on the 8th July and put it to him he could do more for the Republic by propaganda than he could by fighting men of the old Army most of whom thought they were doing their best for the Republic and who would never countenance the King, as in the constitution, and also that although he had the moral right to fight it was bad tactics, since he could only fight for a few months or years without any chance of a successful revolution.[27]

These arguments apparently had little effect, though Lynch's reception may not have been as unenthusiastic as that of Mulcahy. Aiken remained in the city in the days that followed and, with his status as a neutral, acted as a liaison between the two factions for the duration of the locally agreed truce.[28]

This truce was short-lived, however. The provisional government was opposed to the agreement. It also appears that the main objective of the local pro-Treaty commanders in subscribing to the deal was to buy time so that reinforcements could be sent to the city in order to push ahead with an offensive.[29] The truce ended on 11 July. Aiken was with Lynch when they received the news. He attempted to intervene in the situation, but to no avail. He later related that 'Lynch's attitude was that the other people had started the fight and that it was up to them to take steps to stop it.'[30] Brennan, meanwhile, indicated that the decision was no longer his, and that General James Hogan was now in charge. The fighting resumed within hours, and Aiken left the next morning.[31]

Probably the most striking feature of Aiken's peace mission was the basic principle he came to espouse during it; that the government should get rid of the oath, and thus provide the anti-Treaty faction with 'a constitutional way to carry on working for a Republic in the Army, and in the Civil Government'.[32] This differed little from the stance he endorsed after the civil war as a supporter of de Valera and a founder member of Fianna Fáil.[33] It also demonstrated a key difference between Aiken's outlook, and that of anti-Treaty republicans. It is often suggested that the latter, the IRA in particular, were 'basically undemocratic'.[34] This perception has developed largely as a result of the faction's rhetoric during the split, as well as its willingness to go to war over the Treaty despite the popular endorsement of the agreement at the June elections. It is also viewed as an extension of the IRA's elitism during the war for independence, and the disdain with which many of those in the organisation had viewed constitutional politics and politicians.[35] As Garvin observes, many volunteers 'saw themselves as having created the Republic and no one had the right to give it away, democratically or otherwise.'[36]

Aiken differed significantly from his peers in this respect. From an early stage he had shown an interest in politics and a respect for constitutional methods. As a result, he did not demonstrate the same 'undemocratic' – or perhaps 'a-democratic' – tendencies as many of the Treaty's opponents.[37] Unlike many anti-Treatyites, he accepted the results of the June election. The peace proposals that he submitted to Mulcahy in the first weeks of the civil war called for the convening of the Third Dáil, elected in June, rather than a reconstituted Second Dáil. Nevertheless, he did hold a different view of what the results represented: 'the people want peace between Irishmen. They returned a large majority of the Third Dáil on the platform of peace between the civil and military organisation.'[38] He did not contest the validity of the election, or the composition of the Third Dáil. He merely believed that under the terms of the Collins-de Valera pact, the people had voted for the establishment of a coalition government and that to obtain this the oath would have to be removed.

'FRANK YET HAD HOPES OF PEACE'

Before leaving Dundalk, Aiken had successfully reunited the Fourth Northern Division's pro- and anti-Treaty units under his policy of neutrality.[39] As a result, the opening weeks of the civil war were relatively peaceful in north Louth. Shortly after Aiken's departure, however, his division's neutral stance faced a sustained challenge from the provisional government army GHQ at Beggars Bush. Upon learning of Aiken's peace mission, O'Duffy had sent him a confrontational communiqué demanding that he return to Dundalk.[40] Orders were also sent directly to Dundalk Barracks demanding that all anti-Treaty posts in the area be attacked immediately. In Aiken's absence, John McCoy responded that 'the division was united as constituted prior to the 26 March 1922.' A tense stand-off developed, with McCoy and his fellow divisional officers attempting to hold their ground amidst a flood of warnings and threats from Beggars Bush as to the dire consequences of refusing to follow orders.[41] To make matters worse, no one in Dundalk was entirely certain of Aiken's whereabouts. He apparently had not received O'Duffy's message before leaving for Limerick, and was clearly unaware of the threat that his division now faced.

The Fourth Northern Division's precarious position was further complicated by internal issues. In Aiken's absence, a wage dispute developed. This came as a direct result of his unique policy of neutrality. Although the Fourth Northern Division had remained under the authority of the department of defence, Aiken had refused to pledge his men for service in the fledgling provisional government army. As a consequence, Beggars Bush refused to provide full financial assistance to the division, and it was not possible to pay the standard wage then being received by attested pro-Treaty soldiers. Divisional officers, and some brigade ranks, were not affected by this, however, and continued to receive a wage from a weekly sustenance allowance. This situation held clear potential for conflict, yet it did not become an issue until after the outbreak of hostilities in Dublin, when a number of officers in Dundalk Barracks became increasingly resentful and refused to carry out their assigned duties.

The disaffected officers presented a very different view of the dispute. One of those apparently involved later gave his version of events after being arrested in Northern Ireland in October 1922:

> They thought they were Free Staters and also that Aiken was a Free Stater. At first they were paid fairly regularly, but after a time received no pay at all. There was a good deal of grumbling and it was eventually found out that Aiken had received the money to pay his men, but had spent it on buying arms and ammunition for the irregulars [anti-Treaty IRA].[42]

These claims are highly suspect, however. No one in the Fourth Northern Division was misled as to its status throughout early 1922. At least two memos were circulated during these months that clearly explained the policy of neutrality then adopted. The allegation that Aiken had diverted money to buy arms for the anti-Treatyites is also entirely without foundation, and runs contrary to all other available evidence for events within the division during this period.

In an attempt to quell the indiscipline, McCoy and his fellow divisional officers addressed the garrison, explaining the financial situation and pledging that, although a wage could not be paid, clothing, boots and accommodation would continue to be provided free of charge. According to McCoy, the majority of the men were placated by this, and only four rejected these terms of service.[43] Nevertheless, the disaffected officers proved extremely troublesome. On 12 July, they broke into the divisional stores. Having stolen weapons, supplies, and a car, they then set out for Dublin to join the provisional government army. McCoy quickly raised a small force and eventually apprehended the men at Drogheda. With the agreement of the local provisional government commander, they were subsequently brought back to Dundalk to be disciplined. The barracks O/C, Dominic Doherty, was also demoted as a result of the incident when it emerged that he had taken no action when he learned of the thefts.[44]

At first, this dispute over wages seems a rather trivial issue. Yet on closer inspection, it becomes clear that it marked the beginning of a new split within the division. This time the discontent emanated from the south Down contingent. All those who became embroiled in the dispute were south Down officers, the most notable amongst them being Patrick Casey, Charlie Grant and Dominic Doherty.[45] With the possible exception of Doherty, all eventually ended up serving in the provisional government army. Casey, in particular, also appears to have been instrumental in later convincing as many as twenty companies from across south Down to pledge their loyalty to the Irish Free State in return for continued financial assistance.[46] The geographic dimension of this new split was not as pronounced as that involving the First Brigade earlier in the year, however. The south Down units were better integrated into Aiken's command than their counterparts in north Louth. A number of influential south Down officers also remained loyal to Aiken, most notably Seán and Padraig Quinn, Andy O'Hare and Ned Fitzpatrick.

The new split was influenced by various factors. Before the outbreak of hostilities in Dublin there were indications that a number of south Down volunteers were opposed to Aiken's neutral stance and held unreservedly pro-Treaty views.[47] Yet this appeared to pose few problems so long as fighting continued in the north. The dispute over wages itself was undoubtedly a factor, but it may also have simply provided a focal point for various personal grievances. Doherty, for example, only appears to have become involved after his demotion. Casey, meanwhile, was apparently unhappy with Aiken's leadership following the division's withdrawal from the joint-IRA offensive and (possibly) the carnage at Altnaveigh.[48] A divergence of views regarding the Treaty, therefore, was not necessarily the most important issue.

It was to this tense situation that Aiken returned on 14 July. While making his way back to Dundalk he had received a summons for a meeting with Mulcahy the following day. In preparation he convened a divisional council at which an official position was agreed upon and a number of precautions were ordered in case of a break with GHQ. Arms and war material were concealed. All posts were abandoned. Yet there was no intention to fight. Rather, it was Aiken's hope that the division could be kept intact 'until – an ordered state of government obtaining in the south – we could attack the north with a chance of getting a united Ireland.'[49] At the meeting with Mulcahy, Aiken set forth the agreed position and a representative assortment of divisional officers pledged their support for the policy. Mulcahy asked that Aiken present the points he had raised in a memorandum to Collins, as commander-in-chief of the army, and Griffith, as president of the provisional government. As McCoy recalled, he also warned 'that our position was creating a critical situation for him and his associates'.[50]

Aiken returned to Dundalk that evening with a few of his fellow officers and set to work on his memorandum. In the early hours of the following morning, however, the Fifth Northern Division, under the leadership of Dan Hogan, entered Dundalk and quickly captured all the main positions in the town in a surprise swoop. No resistance was offered, although one volunteer was killed and another wounded while attempting to escape.[51] At the military barracks, Aiken and his men were taken by surprise. As he colourfully put it,

> I awoke with two Thompsons at my nose. An officer who had been reduced for inefficiency, some men who were under arrest for drunkenness, opened the gates and so – Brilliant Victory of National Army! 300 Irregulars Arrested! Not a Shot Fired![52]

The handful of south Down officers that had come to oppose the division's stance had conspired with the provisional government forces for the handover of the barracks.[53]

There is some confusion as to who within the pro-Treaty leadership authorised the capture of Dundalk and why. Aiken was quickly granted a meeting with Mulcahy, who claimed that he had no knowledge of the plans. Yet he also went on to say that intelligence had been received that suggested that the division had abandoned its neutral status and intended to attack provisional government forces. This had been passed on by Dominic Doherty, the former barracks O/C at Dundalk. Following his demotion he had sought leave, stating the intention of taking a break in Galway. Instead, he made contact with Beggars Bush and reported details of a divisional staff meeting that had occurred shortly before Aiken's return.[54] McCoy later admitted that during this meeting 'many of our officers appeared to favour the idea that we should depart from our neutral attitude and join the executive forces.'[55] Ultimately, however, no decision had been taken and when Aiken later arrived they instead agreed to his policy.

Contemporaries and historians alike have agreed that Hogan acted on his own initiative in capturing Dundalk.[56] Mulcahy is certainly believed to have had no part in the operation. Aiken himself was suitably convinced of this.[57] Yet others within the divisional staff were much more sceptical. McCoy later claimed that after the meeting with Mulcahy on 15 July, he had taken away 'the impression that a decision had already been taken in connection with the problem our neutrality presented.'[58] Padraig Quinn later recorded that he had similar suspicions, believing that Mulcahy's summons for a meeting that required the attendance of the entire divisional staff and all brigade officers was a ruse aimed at the mass arrest of the Fourth Northern Division leadership. As a result of these concerns, he claimed, it was decided to leave a 'considerable number of reliable men behind.'[59] It is suggested elsewhere, moreover, that while Aiken was in Limerick, Mulcahy had sent Emmet Dalton to Dundalk to assess the situation there. Dalton had subsequently placed the Fourth Northern Division's area of operations under Hogan's command.[60]

Mulcahy, therefore, may have inadvertently created the conditions for Hogan's supposedly independent actions. Hogan's close relationship with O'Duffy would also suggest that the latter was in some way involved. He had made clear in previous weeks that he had no intention of observing Aiken's neutrality and, as chief-of-staff, it seems likely that he sanctioned the operation.

An important point regarding the capture of Dundalk that is often overlooked is that the provisional government had motives for the operation that went beyond the issue of the Fourth Northern Division's neutrality. Aiken and his men were, in theory at least, under the provisional government's authority and held a military barracks on its behalf. They were, however, using this base to hold a number of northern unionist hostages, both civilians and members of the USC. The governments in Belfast and London were fully aware of this and placed considerable pressure on Collins and his colleagues for their release. The issue was particularly pertinent in early July 1922, following a speech by Churchill at Westminster in which he attacked the provisional government for its maintenance of IRA divisions in Northern Ireland.[61] Although references to the hostage issue are sketchy, it does appear to have created further tension between the Fourth Northern Division and Beggars Bush. McCoy recalled that Aiken was under pressure from both Mulcahy and O'Duffy to release the prisoners in the weeks before the barracks was captured.[62] Aiken also apparently felt the issue to have been crucial in leading to the capture of Dundalk, and later expressed the opinion that the hostages should have been released earlier, as in holding them he had merely played into the hands of Hogan and O'Duffy.[63]

Despite his arrest Aiken still had little intention of fighting the provisional government. When Mulcahy offered that Aiken and his men could be released in return for a signed pledge that they would not take up arms against the state, Aiken said he could guarantee that they would not, but refused to sign the form and doubted if any of his men would either. He was, therefore, returned to Dundalk with assurances that he and his men would be given the status of 'officers confined to barracks.'[64] The Fifth Northern Division disregarded this order, however, and instead held Aiken and his men in Dundalk Gaol. His subsequent requests to speak to Mulcahy in relation to the situation were denied by his captors, as was his plea for permission to speak to those divisional officers who remained at large, in an attempt to prevent any retaliatory attacks in Dundalk. Exasperated by the intransigent attitude with which he was faced, Aiken washed his hands of the situation and in the days that followed wrote to Mulcahy stating his belief that 'someone wants to goad our division into resistance.'[65]

Indeed, resistance soon followed. A number of Fourth Northern Division officers had remained at large after the capture of Dundalk, amongst them

John McCoy, Seán Quinn and Eiver Monaghan, the divisional engineer. Having regrouped, these men held a meeting in the rather dramatic setting of Faughart graveyard, 'using as a desk the flat tombstone which tradition holds covers the grave of Edward Bruce who fell in the Battle of Faughart in the year 1318.'[66] It was decided that preparations should be made for an assault on the provisional government forces at Dundalk, and the rescue of Aiken and his companions from Dundalk Gaol.[67] The latter operation took place on 27 July and proved a remarkable success. At around seven o'clock that morning a large mine was detonated at the gaol wall.[68] This was timed to coincide with the prisoners' morning exercise and, as a result, 105 men escaped, including Aiken and the other incarcerated divisional officers.[69] To ensure the successful withdrawal of the rescue party and the freed prisoners, two ambushes were set along the main routes to the gaol to attack any relief party. Two provisional government soldiers and one IRA man were wounded as a result of these brief skirmishes.[70] In the confusion, a number of IRA men were also captured, most notably McCoy, and it was reported in the following days that up to 50 of the released prisoners had quickly been returned to custody.[71]

Now free, Aiken set his sights on re-capturing Dundalk. Since his arrest he had been smarting over the fact that Hogan's capture of the town was being lauded as a great victory for the provisional government. Indeed, after his arrest he had demanded that Mulcahy have the truth of the situation published 'so that it could not be said that 300 of the IRA meant to fight, and were such military fools or such cowards, as to be arrested without firing a shot.'[72] His decision to launch an attack on the provisional government positions in the town was, therefore, a point of honour rather than a firm indication of his intention to throw in his lot with the anti-Treaty executive.

Aiken's subsequent attack on Dundalk on 14 August was later described by one contemporary as 'by far the most spectacularly efficient carried out by the IRA.'[73] The assault was meticulously planned from a base at Ravensdale, close to the border. Despite the previous week's events Aiken was in a remarkably strong position. Provisional government forces, despite capturing Dundalk, had made no attempt to neutralise the Fourth Northern Division's camps in the north of the county. There was, therefore, a plentiful supply of material and manpower available. Furthermore, Aiken and his men had extensive knowledge of the town and the military positions, and this was further supplemented by intelligence from planted individuals and 'deserters'. The latter were men who had taken up the offer of joining the provisional government army after the capture of Dundalk.[74] Many had subsequently changed their minds and were allowed to go free.[75]

Aiken mobilised his men, many of whom were unaware of what was planned, at Omeath.[76] They then crossed to Dundalk by boat, landing at

Soldiers Point. The attack commenced at approximately four o'clock in the morning. The barracks was stormed by two parties, each consisting of 14 men. Each man carried a revolver, a bomb and a battery, and each group was armed with eight 'petrol can mines', one 30-pound mine, and detonation equipment. These men were charged with blowing in the gates at the front and rear of the barracks. They were then to enter and set off explosions at a number of predetermined points. Each party was then to be followed by a group of rifle-men who would advance upon hearing the first explosion.[77] Despite claims later made by the provisional government army, the Fourth Northern Division had not secretly mined the building during their previous occupation.[78]

The plan did not go as smoothly as was hoped. A mine placed at the front gate failed to detonate and both parties were forced to enter through the back. Despite this setback, however, the military barracks was soon subdued. The attack focused primarily on the officers' quarters and a quick surrender was obtained.[79] Having captured the barracks, Aiken refused to allow the com-manding officer of the provisional government troops to help the survivors in the rubble until all other military posts in the town were ordered to surrender. At the outset of the attack these positions had been surrounded and kept under sustained fire. Aiken's ultimatum was quickly accepted and the town was now in the hands of the Fourth Northern Division.[80]

Despite the impressive scale of the operation the casualties were surprisingly few. In all, four provisional government soldiers were killed and 13 wounded. Two further casualties were recorded within the Fourth Northern Division. Patrick McKenna, O/C of the First Brigade, was killed accidentally after capturing an armoured car. His comrades, not realising that the vehicle was no longer a threat, detonated a mine as it passed.[81] Tom Rogers, a divisional officer, was also wounded during a gunfight in one of the guard rooms. It was later claimed that he was shot after the provisional government soldiers with whom he was engaged offered a false surrender.[82]

Having captured Dundalk, Aiken and his men occupied the town for three days. The provisional government soldiers were made prisoner, in place of around 250 republicans, and efforts were directed towards removing the impressive haul of arms and war material captured in the operation.[83] Immediate defensive action was also taken to slow any advance by the provisional govern-ment army. At Carlingford harbour, mines were positioned to fend off any attempt at a landing. A party of men also headed south, by train, towards Drogheda to destroy bridges. In the process a brief panic was created in the town, as it was feared that Aiken was intending to advance.[84] He had no such plans, however, and did not even intend on trying to hold Dundalk. As Mick O'Hanlon recalled, 'Frank yet had hopes of peace.'[85]

A public meeting was called at Market Square in Dundalk and addressed by an assortment of republicans from Armagh and Newry; amongst them such figures as James McGuill, Robert Kelly and Patrick Lavery. Significantly, Aiken did not address the crowd, and instead sent a letter expressing his regret that he could not attend 'owing to military matters.' A statement from the divisional officers was read to the crowd and a resolution proposed; that the Dáil be summoned either to 'arrange an honourable peace' or, failing that, to dissolve the Third Dáil and hold another election on the issue of 'the present constitution'. Thereafter, the assortment of speakers further espoused the need for a truce and for a constitutional means for republicans to be involved in the new state. Their views were, it seems, not shared by the majority of local residents. Press reports noted that when the proposals were put to the crowd 'a good number replied in the negative.'[86] The *Dundalk Democrat* appeared to have accurately captured the public mood when it observed that, whatever good intentions Aiken and his comrades may have had, they had rejected the public's verdict as expressed in the June elections.[87]

The provisional government's reply came two days later when, on the evening of 16 August, its forces arrived to re-capture Dundalk. By this time, the majority of Fourth Northern Division units had already moved north. To cover their withdrawal, they detonated a large bomb in the town centre, and cut all power. A small IRA force also remained in the town, to harass and further hold up the incoming troops. The explosion, and a number of small skirmishes, resulted in considerable casualties. Four provisional government soldiers were wounded. One republican was killed, and another seriously injured. The first civilian casualties of the conflict were also reported, with one dead and four wounded.[88] Having re-occupied Dundalk, provisional government troops swiftly moved north to round up the Fourth Northern Division's camps closer to the border, taking a number of prisoners in the process.[89] Aiken and a considerable number of his men had already crossed the border into south Armagh and south Down. With all hopes of peace finally eroded, they now faced a difficult decision as to what to do next.[90]

WAR

Aiken is often portrayed as a reluctant participant in the civil war, not only on account of his early neutrality in the conflict, but also for the hesitancy with which he joined the anti-Treaty cause. Following his escape from Dundalk Gaol in late July, the anti-Treaty leadership were hopeful that Aiken would quickly align his division with the IRA executive. Indeed, as early as 6 August,

Ernie O'Malley, the assistant chief-of-staff, had sent a messenger to Aiken in order to determine his intentions. At this stage, however, it was found that Aiken 'has not made up his mind to act as yet [. . .] he is still a kind of neutral but I believe will be eventually forced into it more by the actions of the Free Staters.'[91] Nevertheless, O'Malley persisted, and sent another messenger, Todd Andrews, to Dundalk a week later to see if there had been any change in Aiken's outlook. Andrews's recollection of what occurred provides some indication of the coolness with which these approaches were met:

> He [Aiken] was sitting on the bed and made no attempt to make me welcome. There was a chair in the room but I was not invited to sit down. He did not ask what I wanted. He looked at me in what he may have thought was a questioning manner but the muscles of his face did not appear to move. Finally a grunted 'Well?' indicated that discussion should get under way. I explained the purpose of my visit. He told me as laconically as possible to go back and tell O'Malley that he intended to attack and re-capture Dundalk. I asked feeling, but I hope not showing, some scepticism 'When?' 'In a few days' was the reply. The conversation was beginning to resemble a Red Indian pow-wow.[92]

Aiken eventually warmed to Andrews somewhat, and the latter stayed on to participate in the attack on Dundalk Barracks. Yet there was still no clear idea of Aiken's views or intentions, although he did offer to provide some arms and material for other anti-Treaty units.[93]

   Aiken finally aligned with the executive at the end of August 1922, but this formalisation of his position did not lead to any improvement in his relations with O'Malley, or the chief-of-staff, Liam Lynch.[94] During September, Aiken remained distant. Upon joining the anti-Treaty effort he was immediately offered the position of O/C of a new 'Northern Command'.[95] By 7 September, however, despite O'Malley's numerous attempts to make contact, he had still not indicated his acceptance.[96] O'Malley was also frustrated with Aiken's failure to provide any indication of his views on the conflict: 'I do not know his outlook on the general situation, nor has he forwarded me his impressions on the northern situation though I have asked him to do so.'[97] In the following days Aiken did finally contact O'Malley, but it is clear that there was mounting concern regarding his reliability, and Lynch decided that 'we will not fix up with regard to the Northern Command until we are more certain of the officer concerned.'[98]

   Aiken's lack of enthusiasm for the conflict was evident in his relations with the anti-Treaty leadership. It might be argued that his attitude reflected an understandable reluctance to go to war with former comrades. Yet as the attack on Dundalk Barracks clearly suggests, Aiken was not unwilling to fight the Free State, particularly in light of the way he had been treated by the pro-Treaty leadership. Rather, his reluctance reflected his uneasiness about committing to the anti-Treaty cause. Throughout early 1922 he had done his utmost to avoid becoming embroiled in the split and, subsequently, the civil war, and he was clearly very passionate about his policy of neutrality. He had, moreover, shown no particular predilection towards the anti-Treaty standpoint. If anything, he had shown a greater solidarity with the pro-Treaty faction, particularly amid the various attempts to secure army unity. In this context, his transition to fully fledged anti-Treatyite represented a radical step-change; one made all the more difficult by the stress and trauma of the events that had prompted it.

Indeed, events from mid-July onwards had taken their toll on Aiken, and there are signs that he was suffering severe emotional strain. Similar obser- vations have been made with regard to various figures embroiled in the civil war. Events in 1922 were said to have 'induced a nervous breakdown in de Valera' while in the same period Kevin O'Higgins was described as being 'in some ways quite disturbed.'[99] In Aiken's case the evidence is intriguing, but incredibly thin and circumstantial. The stress of the preceding months (and indeed years) had almost certainly affected him physically. This can be deduced from a description recorded in the Dundalk Gaol register upon his incarceration in July. In contrast to the other young 'fresh' faced divisional officers, he was described as having a 'sallow' complexion, and was listed as being 38 years old, a full 14 years older than his actual age of 24.[100] Events also seem to have affected him emotionally. The clearest indication of this comes in a letter to Mulcahy upon the death of Collins in August, in which Aiken appears to offer himself as a sacrifice through which to end the war:

> If you believed absolutely in the sincerity of the men opposed to you, you would stop the struggle. If that is true I'll prove to you if you wish. I'll die in order to prove to you if you guarantee to me that you'll stop this Civil War if I do so. For God's sake Dick, agree to this and let one death end it all.[101]

It is difficult to say if this was a genuine plea, or if Aiken was being uncharacteristically melodramatic. Mulcahy clearly believed the former, and attributed the letter to an 'entirely unstrung state of mind.'[102] Whatever the truth, Aiken was certainly traumatised by the conflict. Comrades such as Andrews later remarked on how 'horrified' and 'saddened' he was over the civil war.[103] Family members have also recalled his emotional response to discussion of the conflict in later life: 'my dad absolutely hated the Civil War [. . .] I still get emotional when I remember how much he hated it.'[104]

Regardless of Aiken's state of mind at this time, and irrespective of the initial uncertainty concerning his division's commitment to the anti-Treaty cause, the conflict had continued unabated in north Louth. The re-occupation of Dundalk by provisional government forces (now more popularly known as the National Army) brought an end to the 'conventional phase' of the civil war in the area. This was in keeping with events throughout the country. As the National Army successfully established control in the towns and cities, anti-Treaty IRA units increasingly reverted to guerrilla warfare. On the day that the Fourth Northern Division attacked Dundalk Barracks, the propaganda sheet, *Poblacht na hÉireann War News*, announced the beginning of this '2nd or principle phase of the resumed war of independence.'[105] The shift in tactics was made official in the week that followed when orders were issued calling for the establishment of ASUs.[106] Now on the run, both north and south of the border, Aiken and his remaining supporters duly followed suit.

The resulting guerrilla campaign in north Louth is difficult to discuss in detail. Those involved left little record of their activities, and contemporary documentation is sparse. The Bureau of Military History statements of Fourth Northern Division members typically end with the attack on Dundalk Barracks, while some include brief accounts of time spent in internment camps either north or south of the border. This reflects the fact that after the Dundalk operation many men returned home and refused to take any further part in the conflict. In November 1922, for example, a USC commandant in Armagh noted that since the previous July he had received 'various visits from the people who had relatives on the run in the Free State, asking if they would be allowed to return and if they would be free from molestation.'[107] In his area alone four men had returned on the condition that they submit to close monitoring.[108] Others, like Edward Fullerton, saw no possibility of returning home and found themselves stranded in Dundalk, living off the charity of friends.[109] Still others, like John Grant, who were actively involved, simply refused to give any account of their activities: 'I have no desire to deal in any more detail with any of the engagements I had with former comrades during the civil war, but I do want to place on record that I took the republican side.'[110]

Nevertheless, despite the absence of detailed evidence, it is possible to provide some idea of the dynamics of the campaign over which Aiken presided in 1922 and 1923. Broadly speaking this can be divided into two phases, the first of which began after the attack on Dundalk Barracks in mid-August and lasted until the end of December 1922. It was characterised by persistent low-level operations, such as sniping and the destruction of bridges, interspersed with the occasional large-scale attack on military posts and patrols, as Aiken and his men fell back on the tactics with which they were most familiar.

During the autumn, there were four set-piece ambushes in Dundalk and the surrounding area.[111] These differed little from the division's ambushes earlier in the revolutionary period. Although there was a more effective use of land mines during the civil war, this was an old tactic. Its newfound success simply reflected the greater availability of explosives, and the fact that local units had more luck in engaging their opponents than in earlier periods of fighting. As with earlier ambushes, it was also rare for either side to claim a decisive victory. Attacks tended to be short, resulting in few casualties, before one or other force withdrew. One remarkable exception was an ambush on the main route between Dundalk and Carrickmacross on 21 November, when up to twelve soldiers were wounded, one mortally. The attack began with a road-side explosion that effectively neutralised the entire National Army patrol. The IRA ambush party then began their attack, but quickly accepted the surrender of their dazed and injured opponents.[112]

Large-scale attacks on National Army posts also occurred during this period, but they are difficult to quantify. Throughout these months, sustained sniping attacks occurred in Dundalk almost every night, and it is often difficult to identify the more serious IRA operations. Nevertheless, there appear to have been at least four determined assaults on National Army barracks and outposts before the end of 1922. As was the case with ambushes in the region, these were strikingly similar to the Fourth Northern Division's barracks attacks earlier in the revolutionary period. Although the capture of Dundalk had hinted at the division's potential for tactical innovation, these later operations showed little originality. An attack on a National Army post in Omeath in October 1922 is illustrative in this respect. The area was isolated before the operation commenced, with roads blocked, railway lines cut, and all means of communication disrupted. The building was then subjected to a sustained attack with rifle and machine gun fire from three positions. The IRA party finally withdrew at dawn, having failed to capture the position, and having inflicted only one (civilian) casualty.[113] This bore more than a passing resemblance to earlier barracks attacks in south Armagh, and achieved similarly poor results.

One notable difference between the Fourth Northern Division's civil war campaign and its earlier operations in Ulster was a more effective use of sabotage. This reflected the strength of the division's engineering department, which was judged by Paddy Coughlan (director of engineering) to be the best organised in the IRA's northern and eastern command area.[114] The division used this to full effect during the conflict, and the results were most visible on the railway. Between mid-November and early January, the IRA derailed five trains in north Louth, two of which were destroyed in one spectacular operation on 20 December.[115] There was also a greater use of sabotage for tactical advantage. During an operation in Dundalk on 15 September, for example, an IRA party first seized the local power station and plunged the town into darkness. Attacks were then carried out on National Army posts and patrols, resulting in the death of one soldier.[116] Plans for booby-trap bombings were also mooted. Documents captured in the final days of the conflict contained references to the planting of concealed mines in buildings likely to be commandeered by the National Army. The idea was that, once the building was occupied, these could be detonated by an engineer using a pre-positioned cable with a minimal risk of capture.[117] A successful operation of this nature may even have occurred in Ardee in October 1922, when a bomb hidden behind a fireplace in the local barracks exploded and injured three soldiers.[118]

Overall, the Fourth Northern Division's performance in north Louth during late 1922 was consistent with that which it had achieved in Armagh and south Down during earlier bouts of fighting. This is perhaps best illustrated by the number of enemy casualties it inflicted. In the five months between August and December 1922, the division was responsible for the deaths of 13 soldiers and the wounding of a further 34. These figures are broadly in keeping with the number of casualties the division inflicted on enemy forces during two comparable periods of conflict earlier in the revolutionary period; the first six months of 1921 (seven dead, 14 wounded), and the first six months of 1922 (13 dead, 16 wounded). The only significant difference is the greater number of those wounded, which was more than double that of the earlier periods of conflict.[119] This was, however, primarily a reflection of the greater impact of low-level operations, such as sniping, and the division's more efficient use of explosives. The aforementioned ambush near Dundalk in November 1922, which resulted in the wounding of 12 soldiers, is a particularly good illustration of this.[120]

Aiken appears to have maintained a firm control over the Fourth Northern Division's new campaign, initially at least. Certainly in later years he claimed to have 'commanded all significant operations in the Fourth Northern Divisional area'.[121] This is corroborated, to an extent, by Ernie O'Malley's recollections of a visit to Dundalk sometime in September or October 1922, where he witnessed Aiken presiding over the preparations for an attack on Free State posts in the town. Evidently impressed, he later recounted the scene in his characteristically literary style, and provides a rare glimpse into Aiken's working relationship with his men:

> The officers for each specific operation were present, most of them young boys. Frank Aiken puffed slowly at his pipe. His quiet brown eyes glanced over operations maps; he held up a finger to emphasise points. The officers received

instructions, asked questions, made suggestions, then outlined their plan of action. They seemed well trained, eager, capable of responsibility without much supervision.[122]

Aiken's continued centrality to the planning and direction of the local campaign at this point of the conflict might also be indicated by a brief upsurge of republican violence in Armagh and south Down in the autumn of 1922, during which there were seven attacks on the RUC and USC resulting in the death of one civilian and the wounding of four special constables.[123] The available evidence certainly suggests that Aiken had remained fixated on the north. Sean McConville, an Armagh officer, later recalled his belief that Aiken 'had no liking for the activities in the south of Ireland' in this period, and that 'he was more keenly interested in the republican position in the north'.[124] Nevertheless, it is also possible that the fresh attacks north of the border were actually the work of disillusioned volunteers who, unable to return home, remained 'on the run' in and around the border, sustained by republican supporters and raids on unfortunate locals. Indeed, intelligence reports in Northern Ireland suggest that these 'armed gangs' continued to operate in areas such as Ravensdale until as late as 1923.[125]

By October 1922, there were signs that Aiken's role was beginning to change. As O'Malley's visit to Dundalk might suggest, Aiken's relations with the IRA leadership had improved considerably. Accordingly, that month, he was finally appointed as officer commanding (O/C) of the 'Northern Command'. In theory at least, he was now in charge of all northern IRA divisions, as well as parts of south Louth, north Meath and Leitrim.[126] As a result, both he and a number of his most trusted divisional officers – such as Mick O'Hanlon and Padraig Quinn – were increasingly preoccupied with organisational work as they travelled around the new commands and attempted to instigate activity; though wherever possible Aiken tried to remain active in the fighting.[127] That same month Aiken also became a member of the IRA army council. His appointment was announced during the same executive meeting at which it was decided to call upon de Valera to form a republican government.[128] Yet this was no coincidence. As Aiken later explained,

> When I was first asked to act on the executive I refused to agree unless steps were taken to set up some civil authority and it was after that at the next meeting of the executive that it was agreed to ask de Valera to form a government.[129]

It is unclear if this pressure from Aiken was responsible for the IRA's decision to call for the formation of a republican government. Indeed, the logic for the move most likely derived from a desire to respond to the convening of the Third Dáil during September, as well as hopes that it might provide a legal basis through which the unused funds of the Second Dáil could be claimed.[130] Nonetheless, it is significant that Aiken felt the need for civil control over the IRA, especially as this issue raised few concerns amongst other anti-Treaty leaders.

Despite the improvement of relations between Aiken and the IRA leadership tensions still remained. In December, the 'director of organisation' (most likely Seán Dowling) launched a scathing attack on Aiken's conduct in a communication to the chief-of-staff. He called for an 'immediate investigation' into the situation within Aiken's command. It was claimed that IRA units in Belfast were, as yet, unaware of the formation of a Northern Command area, and that Aiken's only contact with these units was to 'ask for arms and ammunition, of which he has plenty already.' His efforts to organise the area were described as consisting of little more than his 'moving around in one or two brigade areas in Dundalk exhorting the men to fight by his personal influences.' Criticisms were also made about his continued failure to reply to communications. The list of complaints ended with a statement which summed up much of the criticism that Aiken received from his fellow anti-Treaty officers during the civil war period:

> Aiken's position is extraordinary. He has over 2000 [men] and must have 6 or 700 rifles and about 20 machine guns but apparently he imagines that he is short of men and arms [. . .] it seems to me that Aiken's eyes are on the Six-Counties in which he has about 1500 men and he is saving himself to attack the Specials who are not doing us any harm at all.[131]

Responding to the allegations, Aiken replied simply that, 'Monaghan, Cavan, North and South Louth have not done anything like what they should have done. For this of course I, being O/C am responsible, though I can honestly say I tried to do the best according to my ability.' He also defended his attempts at re-organising his area:

> I thought it was going to be a long drawn out war, and seeing that most of these areas had failed before when outsiders were put in I tried to develop officers that were natives of the areas, and by keeping in close touch with them myself and sending engineers into them, to make the most possible out of them. Outside flying columns failed being mopped up in a short time, because the local organisation was hopeless.[132]

Probably the most remarkable element of this episode is that despite the criticisms levelled against him, Aiken was promoted to the position of deputy chief-of-staff the following month.[133]

Aiken's continued advance within the IRA, despite the obvious concern over his conduct, demonstrates the leadership vacuum that existed within the anti-Treaty IRA throughout the civil war. The split had removed many of the most effective revolutionary leaders, such as Collins, Mulcahy and O'Duffy, from the IRA. Of those who remained, a number of the more senior officers were captured or killed early in the conflict. In Dublin, for example, Rory O'Connor and Liam Mellows were imprisoned (and later executed) after the fall of the Four Courts. In the months that followed there were further arrests, including that of O'Malley in November, and Liam Deasy in January 1923. Aiken became one of the few remaining officers to have held a senior position prior to the signing of the Treaty. As a result, he continued to advance, despite the reservations of his peers.

From January 1923 onwards, Aiken's activities become ever more unclear, and what little information can be pieced together tends to revolve around contemporary rumour and speculation. Intriguingly, much of this concerns his health. In January, there were claims that he had been wounded in the jaw and was being treated in a private hospital.[134] A few months later, in March, intelligence reports from Northern Ireland also reported that he was taking refuge in a house in Dundalk where he was suffering from a serious internal complaint and was not expected to recover.[135] The former report was likely false as there is little evidence to suggest that Aiken was ever wounded. The latter is perhaps more plausible. Given that Aiken was treated for suspected tuberculosis in 1926, it is entirely possible that he was suffering from an earlier bout of respiratory illness.[136] In February, meanwhile, the Free State minister for justice, Kevin O'Higgins, named Aiken as the leader of an IRA reprisal raid at Ballyconnell, Co. Cavan, during which two civilians were killed and a number of properties burned. Yet the accusation appears to have little sub-stance, and is not corroborated by any other source. Indeed, in making the claim during a speech in the Dáil, O'Higgins admitted that he had little information on the incident, other than that publicised in press reports. It seems likely, therefore, that his accusation against Aiken was due to the fact that Cavan fell within the IRA's 'Northern Command' area.

The Ballyconnell accusation was not the most remarkable aspect of O'Higgins's speech, however. That dubious honour went instead to his accompanying claim that Aiken was being sheltered by the Northern Ireland government. In a scathing attack he referred to Aiken as,

That mad dog who has been rushing in and out across the border for many months – not that he is quite a mad dog when he is on the six county side of the border line [. . .] he is very glad of the benevolent protection of the border and of this government in the north east which presumably he does not recognise.[137]

These comments were undoubtedly little more than an opportunistic propaganda exercise, but they also reflected a general view within the Free State government, and the National Army, that Aiken and his men faced little threat of arrest in Northern Ireland, and that they exploited this in pursuit of their campaign in the south. In August 1922, Dan Hogan had similarly reported that 'the six-county forces are at present facilitating the Irregulars along the Armagh Border'.[138] There was little foundation for such claims. Arrests of IRA men in Northern Ireland continued well after the collapse of operations there.[139] The Northern Ireland government was, however, unwilling to share intelligence on Aiken with the Free State. In March 1923, for example, the ministry of home affairs decided not to pass on intelligence to the Free State regarding Aiken's whereabouts in Louth as they were 'against making any overtures.'[140] O'Higgins's accusations did, however, spark fresh vigour in the pursuit of Aiken in Northern Ireland, and perhaps prompted the arrest and internment of Nano Aiken a few days later.[141] Direct orders were also issued on 26 February to arrest Aiken if he was found in Northern Ireland. One day later it was reported that he was indeed almost captured during a raid in Newry.[142]

It was against this backdrop that the second (and final) phase of the Fourth Northern Division's guerrilla campaign in north Louth became discernable in late December 1922. Characterised by a gradual de-escalation of violence, it effectively marked the division's last stand as it slowly collapsed, and its military capability weakened. Rather ominously, perhaps, the most noteworthy feature of this new phase of activity was the IRA's increased aggression towards civilian targets. Although there had been a considerable number of civilian casualties in the region between July and December 1922, the victims were usually unfortunate bystanders caught up in the fighting between the IRA and the National Army. This was particularly true in July and August during the struggle for control of Dundalk. From late December 1922 onwards, however, civilian victims of violence in the region were more likely to have been purposely attacked. As December 1922 drew to a close the first alleged informer of the conflict was executed near Castlebellingham. The Dundalk Brigade claimed responsibility for the shooting, and it was believed that the victim was targeted for having pointed out the location of a house to a National Army patrol.[143] A second man was also found shot to death outside Dundalk in early January, but responsibility for this killing is unclear, with press reports indicating IRA involvement, and Fourth Northern Division reports suggesting the culpability of the National Army.[144]

The targeting of civilians in these final months of the conflict, however, was more noticeable in terms of attacks on property. These occurred in late January and early February in reprisal for the executions of six republican

prisoners in Dundalk. These executions were carried out under the controversial Public Safety Act, which became law in late September 1922 and allowed
military courts to pass the death sentence for offenses such as possession of a
weapon, or aiding and abetting attacks on government forces.[145] The first
executions took place in November 1922. Yet, as Kissane has observed, the
numbers rose sharply at the beginning of 1923 with 34 executions occurring in
January alone.[146] In response, IRA units throughout the country responded
with reprisal attacks on property belonging to government officials and supporters. 'Big houses', the mansions of the ascendancy class, were a particularly
prevalent target.[147]

In north Louth, the IRA carried out five reprisal attacks. The ascendancy
homes of the local sub-sheriff, and the clerk of peace, were burned.[148] At
Dundalk, the home and business premises of Peter Hughes, a pro-Treaty TD,
were damaged in a bomb attack. At nearby Carrickmacross, Co. Monaghan,
a house was burned as part of the reprisals because members of that family had
joined the Civic Guards, the Free State's new unarmed police force.[149] The
editor of the *Dundalk Democrat*, T. F. McGahon, was also targeted. His newspaper had been criticised by republicans in previous months for its perceived
Free State bias.[150] During the reprisals, his home at Dundalk was attacked
without success. This was, however, followed up with the destruction of
two holiday cottages at nearby Blackrock that were regularly used by the
McGahon family.[151]

This spate of reprisals soon ended and with no further executions in
Dundalk, it effectively ceased. Despite the brief rise in attacks on civilians
there was, as Hart has observed, no turn towards 'terrorism'. Rather, this brief
reversion to attacks on civilians and civilian property 'was due to the collapse
of the republican military campaign.'[152] This is borne out by events in the
following months. IRA attacks on the Free State army were reduced to two
opportunistic shootings of individual soldiers in March and April.[153] Other
'operations' included small scale nuisance attacks on the Free State administration such as the seizure of rates books from a tax collector in mid-April.[154]

A report dated 7 April 1923 provides a strong indication of the problems
that the Fourth Northern Division was facing.[155] The division was still relatively
well armed, with 150 rifles, seven Thompson sub-machine guns, and around
9,000 rounds of ammunition. Yet it is clear that the large amount of arms and
material available at the beginning of the conflict had been significantly reduced
by successful National Army raids.[156] A more significant issue, however, was
the shortage of manpower. The division's membership was estimated at a
mere 350 men, of whom only 50 could be considered active. It is most likely
that this situation was created by the continued exodus of volunteers who had
become disillusioned with the conflict, though arrests and internment had

also taken their toll. Amongst those who remained, moreover, discipline could only be described as 'very poor with few exceptions.'[157]

Declining numbers were further exacerbated by the fact that many of the division's most experienced men had been captured at Dungooley camp, shortly after the National Army re-occupied Dundalk. A number of key divisional officers had also been arrested or interned. John McCoy, who had been captured during the Dundalk gaol break, had already been transferred to another facility by the time Aiken's forces re-occupied Dundalk on 14 August. Others such as Mick O'Hanlon and Eiver Monaghan were arrested in the months that followed. Indeed, as the conflict reached its end only a handful of the division's pre-civil war staff remained – notably Seán and Padraig Quinn, Tom Rogers and Ned Fitzpatrick – and whatever semblance of republican opposition continued to exist in north Louth rested largely on their efforts.

It was not long, however, until the division experienced a final devastating blow which effectively marked the end of the conflict in north Louth. On 22 April, Séan and Padraig Quinn – now divisional commandant and divisional adjutant respectively – were severely wounded and captured at Tallanstown, near Castlebellingham. The house in which they had been staying was surrounded by Free State soldiers. They tried to fight their way out, but were quickly shot down. Seán died from his wounds a month later. Padraig ended up losing one of his legs.[158] In the weeks that followed rumours circulated that the men had been anxious to give up the fight 'but were intimidated from doing so, owing to a threat of death received from some of their followers'.[159] Yet there was little substance to this claim.

The Fourth Northern Division's position in north Louth in April 1923 was representative of the more general situation within the IRA at this time. In Sligo, Michael Farry has noted that 'only a few incidents of sniping at town posts were reported between February and April'.[160] In Limerick and north Tipperary, meanwhile, Hopkinson has observed that republicans were limited to a 'defensive harassment role'.[161] Only in a few areas – notably Longford and south Wexford – had republican activity managed to gain any momentum in early 1923, and these were rare exceptions.[162] Indeed, it was painfully clear to most within the anti-Treaty leadership that the conflict was all but lost, and, accordingly, internal discussions commenced as to the possibility of negotiating peace with the Free State government. Yet these efforts ultimately faltered on account of Lynch's delusions that victory was still possible, and his opposition to any terms that would result in the surrender of the 'Republic'.[163] Given the lack of evidence of Aiken's activities in early 1923, it is perhaps no surprise that there is little indication of his specific views on these developments. It seems most likely that he would have been among the majority who accepted that there was no chance of an anti-Treaty victory, particularly in light of his continuing distaste for the conflict. Nevertheless, he was not willing to accept peace at any price, and this became evident once he succeeded Lynch as chief-of-staff in April 1923.

In late March 1923 a meeting of the IRA executive was convened in Co. Waterford to assess its position in light of the increasingly frequent calls for peace negotiations. Various proposals were put forward during the four days of talks but opinion was divided and eventually led to a three-week adjournment while de Valera tried to assess the likelihood of negotiations based on his stated prerequisites of the acknowledgement of Irish sovereignty and the abolition of the oath.[164] Another meeting was scheduled for 10 April. On the morning on which this meeting was to take place a number of officers, including Aiken and Lynch, were surprised at their billet at the foot of the Knockmealdown Mountains by the National Army, who had learned of the planned gathering and were conducting a large-scale sweep of the area. As the republican leaders attempted to make their escape Lynch was mortally wounded. He died in captivity that evening. Aiken described the incident in a letter to de Valera the following day:

> There were six of us under fire from forty rifles and machine gun for half [an] hour on a bare mountain, and only he got hit. We carried him a short bit but he insisted on our leaving him. It was damned hard to do but there was nothing else to be done. The rest of us sighted 8 more columns of Staters that day and had two encounters.[165]

In the days that followed there were further arrests, including that of the IRA adjutant general, Tom Derrig, Austin Stack, and four other anti-Treaty commandants.[166]

Owing to Lynch's death, and the sustained military activity in the region, the reconvened meeting did not take place until 20 April. Aiken, who had been acting chief-of-staff for the previous ten days, was unanimously elected as Lynch's successor. As Hopkinson has noted, in some respects 'Aiken was a strange choice given his peripheral role in the war and his sceptical attitude to it.'[167] It is unclear exactly why he was chosen. It may have been hoped that, in light of his moderate attitude, his selection might hasten the end of the war. That said, however, Aiken could prove remarkably difficult to read. Indeed, even his closest remaining Fourth Northern Division comrades, Séan and Padraig Quinn, appeared unsure of his attitude: 'poor Liam is gone [. . .] I suppose the DCS [Aiken] becomes chief now, perhaps he will get the southerners to carry on.'[168] As Aiken was already deputy chief-of-staff it is likely that he was chosen as a result of his seniority. As with his previous anti-Treaty IRA positions, however, he appears to have been somewhat unenthusiastic about the role, and later wrote to Molly Childers that 'I have undertaken a great responsibility which I was very reluctant to undertake.'[169]

This change in the leadership was swiftly followed by another, with the adoption of a three-man army council composed of Aiken, Tom Barry and Liam Pilkington. This further confirmed the ascent of the moderate opinion within the executive as Barry's views in favour of ending the conflict were well known.[170] Aiken then proposed a resolution that peace be made on the basis that 'the sovereignty of the Irish nation and the integrity of its territory are inalienable' and 'that any instrument purporting to the contrary is, to the extent of its violation of [the] above principle, null and void.' The resolution was passed by a vote of nine to two, with Barry abstaining. An amendment proposed by Barry to the effect that 'in view of the position of the army that we direct the government and army council to call off all armed resistance against the Free State "government" and Free State forces' was defeated by the same margin of nine to two, with one abstaining.[171] Following on from this resolution, a joint meeting of the army council and the republican government was held on the night of 26–7 April, at which it was agreed to suspend the IRA's offensive and pursue negotiations with the Free State government.[172]

Aiken was certainly in favour of bringing an end to the civil war, but unlike figures such as Barry he was not willing to do so unconditionally. At the meeting of the army council on 20 April, for example, he had proposed that the war should continue if the Free State rejected their terms. The vote on the issue was split, however, and the resolution ultimately did not pass. Further evidence of the complexity of his attitude towards ending the conflict is visible in his correspondence with de Valera during the negotiations with the Free State in the month that followed. On 8 May, for example, he raised the possibility of cancelling the 'suspension of offensive' order – which had been duly issued on 27 April – in response to suggestions that the Free State government was intent on negotiating terms with individual anti-Treaty commandants to avoid recognising the republican government or the IRA leadership.[173] In other letters he was also scathing of Barry's alleged attempts to negotiate peace with the Free State independently, and claimed that he forced the latter to resign in July because of this alleged breach of discipline.[174] In 1935, further comments by Aiken on this matter led to a brief, if uneventful, public spat with Barry in the letters pages of the *Irish Independent*.[175]

Peace negotiations between the anti-Treatyites and the Irish Free State were ultimately unsuccessful. The Free State government was adamant that there could be no negotiation without the decommissioning of IRA weapons and the anti-Treatyites' acceptance of majority rule. Aiken, for one, was not willing to meet these conditions. Speaking in later years he explained that, 'I wanted to hold out until Mr Cosgrave would agree to abolish the oath. I stood against surrendering arms while the oath remained.'[176] Such an unrealistic suggestion would further suggest a degree of political naivety on Aiken's part at this time.

The issue was finally overcome at a meeting of the republican government and the army council on the night of 13–14 May. De Valera outlined the situation to those present, telling them that it was quite evident that the Free State government 'wanted submission pure and simple.' A unanimous decision was then taken that, rather than concede to the Free State demands, orders would be issued to ceasefire and dump arms.[177] Aiken subsequently issued these orders on 24 May, with instructions that the dumping of all arms was to be completed within four days. In an accompanying statement he defiantly declared, 'our enemies have demanded our arms. Our answer is "we took up arms to free our country, and we'll keep them until we see an honourable way of reaching our objective without arms".'[178] This was followed two days later with a memo to all officers and men titled 'our duty in future', in which Aiken addressed the challenges that lay ahead. 'The dumping of arms does not mean that the usefulness of the IRA is past', he wrote, 'on the contrary, a disciplined Volunteer force, ready for any emergency, will be a great source of strength to the nation in its march to independence. It is clearly our duty to keep the Army organisation intact'. Yet the overriding emphasis on the immediate welfare and security of active men, the preparations to assist their demobilisation and return to civilian life, and the encouragement that all volunteers should 'join Sinn Féin', was rather more reflective of the situation in which they now found themselves.[179] The civil war was over. Though in the absence of a truce or a negotiated peace, the Irish Free State officially remained in a state of war.[180]

AFTERMATH

For Aiken the ceasefire and dump arms orders of May 1923 marked the end of the Irish revolution, and he himself seems to have been aware of this. Writing to de Valera in June 1923, he expressed his view that 'having clearly defined the basis on which we must work and our objectives, the work to our hand is to organise the national forces as they were organised after Easter Week.'[181] In his mind, at least, the struggle that lay ahead was not a simple continuation of the previous conflict, rather it represented the beginning of something new.

In the more immediate term, however, now that he was chief-of-staff, Aiken was consumed with the tasks of demobilising a thoroughly defeated IRA and securing the release of republican prisoners. With regard to the latter, his main responsibility was – in de Valera's words – 'to shepherd our men back to employment in civil life.'[182] To this end he contributed to the creation of a republican 'employment bureau', a scheme that aimed to find IRA volunteers work with sympathetic employers, and thus assist their transition back to civilian life.[183] With regard to the prisoner issue, meanwhile, he backed various schemes north and south of the border. In the Free State, he advocated the use of hunger strikes as early as June 1923. He even intended to lead such an effort personally by allowing himself to be arrested. His belief that officers should lead by example, and be willing to take the greatest risks, had clearly not diminished, though he was eventually talked out of the idea by de Valera.[184] When hunger strikes did eventually begin in October 1923, apparently on the initiative of the prisoners themselves, Aiken fully supported the effort, impressing upon those involved that 'under no circumstances, even should a comrade die, are you to call off the hunger strike.'[185] The effort very quickly collapsed, however, leaving the movement further demoralised, though in its aftermath the Free State government began a slow process of prisoner releases which was eventually completed the following summer.

In Northern Ireland, hunger strikes were also utilised in an effort to secure the release of republican prisoners.[186] Perhaps realising that such an action might not exert the same pressure in Belfast as it would in Dublin, however, plans were also drawn up to assist attempted gaol breaks. The most notable, ordered by Aiken in 1924, involved providing boats to aid the escape of men held at the Larne workhouse internment camp. Seán MacBride was placed in charge of the operation, though it ultimately came to nothing when the prisoners' tunnel was discovered by their guards.[187] That same year, Aiken also instigated an operation aimed at rescuing his sister Nano from Armagh Gaol. An attempt was eventually made, though quickly aborted in confusion. Coincidentally, she was released only a few days later on medical grounds.[188]

As Aiken grappled with these issues, his former comrades in the Fourth Northern Division were facing their own difficult transitions back to civilian life. As has already been observed, many had no other option than to continue living as fugitives along the border until such a time as they might safely return home. In Northern Ireland, however, any such security was a long way off, as the case of Thomas Carr – an IRA fugitive shot dead by police in Newry in February 1925 – clearly demonstrated.[189] Many others remained imprisoned north and south of the border until as late as 1924, enduring the abysmal conditions of internment facilities such as the notorious prison-ship *Argenta*, moored in Belfast Lough, as well as periods of hunger strike.[190] Upon their release they often faced a difficult decision as to where they should go next. After being freed from southern camps, some men – notably Jack McElhaw and Charles McGleenan – returned to Northern Ireland where they were again arrested and interned, and ended up facing a protracted battle with the ministry of home affairs to be allowed to live in their home districts. Others, such as John McCoy and John Grant, chose instead to build new lives in the south; the former becoming a high ranking civil servant, the latter a member of the Garda Síochána. For many former members, however, it proved preferable to leave Ireland all together. Company rolls collected in the 1930s to aid the verification of applications for military service pensions show that large numbers emigrated to the United States or England. The Meigh Company was a particularly striking illustration of this trend, with 27 of its 63 former members listed as living outside Ireland by 1936.[191]

As an entity, the Fourth Northern Division survived the civil war, though only barely. Severely weakened by deaths and arrests, its structures were maintained by a handful of dedicated officers, such as Mick O'Hanlon who, having narrowly avoided execution after his arrest in late 1922, had returned to the division in May 1923 after a daring escape from the Curragh internment camp.[192] Yet reports and correspondence from the division – captured by the authorities in Northern Ireland – reveal just how feeble and disorganised the unit had become. Even the most basic lines of communication were weak, and the remaining rank and file members were reluctant to engage in any activity involving an element of risk. Indeed, it now proved difficult to carry out even the simplest of tasks, such as Aiken's request that a three-volley salute be fired over the grave of the late Séan Quinn on the night of his funeral ceremony in Newry.[193] As time passed the unit became increasingly moribund and irrelevant. Indeed, it is significant that as former members were released throughout 1924, few appear to have taken any further interest in it, or the IRA in general. In view of such decline, it came as no surprise when the Fourth Northern Division – along with all other remaining divisional units – was finally dissolved amid an extensive reorganisation of the IRA instigated by Aiken in 1924 and 1925.[194]

By 1925, there were also signs that Aiken's own role in the IRA had run its course. With the conflict at an end, he was now in a position to reengage in politics. In the general election of August 1923 he was successfully elected as a republican TD for Louth, and briefly served as minister for defence in the 'Comhairle na dTeachtaí' – or 'council of deputies' – a provisional republican assembly convened in August 1924 by de Valera and consisting of both the surviving anti-Treaty members of the Second Dáil and recently elected abstentionist republican TDs.[195] A devoted follower of de Valera, he became increasingly identified with the latter's moves to abandon the policy of abstention from the Dáil so long as the contested oath of allegiance was removed. That Aiken came to support this stance was hardly surprising. If anything it was a mark of consistency, given the views he had expressed in the early weeks of the civil war as he desperately sought to broker peace.[196] Within the IRA, however, it prompted considerable discord. Matters eventually came to a head at a convention on 14 November 1925, where Aiken admitted that there had been discussions about the possibility of entering the Dáil if the oath was removed. He subsequently failed to win re-election as chief-of-staff, although he did retain a position on the army council. He and the other officers supporting his stand were – on his suggestion – allowed to retain their positions on the body in order to avoid a split.[197]

The 1925 convention marked the beginning of the end of Aiken's personal involvement in the IRA. Though he officially remained a member until 1927, and maintained cordial relations with key figures in the organisation until well into the 1930s, so far as he was concerned it was now a time for politics to take precedence over armed struggle.[198] In 1926, he became a founding member of de Valera's new republican political party, Fianna Fáil. When hopes of forcing the abolition of the oath through a constitutional referendum were scuppered the following year – as a result of government policy changes prompted by the assassination of Kevin O'Higgins – he followed de Valera and his fellow deputies into the Dáil, dismissing the oath as little more than an 'empty formula'. None of this, however, constituted a dramatic conversion to constitutional principles. Nor did it mark much of a step-change in his ideological views. His predilection for politics was – and always had been – as much a part of his character as his propensity for violence.

NOTES

1.   M. Hopkinson, *Green Against Green: The Irish Civil War* (Dublin, 1988), p. 55; D. Fitzpatrick, *Harry Boland's Irish Revolution* (Cork, 2003) pp 294–7; M. Gallagher, 'The pact general election of 1922', in *Irish Historical Studies*, 22: 84 (Sept., 1979), pp 404–6.

2.   The substance of their arguments was also submitted as a memorandum, 'Six county position in the present crisis', *c*.May 1922, University College Dublin Archives (hereafter, UCDAD), Mulcahy papers, P7a/145.

3.   Aiken to O'Donoghue, 9 Mar. 1953, National Library of Ireland (hereafter, NLI), O'Donoghue papers, Ms 31,421.

4.   Hopkinson, *Green Against Green*, p. 96.

5.   See, for example, Aiken to O'Donoghue, 9 Mar. 1953, NLI, O'Donoghue papers, Ms 31,421; Frank Aiken, UCDAD, O'Malley notebooks, P17b/90; *Dáil Éireann Debates* (hereafter, *DÉD*), vol. 208 (9 Apr. 1964), col. 1377.

6.   Aiken to O'Donoghue, 9 Mar. 1953, NLI, O'Donoghue papers, Ms 31,421.

7.   Hopkinson, *Green Against Green*, p. 109.

8.   J. M. Regan, *The Irish Counter-Revolution, 1921–1936: Treatyite Politics and Settlement in Ireland* (Dublin, 1999), p. 60; P. Hart, *Mick: The Real Michael Collins* (London, 2005), p. 389; B. Kissane, *The Politics of the Irish Civil War* (Oxford, 2005) p. 73; B. Kissane, *Explaining Irish Democracy* (Dublin, 2002), p. 121.

9.   Hart, *Mick*, pp 392–3.

10.   Hopkinson, *Green Against Green*, pp 105–8.

11.   Kissane, *Politics of the Irish Civil War*, p. 33; figures provided represent all successful candidates (national coalition panel, independents etc).

12.   D. Hall, 'Violence, political factionalism and their effects on North Louth' (PhD, National University of Ireland Maynooth, 2010), pp 74–5.

13.   Hopkinson, *Green against Green*, pp 110–111; Hart, *Mick*, pp 393–4; M. Laffan, *The Resurrection of Ireland: The Sinn Féin Party, 1916–1923* (Cambridge, 1999), pp 404–11; Gallagher, 'The pact general election of 1922', pp 413–19.

14.   Padraig Quinn memoir, Kilmainham Gaol Museum (hereafter, KGM), McCann Cell Collection, 20/M5/IP41/08.

15.   Aiken to Mulcahy, 6 July 1922, UCDAD, Aiken papers, P104/1239.

16.   Johnnie McKay [McCoy], UCDAD, O'Malley papers, P17b/90.

17.   Aiken to Molly Childers, 18 Apr. 1924, Trinity College Dublin Archives (hereafter, TCD), Childers papers, Ms 7,847.

18.   Untitled statement by Frank Aiken, *c.*1925, UCDAD, Aiken papers, P104/1308.

19.   Padraig Quinn memoir, KGM, McCann Cell Collection, 20/M5/IP41/08.

20.   Mick O'Hanlon, UCDAD, O'Malley notebooks, P17b/106.

21.   Aiken to Mulcahy, 6 July 1922, UCDAD, Aiken papers, P104/1239.

22.   See, for example, Hopkinson, *Green Against Green*, p. 101; Kissane, *Explaining Irish Democracy*, p. 133.

23.   Hopkinson, *Green Against Green*, p. 102.

24.   'Position of the Fourth Northern Division, Jan. 1922–17th July 1922', *c.*July 1922, NLI, Johnson papers, Ms 17,143.

25.   Mick O'Hanlon, UCDAD, O'Malley notebooks, P17b/106.

26.   Hopkinson, *Green Against Green*, p. 148.

27.   'Position of the Fourth Northern Division, Jan. 1922–17th July 1922', *c.*July 1922, NLI, Johnson papers, Ms 17,143.

28.   R. Fanning, 'Aiken, Francis Thomas (Frank)', in *Dictionary of Irish Biography* (hereafter, *DIB*), www.dib.cambridge.org/ (accessed 10 Jan. 2010).

29.   Hopkinson, *Green Against Green*, p. 148; C. Younger, *Ireland's Civil War* (London, 1968), pp 362–9.

30.   'Notes of interview with Frank Aiken at Leinster House', 18 June 1952, NLI, O'Donoghue papers, Ms 31,421.

31.   Aiken to Molly Childers, 22 Apr. 1924, UCDAD, Aiken papers, P104/1317.

32.   Aiken to Mulcahy, 15 July 1922, Irish Military Archives (hereafter, IMA), Bureau of Military History Contemporary Documents (hereafter, BMH CD) 6/36/14.

33.   See, for example, Aiken to the Chairman of the Army Council, 18 Nov. 1925, UCDAD, Twomey papers, P69/181.

34.   Kissane, *Explaining Irish Democracy*, p. 128.

35.   See, for example, P. Hart, *The IRA and its Enemies: Violence and Community in Cork* (Oxford, 1998), pp 236–7.

36.   T. Garvin, *1922: The Birth of Irish Democracy* (Dublin, 2005), p. 34.

37.   For a discussion of the IRA as 'a-democratic', rather than 'undemocratic', see P. Hart, *The IRA at War* (Oxford, 2003), p. 97.

38. Aiken to Mulcahy, 20 July 1922, UCDAD, Aiken papers, P104/1208.

39. MacEoean [McCoy] to Mulcahy, 8 July 1922, UCDAD, Mulcahy papers, P7a/175.

40. O'Duffy to Aiken, 7 July 1922, UCDAD, Aiken papers, P104/1204.

41. John McCoy, IMA, Bureau of Military History Witness Statement (hereafter, BMH WS), 492.

42. 'Frank Aiken' file, The National Archives (hereafter, TNA), War Office (hereafter, WO) 35/206.

43. Padraig Quinn memoir, KGM, McCann Cell Collection, 20/M5/IP41/08; John McCoy, IMA, BMH WS 492.

44. John McCoy, IMA, BMH WS 492.

45. Padraig Quinn memoir, KGM, McCann Cell Collection, 20/M5/IP41/08.

46. Aire Chosanta to Director of Organisation, 15 Sept. 1923, IMA, Department of Defence, A/6885.

47. See, for example, Hugh Gribben, IMA, BMH WS640.

48. Patrick Casey, ibid., 1148.

49. 'Position of the Fourth Northern Division, Jan. 1922–17th July 1922', c.July 1922, NLI, Johnson papers, Ms 17,143.

50. John McCoy, IMA, BMH WS492.

51. *Irish Times*, 17 July 1922.

52. 'Position of the Fourth Northern Division, Jan. 1922–17th July 1922', c.July 1922, NLI, Johnson papers, Ms 17,143.

53. Padraig Quinn memoir, KGM, 20/M5/IP41/08; Edward Fullerton, IMA, BMH WS 890.

54. 'Position of the Fourth Northern Division, Jan. 1922–17th July 1922', c.July 1922, NLI, Johnson papers, Ms 17,143; Padraig Quinn memoir, KGM, McCann Cell Collection, 20/M5/IP41/08; Edward Fullerton, IMA, BMH WS 890.

55. John McCoy, IMA, BMH WS 492.

56. Hopkinson, *Green Against Green*, p. 170; Seamus Woods as quoted in R. Lynch, *The Northern IRA and the Early Years of Partition* (Dublin, 2006), p. 188.

57. 'Position of the Fourth Northern Division, Jan. 1922–17th July 1922', c.July 1922, NLI, Johnson papers, Ms 17,143.

58. John McCoy, IMA, BMH WS 492.

59. Padraig Quinn memoir, KGM, McCann Cell Collection, 20/M5/IP41/08.

60. C. Younger, *Ireland's Civil War* (London, 1982), p. 375.

61. *Irish Times*, 27 June 1922.

62. Johnnie McKay [McCoy], UCDAD, O'Malley notebooks, P17b/94.

63. Interview with Dr Eoin Magennis, 19 May 2010.

64. 'Position of the Fourth Northern Division, Jan. 1922–17th July 1922', c.July 1922, NLI, Johnson papers, Ms 17,143.

65. Aiken to Mulcahy, 23 July 1922, UCDAD, P7a/175; 'Position of the Fourth Northern Division, Jan. 1922–17th July 1922', c.July 1922, NLI, Johnson papers, Ms 17,143.

66. John McCoy, IMA, BMH WS492.

67. Ibid.

68. *Irish Times*, 28 July 1922.

69. John McCoy, IMA, BMH WS492.

70. *Irish Times*, 28 July 1922.

71. John McCoy, IMA, BMH WS 492; *Irish Independent*, 29 July 1922.

72. 'Position of the Fourth Northern Division, Jan. 1922–17th July 1922', c.July 1922, NLI, Johnson papers, Ms 17,143.

73. C. S. Andrews, *Dublin Made Me: An Autobiography* (Cork, 1979), p. 243.

74. 'Report of the capture of Dundalk town 13 Aug. 1922', c.Aug. 1922, NLI, Ms 43, 123.

75. Edward Fullerton, 16 Sept. 1953, IMA, BMH WS 890.

76. Jack McElhaw, ibid., 634.

77. 'Report of the capture of Dundalk town 13 Aug. 1922', NLI, Ms 43,123.

78. 'Report to C/S', 17 Aug. 1922, UCDAD, Mulcahy papers, P7/B/16.

79. *Dundalk Examiner*, 19 Aug. 1922.

80. Report to C/S, 17 Aug. 1922, UCDAD, Mulcahy papers, P7/B/16.

81. Edward Boyle, IMA, BMH WS 647; *Dundalk Examiner*, 19 Aug. 1922.

82. *Dundalk Examiner*, 19 Aug. 1922; Aiden Rogers interview, 27 Jan. 2006, Louth County Archives (hereafter, LCA), Oral History Archive (hereafter, OHA) 0149.3 (2); 'Report of the capture of Dundalk town 13 Aug. 1922', c.Aug. 1922, NLI, Ms 43,123.

83. 'Report of the capture of Dundalk town 13 Aug. 1922', NLI, Ms 43,123.

84. *Dundalk Examiner*, 19 Aug. 1922; *Irish Times*, 15 Aug., 17 Aug. 1922.

85. Mick O'Hanlon, UCDAD, O'Malley notebooks, P17b/106.

86. *Frontier Sentinel*, 26 Aug. 1922.

87. *Dundalk Democrat*, 19 Aug. 1922.

88. *Irish Times*, 18 Aug. 1922.

89. Jack McElhaw, IMA, BMH WS 634; Charles McGleenan, ibid., 829.

90. Fifth Northern Division Report on Operations, 21 Aug. 1922, UCDAD, Mulcahy papers, P7/B/59.

91. O'Malley to Lynch, 6 Aug. 1922, in E. O'Malley, *No Surrender Here: The Civil War Papers of Ernie O'Malley 1922–1924*, eds C. O'Malley and A. Dolan (Dublin, 2007), p. 162.

92. Andrews, *Dublin Made Me*, p. 241.

93. Andrews to O'Malley, 11 Aug. 1922, in O'Malley, *No Surrender Here*, p. 97.

94. An exact date is unclear, but communications between Lynch and O'Malley indicate that the Fourth Northern Division was firmly aligned with the executive by the end of Aug. 1922; see, Lynch to O'Malley, 30 Aug. 1922, in ibid., pp 526–7.

95. See, for example, Lynch to O'Malley, 30 Aug. 1922, in ibid., pp 134–5.

96. O'Malley to Price, 7 Sept. 1922, in ibid., p. 162.

97. O'Malley to Lynch, 13 Sept. 1922, in ibid., pp 179–80.

98. Lynch to O'Malley, 17 Sept. 1922, in ibid.

99. Kissane, *Politics of the Irish Civil War*, p. 65.

100. Dundalk Gaol Register (microfilm copy), 1920–2, LCA, PP/11/4.

101. Aiken to Mulcahy, 27 Aug. 1922, UCDAD, Mulcahy papers, P7a/81.

102. Mulcahy to Aiken, 31 Aug. 1922, ibid., P7a/173.

103. Andrews, *Dublin Made Me*, p. 244.

104. *Irish Times*, 13 Nov. 2008.

105. *Poblacht na hÉireann War News*, 14 Aug. 1922.

106. 'General Order no. 3: selection of men for Active Service Units', 14 Aug. 1922, in O'Malley, *No Surrender Here*, p. 502; 'Operational Order No. 9: organisation and activities of Active Service Unit', 19 Aug. 1922, in ibid., pp 526–7.

107. Major Fillery to CI Armagh, 29 Nov. 1922, Public Record Office of Northern Ireland (hereafter, PRONI), HA/32/1/306.

108. 'Supervision of suspected IRA members by Police' file, c.PRONI, HA/32/1/306.

109. Edward Fullerton, IMA, BMH WS 890.

110. John Grant, ibid., 658.

111. *Irish Times*, 22 Sept., 19 Oct., 6 Nov., 22 Nov. 1922.

112. *Freeman's Journal*, 22 Nov. 1922; the number of casualties is unclear with various reports estimating a figure somewhere between seven and twelve.

113. *Irish Times*, 4 Oct. 1922.

114. O'Malley to Coughlan, 24 Sept. 1922, in O'Malley, *No Surrender Here*, p. 224.

115. *Irish Times*, 11 Nov., 16 Dec., 21 Dec. 1922; *Irish Independent*, 5 Jan. 1923.

116. *Irish Times*, 16 Sept. 1922; the same tactic had been used during a similar attack on the town a month earlier, see *Freeman's Journal*, 15 Aug. 1922.

117. 'Copy of Documents on Quinn Div. QM Irregulars', undated, UCDAD, Mulcahy papers, P7/B/90.

118. *Irish Times*, 25 Oct. 1922.

119. See Aappendix II, Table IX.

120. See above, p. 187.

121. Frank Aiken, IMA, Military Service Pensions Collection (hereafter, MSPC), MSP34REF59339.

122. E. O'Malley, *The Singing Flame* (Dublin, 1978), p. 165.

123. For details see, *Freeman's Journal*, 19 Aug., 5 Sept., 13 Oct. 1922; *Irish Independent*, 19 Sept., 10 Oct. 1922; *Irish Times*, 22 Sept., 21 Nov. 1921.

124. Sean McConville, IMA, BMH WS 495.

125. Bi-monthly Intelligence Report, 31 Oct. 1923, PRONI, HA/32/1/212.

126. Lynch to O'Malley, 1 Oct. 1922, in O'Malley, *No Surrender Here*, pp 244–5.

127. For growing preoccupation with organisational work see Aiken to O'Malley, 16 Sept. 1922, in ibid., pp 186–7; Andrews to O'Malley, 30 Sept. 1922, in ibid., pp 239–40. For Aiken's continued participation in operations see O'Hanlon's references to activities in Cavan; Michael O'Hanlon, IMA, MSPC, MSP34REF20993.

128. 'Minutes of the IRA Executive Meeting', 16–17 Oct. 1922, in O'Malley, *No Surrender Here*, pp 493–8.

129. 'Notes of interview with Frank Aiken in Leinster House', 18 June 1952, NLI, O'Donoghue papers, Ms 31,421.

130. Kissane, *Politics of the Irish Civil War*, p. 90.

131. D/O [Dowling?] to Lynch, 22 Dec. 1922, UCDAD, Twomey papers, P69/35.

132. Aiken to Lynch, undated, UCDAD, Twomey papers, P69/35.

133. Lynch to Aiken, 18 Jan. 1923, ibid.

134. *Irish Independent*, 5 Jan. 1923.

135. Inspector General's Department to Secretary Home Affairs, 23 Mar. 1923, PRONI, HA/32/1/281.

136. T. Mahon and J. J. Gillogly, *Decoding the IRA* (Cork, 2008), p. 230.

137. *DÉD*, vol. 2 (7 Feb. 1923), cols 1358–9.

138. 'Report on Operations', 21 Aug. 1922, UCDAD, Mulcahy papers, P7/B/59.

139. See, for example, *Weekly Irish Times*, 30 Sept. 1922; Edward Boyle, IMA, BMH WS 647.

140. Minute Sheet, 29 Mar. 1923, PRONI, HA/32/1/281.

141. For details see, 'Nano Aiken' file, ibid., /5/2303.

142. County Inspector to Secretary of Home Affairs, 24 June 1927, PRONI, HA/32/1/281; 'Frank Aiken' file, TNA, WO 35/206.

143. *Freeman's Journal*, 30 Dec. 1922; 'Dundalk Brigade Report for Dec. 1922', *c.*Jan. 1923, NLI, Ms 43,123.

144. O/C Fourth Northern Division to A/G, 2 Feb. 1923, UCDAD, Twomey papers, P69/35.

145. Hopkinson, *Green Against Green*, p. 181.

146. Kissane, *Politics of the Irish Civil War*, p. 85.

147. In Co. Longford, for example, fifty–five per cent of the 'big houses' targeted during the Civil War were destroyed between Jan. and Mar. 1923. See M. Coleman, *County Longford and the Irish Revolution* (Dublin, 2001), p. 145.

148. *Freeman's Journal*, 31 Jan., 5 Feb., 6 Feb. 1923; *Irish Independent*, 13 Feb. 1923.

149. For info on both incidents see, *Irish Independent*, 3 Feb. 1923.

150. *Freeman's Journal*, 21 Dec. 1922.

151. Ibid., 7 Feb. 1923; *Irish Independent*, 9 Feb. 1923.

152. Hart, *The IRA and its Enemies*, p. 120.

153. *Irish Independent*, 13 Mar. 1923; *Freeman's Journal*, 3 Apr. 1923.

154. *Irish Independent*, 10 Apr. 1923.

155. Séan Quinn to Padraig Quinn, 7 Apr. 1923, UCDAD, Twomey papers, P69/35.

156. For details on some of the largest hauls see *Irish Times*, 2 Sept. 1922; *Freeman's Journal*, 21 Dec. 1922; *Irish Independent*, 12 May 1923.

157. Séan Quinn to Padraig Quinn, 7 Apr. 1923, UCDAD, Twomey papers, P69/35.

158. *Freeman's Journal*, 23 Apr. 1923; see also Patrick Casey, IMA, BMH WS 1148.

159. Bi-monthly intelligence report, 30 Apr. 1923, PRONI, HA/32/1/212.

160. M. Farry, *The Irish Revolution 1912–23: Sligo* (Dublin, 2013), p. 106.

161. Hopkinson, *Green Against Green*, p. 245.

162. Coleman, *County Longford and the Irish Revolution*, pp 144–7; Hopkinson, *Green Against Green*, pp 245–6.

163. For a detailed discussion of the debate within the anti-Treaty elite see Kissane, *Politics of the Irish Civil War*, pp 105–16.

164. Hopkinson, *Green Against Green*, p. 238.

165. Aiken to de Valera, 11 Apr. 1923, UCDAD, de Valera papers, P150/1752.

166. D. Macardle, *The Irish Republic* (London, 1937), p. 878.

167. Hopkinson, *Green Against Green*, p. 257.

168. Adjutant, 4th Northern Division to O/C, 4th Northern Division, 12 Apr. 1923, IMA, Civil War Captured Documents Collection, A/0994/Lot 6.

169. Aiken to Molly Childers, 31 Aug. 1923, TCD, Childers papers, Ms 7,847.

170. See M. Ryan, *Tom Barry: IRA Freedom Fighter* (Cork, 2003), pp 257–60.

171. 'Minutes of adjourned meeting (from 26 Mar. 1923) held on Apr. 20th 1923', NLI, Ms 10,973.

172. 'Government and Army Council: Minutes of meeting held on the night of 26th–27th Apr. 1923', NLI, O'Malley papers, Ms 10,973.

173. Aiken to de Valera, 8 May 1923, UCDAD, de Valera papers, P150/1752.

174. *Irish Press*, 6 June 1935.

175. See related correspondence, UCDAD, Aiken papers, P104/1285.

176. Aiken to the editor (*Irish Independent*), 8 July 1935, UCDAD, Aiken papers, P104/1285.

177. 'Minutes of meeting held on night of 13–14 May 1923', 30 June 1923, NLI, Ms 10,973.

178. 'Order of the Day', 24 May 1923, NLI, Dixon papers, Ms 35,262/2.

179. 'Our duty in future', 26 May 1923, UCDAD, O'Malley papers, P17A/25.

180. Hopkinson, *Green Against Green*, p. 258.

181. Aiken to de Valera, 1 June 1923, UCDAD, de Valera papers, P150/1752.

182. de Valera to Aiken, 4 June 1923, ibid.

183. 'To O/Cs all battalions', 2 July 1923, NLI, Ms 17,281.

184. Aiken to de Valera, 1 June 1923, UCDAD, de Valera papers, P150/1752.

185. Aiken, as quoted in Hopkinson, *Green Against Green*, p. 269.

186. Lynch, *Northern IRA and the Early Years of Partition*, pp 182–3.

187. S. MacBride, *That Day's Struggle: A Memoir 1904–1951* (Dublin, 2005), pp 97–9.

188. 'Nano Aiken' file, PRONI, HA/5/2303; Patrick Beagan, IMA, BMH WS 612.

189. *Irish Times*, 21 Feb. 1925.

190. See, for example, Edward Boyle, IMA, BMH WS 647; John Cosgrove, ibid., 605.

191. Fourth Northern Division company roles, UCDAD, Aiken papers, P104/1298.

192. O'Hanlon to Aiken, 9 May 1923, UCDAD, Twomey papers, P69/35.

193. Epitome of raid at 13 Aileen Terrace, Newry, c.June 1923, PRONI, HA/32/1/379.

194. Mahon and Gillogly, *Decoding the IRA*, p. 68.

195. T. P. O'Neill and the Earl of Longford, *Eamon de Valera* (London, 1970), p. 240.

196. See above, pp 175–6.

197. B. Hanley, *The IRA 1926–1936* (Dublin, 2002), p. 113; J. Bowyer Bell, *The Secret Army: The IRA 1916–1979* (Dublin, 1979), pp 52–3.

198. Hanley, *IRA 1926–1936*, p. 14, 127, 143; Mahon and Gillogly, *Decoding the IRA*, pp 100–1.

EIGHT

CONCLUSION

—

In an open letter to the voters of Louth on 20 August 1923, Frank Aiken provided the following advice to an electorate emerging from a sustained period of violence and political upheaval:

> Look to the future and forget the past: but in order to know how to act rightly to learn from the past. The history of our nation and the lives of its heroes should be studied in order to learn how its citizens should act.[1]

This was no mere platitude. Aiken sensed the value of history. In this same period, he was himself immersed in books on topics such as the Boer war and the life of Stonewall Jackson; perhaps in search of informative parallels for the circumstances he now faced.[2] It is highly unlikely, however, that he would have counted himself among those national figures deserving of study; especially not on account of his role in the Irish revolution. If anything, his later reticence on the subject suggests that it was something he felt was best left forgotten.

Nevertheless, Aiken's revolutionary past is deserving of greater scrutiny than it has hitherto been afforded. At the very least, when considered firmly within its local and national contexts, his involvement in the conflict offers a window into the relatively obscure experience of grassroots revolutionary republican activism in the six counties that became Northern Ireland; providing a lesser appreciated perspective on a variety of themes and debates concerning the politics, violence and ideology of this turbulent seven-year period. The IRA campaign that he commanded in the borderlands of south-east Ulster, in particular, offers compelling insights into the violence that gripped the province amid the upheaval of partition; a modest contribution towards closing the 'analysis gap' on that subject – so described by Tim Wilson – within which 'lies a wide range of local motivations and behaviours that rarely receive sustained academic attention.'[3] Aiken's personal experience of the conflict, moreover, serves as an illuminating case study of provincial republican leadership, highlighting the crucial contribution of individual activists and officers in forging the movement at the local level, and subsequently shaping its activities as the conflict progressed.

LEADERSHIP

In many respects, Aiken was the quintessential provincial Irish revolutionary leader. Hailing from a wealthy farming background, he certainly fit the social profile of a large section of the republican elite during this period. His early involvement in the movement, and his efforts in organising the Irish Volunteers in particular, suggest that he was typical of the countless 'local opinion makers' and 'self-appointed organisers' that emerged across the country in the early years of the conflict, and who provided the driving force of the organisation and its local leadership in the early stages of its development.[4] That he came to occupy such a position was undoubtedly a reflection of his status within his local community, something that derived from the prominence of his family and the legacy of his father.

Yet social status and economic background alone are not a sufficient explanation for Aiken's rise within the revolutionary movement. Many individuals who gained prominence for similarly superficial reasons quickly fell by the wayside as the campaign progressed and it was realised that they were ill suited to their positions. Aiken, however, had genuine organisational ability, a sincere commitment to the republican cause, as well as a readiness to take on new roles and responsibilities as and when they arose. His initial emergence as a member of the local revolutionary elite was undoubtedly influenced by his track record of organisational responsibility in groups such as the Gaelic League, the pre-split Irish Volunteers in 1914, and the local flax scutching co-operative that he helped found in 1917. But it also owed much to his enthusiasm and dependability. Indeed, it was his competency, determination and commitment that captured the attentions of his superiors, particularly within the IRA, where his attainment of higher leadership positions owed much to the esteem with which he was held by leaders such as Michael Collins.

Within the Newry Brigade, and later the Fourth Northern Division, Aiken's philosophy of leadership did much to ensure the loyalty and respect of those serving under him. Throughout the revolutionary period he lived up to his stated belief that officers in a volunteer army should lead from the front and face the greatest dangers. His record as a combatant from 1919 onwards is a testament to this, though his active involvement in the fighting may have declined somewhat during the civil war as he attained further responsibilities within the higher echelons of the IRA leadership. His exploits cultivated a formidable reputation amongst his men, which greatly aided his growing dominance within the Newry Brigade, and eventually led to his displacement of Patrick Rankin as the top local IRA leader upon the creation of the Fourth Northern Division in 1921.

Aiken's central role in the majority of local IRA operations also suggests his importance as a driving force of the campaign in Armagh and south Down. This runs contrary to the assertions of some historians who have rejected the notion that the quality of local leadership was an important factor in determining levels of violent activity.[5] In Armagh and south Down, however, Aiken can be seen to have fulfilled a role similar to that of Seán Mac Eoin in Longford.[6] Like the latter, Aiken, working alongside a relatively small band of dedicated fighters, was crucial in directing and sustaining IRA activity in the region, and the escalation of certain aspects of the conflict often appear to have mirrored his own radicalisation.

In these respects, Aiken resembles other provincial republican leaders who attained a degree of notoriety during the Irish revolution. He embodied the commonly identified attributes of such individuals, combining the organisational abilities of a figure such as Eoin O'Duffy, with the hands-on military leadership of men like Ernie O'Malley and Tom Barry. Although his early emergence within the republican movement in south Armagh may have been influenced by factors such as wealth, or status, Aiken ultimately proved his worth in terms of ability and dedication, and it was this that ensured his continued rise within the IRA.

CONFLICT

That Aiken is, perhaps, a somewhat overlooked provincial revolutionary figure is partly a reflection of the degree to which the IRA campaign in the north has been neglected within the historiography. This is particularly true with regard to the years 1919–21. Although it can be argued that the majority of IRA units in six-county Ulster were inactive and disorganised during this period, there were significant hot spots of militant republican activity in the region, and Aiken's hinterlands of Armagh and south Down were chief among them.

Unlike other areas in what became Northern Ireland, the violence experienced in Armagh and south Down – the Newry and south Armagh area in particular – was driven primarily by the orchestrated efforts of the local IRA. The sporadic inter-communal rioting that erupted elsewhere, in places such as Belfast, Derry and Lisburn, was not much in evidence here. The only notable exception were the burnings and workplace expulsions that occurred in Banbridge in the summer of 1920, yet even this outbreak was somewhat peripheral, given that it occurred at the very edges of the Newry Brigade's area of operations. Indeed, in many respects, the IRA campaign in Armagh and south Down during the war for independence was more akin to that experienced in parts of southern Ireland. In both its evolution and chronology, it broadly conformed with events at the national level. Its form and pace was shaped by the same considerations and pressures that fuelled the conflict beyond Ulster. Furthermore, although IRA violence in the region did not reach the levels experienced in areas such as Cork, Tipperary or Dublin, it did surpass that of many southern units, despite the considerable constraints imposed by the hostility of the majority of the local population, both unionist and nationalist.

Despite such similarities, however, the IRA campaign in Armagh and south Down did differ from that experienced in southern Ireland in a number of respects. Most strikingly, perhaps, there were certain contrasts with regard to the pursuit of violence against the civilian population. In the south, civilians were most likely to be targeted by the IRA as alleged informers, and Protestants, ex-servicemen and other real or perceived outsiders ultimately accounted for a disproportionate share of the victims. In Armagh and south Down, meanwhile, though executions of this nature did occur, they were relatively few in number. Furthermore, although the victims were members of the AOH, the republican movement's constitutional nationalist rivals, they were not communal outsiders. Not only were they well integrated into the same broad Catholic-nationalist population from which the local IRA was itself drawn, at times they had also been allies – in opposing conscription in 1918, for instance, or as fellow anti-partitionists during the 1921 general election.

In Armagh and south Down, IRA attacks on civilians were much more likely to take the form of reprisals targeting members of the unionist community. This sectarian aspect of the local conflict was, however, much more complex than might first be expected. Contrary to the prevailing notions of Ulster's endemic and atavistic tribal hatreds, sectarianism was not an immediate or inherent characteristic of the violence experienced in the region. Rather, it emerged only gradually; the cumulative result of a reciprocal process of radical-isation involving militants on both sides of the communal divide. Beginning as early as 1919, when IRA arms raids prompted the creation of defensive unionist patrols, this course was more frequently determined by the way in which violent actions were perceived than by the motives or intentions that inspired them. Although matters would eventually escalate to the point where civilians were liable to be deliberately targeted for reprisal attacks as real or perceived representatives of the communities from which they hailed, in practice such attacks were relatively uncommon, particularly in the conflict's earlier stages. Prior to the truce in July 1921, for instance, IRA reprisals resulted in only one civilian death. In the same period, those killings perpetrated by the USC were not as indiscriminate as has previously been assumed. The majority of their victims in Newry and south Armagh appear to have been members of the IRA, and the killings of civilians often occurred only after failed attempts to abduct known republicans.

In tracing this process within the Fourth Northern Division, the burnings at Killylea in April 1921, and the shooting of Draper Holmes near Newry the following July, provide the first clear indication that attitudes towards the broader unionist community had radicalised to any great extent. This evidently reflected the hardening of Aiken's own attitudes, following his involvement in reprisals at Rosslea, Co. Tyrone, in March 1921. Any further escalation was subsequently stalled by the announcement of the truce. Likewise, the faltering progress of renewed fighting in early 1922 initially served to stifle the momentum of the now familiar cycle of reprisal and counter-reprisal in the region. It was only in May 1922, when Aiken ordered the kidnappings of prominent unionist civilians and members of the USC, that matters radicalised further. This was shortly followed by the notorious reprisals at Altnaveigh and Lisdrumliska in June, an event which ultimately marked the zenith of the inter-communal conflict in the region, though it is very plausible that it could have been surpassed had the IRA campaign continued.

The targeting of civilians in such circumstances was rationalised through a logic of 'representative violence' that few within the Fourth Northern Division appear to have questioned, or readily recognised as sectarianism. Indeed, in many respects, it does not conform to popular expectations of what constitutes sectarian violence. The victims at Altnaveigh and Lisdrumliska, for instance, were not targeted as Protestants, but as (real or perceived) members of the dominant unionist community in Northern Ireland; and as the Fourth Northern Division's efforts to protect the Protestant community in Dundalk clearly illustrate, this distinction was far from trivial. Religious affiliation was a rudimentary indicator of political allegiance; the fulcrum for a crude system of social, religious and geographic profiling that reflected the local IRA's collective ignorance of their Protestant neighbours, though not necessarily the individual pathologies of those involved. Aiken is a case in point. Despite ordering such operations, there is little to suggest that he was motivated by any particular hatred of Protestants, or indeed unionists; though like many republicans he seemed to have a somewhat one-dimensional understanding of that community's views and attitudes.

All this is not to say that the Fourth Northern Division's reprisals in this period lacked an emotive motivational basis. Indeed, the majority appear to have been driven – to some extent – by a desire to avenge violent attacks on individuals closely connected to the local republican movement. This goes against the claims of former members that such operations were designed to protect or avenge the nationalist population more generally. The killing of

Draper Holmes, for instance, was a response to the killing of four IRA men. Yet there was no attempted reprisal for the killings of two local nationalists – neither of whom had republican affiliations – a week earlier. The carnage at Altnaveigh and Lisdrumliska in June 1922, moreover, was a reaction to the shooting of an IRA volunteer's brother and a sexual assault committed against a Sinn Féin councillor's wife. Furthermore, although the kidnappings of prominent local unionists in May 1922 were subsequently described as an effort to deter the USC from committing atrocities against nationalists in south Armagh and south Down, they were actually an attempt to secure the release of various republican prisoners, many of whom had been interned only weeks earlier.

Aiken's responsibility for sectarian atrocities remains the most controversial aspect of his revolutionary past, and for good reason. Yet his role in the joint-IRA offensive in May 1922 has also proven somewhat contentious. With regard to the latter, however, it is clear that questions can be raised as to his culpability for its failure. Contrary to popular belief, he was not in overall command of the venture. Much of the co-ordination was actually carried out by Eoin O'Duffy, as chief-of-staff of the nascent provisional government army. In later years Aiken was very clear about his refusal to assume the leadership of the offensive; something that is corroborated by the testimony of one of his fellow officers. He was a key player in the initiative, however, and his Fourth Northern Division was central to its planning and preparation. This is evident from the role assigned to the division in the grandiose and highly unrealistic plans for the attack. Aiken, meanwhile, as chairman of the Ulster Council, and one of the more experienced guerrilla leaders in Ulster, was also clearly expected to play an important military role in the offensive once it got underway.

Bearing this in mind, it seems all the more unusual that the Fourth Northern Division ultimately failed to commence its operations once the offensive began. Although it is tempting to speculate as to why, there is only sufficient evidence to support a limited number of scenarios. The claim that Aiken withdrew his division at the last moment due to concerns that one of his brigades was not adequately armed is certainly a possibility. Although some members of the Fourth Northern Division derided such logic, it is clear that Aiken would have had legitimate reasons for concern in this respect, particularly given the ambitious plan of action. As such, any decision Aiken may have made to withdraw from the offensive was certainly justified from a purely military point of view. Despite improvements in training and arms, the division was not in a position to fight a conventional campaign. To press ahead in such circumstances would have amounted to nothing more but a sacrificial gesture.

Another equally plausible theory is that the withdrawal of the division was due to orders from Dublin, most likely from the provisional government

GHQ at Beggars Bush Barracks. The logic for the action would, undoubtedly, have been the same that applied to the withdrawal of the First Northern, Fifth Northern, and First Midland Divisions from the offensive; that fighting should not occur on or around the border, presumably to avoid revealing the provisional government's complicity. It also seems to have been the case, as suggested by the testimony of both Aiken and Padraig Quinn, that the Fourth Northern Division was of the belief that an offensive was still imminent right up until the provisional government's attack on the Four Courts one month later, a view encouraged by pro-Treaty leaders such as Mulcahy and O'Duffy. This suggestion lends credence to the view that the pro-Treaty leadership's involvement in the venture was less than sincere, and was motivated more by a desire to avoid (or postpone) the looming conflict in the south than an aspiration to smash partition. Such a conclusion must, however, remain tentative in the absence of further evidence.

The Fourth Northern Division's experiences in the months leading up to the civil war provide a curious example of the complexities of the IRA split at a local level. Although the vast majority of Aiken's men fell in line with his policy of neutrality, this was due primarily to the unifying effect of plans for the joint-IRA offensive. After the army convention the only units to take the anti-Treaty position were those based in north Louth, which, being secure within the territory of the new Free State, were less concerned about partition than their northern counterparts. There were, of course, a variety of other factors contributing to the independent attitude of the north Louth IRA, though, significantly, they had little basis in ideology. Once the civil war began, and plans for further operations in Northern Ireland were cancelled, it was not long before further ruptures occurred within the division, this time between the Armagh and south Down units. It is difficult to say to what extent this later schism represented a genuine divergence of opinion on the Treaty. The strong regional character of this second split, however, would suggest that non-ideological factors were paramount.

Aiken's reputation as a reluctant civil war protagonist is undoubtedly deserved. He was genuinely horrified by the prospect of the conflict, and his early neutrality and efforts to negotiate peace are evidence of this, though his efforts to promote unity and moderation were driven primarily by his desire to maintain cross-factional support for continued IRA operations in the north. His apparent reluctance to join the anti-Treaty position, even after his spectacular capture of Dundalk, further suggests his lack of enthusiasm for the conflict. Indeed, Aiken's participation in the civil war was due primarily to the way in which he was treated by his former allies within the pro-Treaty leadership, in particular their refusal to accept his neutrality, and to instead view him as an aggressor in spite of his determination not to fight. That is not to say that their attitude was unwarranted. Aiken was attempting to remain neutral in the southern conflict while keeping his division intact, and retaining a substantial arsenal in the hope of resuming operations in Northern Ireland at a later date. The proposition that such a force could be allowed to exist, independent of the civil authority, within an emerging state gripped by war, was untenable and it was inevitable that this position would be challenged.

Aiken's neutrality, and his initial reluctance to join the anti-Treaty faction, ensured that the Fourth Northern Division's involvement in the conventional phase of the civil war was extremely limited. Indeed, the capture and occupation of Dundalk was the only operation to fall within this category, and this was quickly followed by the reversion to guerrilla warfare. Despite the division's improvements in training and equipment, however, it enjoyed no greater success in its military endeavours than it had earlier in the revolutionary period. The number of enemy casualties it inflicted, for instance, was in keeping with that achieved in previous bouts of fighting in Armagh and south Down during comparable periods in 1921 and 1922. Although the division had reached the peak of its fighting ability, and could occasionally demonstrate genuine strategic skill, it was ultimately crippled by arrests, deaths and the demoralising effect of fighting former comrades. As was the case in most parts of the country, IRA violence in Louth was ultimately characterised by its gradual de-escalation, and when Aiken (as chief-of-staff) finally issued the order to ceasefire and dump arms, it did little more than formalise the existing local situation.

For Aiken, on a personal level, the civil war was a highly traumatic experience, but also one that did much to facilitate his later prominence within the republican movement at a national level. The leadership vacuum within the anti-Treaty faction ensured his steady rise through the ranks of the IRA, despite concerns over his dedication to the campaign and his military performance. His appointment as IRA chief-of-staff, and subsequent role in bringing the conflict to an end, also signalled the beginning of his close association with Eamon de Valera. Indeed, Aiken's loyalty and devotion to de Valera became one of the dominant characteristics of his later political career. The fact that he entered into such a relationship was not particularly surprising, however. Though a leader in his own right, he had a history of falling in line behind charismatic superiors. Patrick Rankin, the original commandant of the Newry Brigade and the only local man to fight in the Easter rising, was arguably the first, followed closely by Michael Collins. In this respect, his relationship with de Valera from 1923 onwards was part of a longer established pattern.

The same is ultimately true of Aiken's abandonment of armed struggle in favour of constitutional political methods in the aftermath of the civil war. Though often viewed as a radical step-change in Aiken's ideological outlook, in truth it was a mark of consistency. Unlike many of his peers within the

IRA, Aiken had always displayed a certain predilection for politics. He first became involved in the revolutionary movement through Sinn Féin rather than the Irish Volunteers. Even amid the violence of the war for independence, he had continued to involve himself in republican political activities, actively engaging in local government, attaining various positions of authority within Sinn Féin, and even standing as a candidate in the 1921 general elections in Northern Ireland. His willingness to dabble in politics was also visible in the lead up to the civil war, with his intervention in the Collins-de Valera pact negotiations and his attempts to broker peace between rival factions in the south, though these forays often displayed a degree of naivety and a lack of political nous. It is clear, moreover, that there was a considerable degree of continuity in Aiken's views concerning the potential for republican participation in the governance of the Free State before and after the civil war. The policy he championed as a founder member of Fianna Fáil in 1926 – the removal of the oath of allegiance so that republican representatives could take their seats in the Dáil – was effectively the same course of action he had proposed to Mulcahy as a basis for peace in July 1922.

Furthermore, it must also be recognised that the experience of the civil war – as traumatic as it was for Aiken – did not result in his immediate abandonment of the principle of violent resistance. Despite his less than enthusiastic participation in the war, he was by no means eager to end it without favourable conditions in a negotiated peace with the Free State. Indeed, even after the IRA's ceasefire and dump arms order, he displayed a willingness to reignite the conflict in response to certain Free State actions. It is also clear that he retained a rather ambiguous (albeit informal) relationship with the IRA until well into the 1930s. In the decade after the civil war, therefore, Aiken cannot be considered to have undergone any radical conversion to constitutionalist values. His utilisation of political methods in pursuit of his republican ambitions was nothing new, though it had been obscured by his role in the IRA.

LEGACIES

What, then, is the legacy of Aiken's Irish revolution? In the popular mind his involvement in the conflict is remembered (if at all) for his complicity in sectarian atrocities and (to a lesser extent) his failure to participate in the joint-IRA offensive. The former, of course, has ensured his continued notoriety amongst the northern unionist community, particularly in south Armagh, where he is remembered as a vicious sectarian terrorist and a powerful example of the evils of Irish republicanism. The latter has contributed to his somewhat tainted reputation amongst northern republicans. Indeed, as Day has observed, even in his native south Armagh, this community long regarded him with suspicion on account of the view that he turned his back on the north in favour of a political career in the south.[7] In southern Ireland, meanwhile, his involvement in the Irish revolution was long overshadowed by his later political career; though the decision to rename Dundalk Barracks – his former civil war headquarters – in his honour is some small proof that his role in the conflict was never entirely forgotten. Here too, however, the revelations of his role in the sectarian reprisals at Altnaveigh and Lisdrumliska have reignited interest in his IRA past. He is now remembered as much for the latter as he is for his work in the United Nations, and serves as an uncomfortable reminder of the violent foundations of the state, and the sometimes inglorious pasts of its founding fathers.

Yet there are indications that Aiken's legacy is slowly transforming. In recent years, for instance, he has increasingly come to be viewed as the quintessential republican gunman turned statesman, a notion that has proven particularly popular amongst political commentators who look to him as a forerunner of contemporary northern republican figures such as Gerry Adams or Martin McGuinness.[8] In his native south Armagh, meanwhile, there are signs that his memory is now held with higher regard by some of those within the republican community. In Camlough, he is now commemorated with a small bronze plaque in the main thoroughfare. In April 2011, a much publicised memorial lecture on his life and his involvement in the Irish revolution was also held in the district.[9] All this, perhaps, can be taken as a sign that his legacy is now viewed as holding a greater relevance, particularly in light of the political developments in Northern Ireland over the past decade. Indeed, the same may also be true with regard to the Fourth Northern Division, the legacy of which remains closely tied to that of Aiken. Though long commemorated with monuments in south Armagh and north Louth – and more privately with an annual mass organised by the relatives of former members – in recent years its memory has also been appropriated by dissident republican groups.[10]

Nevertheless, ninety years on, Aiken's revolution remains a contentious and highly sensitive subject. In such circumstances, it is perhaps the words of John McCoy that offer the best summation of its lessons. Writing many decades after the fact, he concluded that much of what occurred,

> Should provide an object lesson to the people in the north who are led to take offensive action against their fellow countrymen who have a different political outlook or who worship at a different church. The resort to force is a two edged weapon which had a persistent habit of recoiling on the user and in the last analysis seldom achieves anything that could not be obtained by reason and peaceful means.[11]

This was a sentiment that Aiken and many of his other comrades would have undoubtedly understood. For whether in pursuit of independence, a united Ireland, or the overthrow of the Irish Free State, their violent path had ultimately achieved nothing.

NOTES

1.   Open letter to the voters of Louth, 20 Aug. 1923, University College Dublin Archives (hereafter, UCDAD), de Valera papers, P150/1752.

2.   Aiken to Molly Childers, 22 Feb. 1924, Trinity College Dublin Archives (hereafter, TCD), Childers papers, Ms 7,847.

3.   T. K. Wilson, *Frontiers of Violence: Conflict and Identity in Ulster and Upper Silesia, 1918–1922* (Oxford, 2010), p. 161.

4.   P. Hart, 'Youth culture and the Cork IRA', in Fitzpatrick (ed.), *Revolution? Ireland, 1917–1923* (Dublin 1990), p. 18.

5.   D. Fitzpatrick, 'The geography of Irish nationalism, 1910–1921', in *Past and Present*, 78 (Feb., 1978), pp 117–20.

6.   M. Coleman, *County Longford and the Irish Revolution, 1910–1923* (Dublin, 2003), p. 162.

7.   C. S. Day, 'Political violence in the Armagh/Newry area, 1912–1925' (PhD, Queen's University, Belfast, 1998), p. 349.

8.   See, for example, *Irish Independent*, 12 Sept. 2011; L. Carke, 'Gerry Adams playing well in the US, but not in Ireland', www.belfasttelegraph.co.uk/debateni/blogs/liam–clarke/gerry–adams–playing–well–in–the–us–but–not–ireland–29733962.html (accessed 26 Jan. 2014); S. Breen 'A path paved with blood', www.dailymail.co.uk/news/article–2041552/Family–IRA–victim–Frank–Hegarty–insist–Martin–McGuinness–lured–death.html (accessed 26 Jan. 2014).

9.   'Frank Aiken Memorial (Camlough)', www.cain.ulst.ac.uk/victims/memorials/static/monuments/1292.html (accessed 10 May 2011); *Irish News*, 25 Apr. 2011.

10.   Email correspondence with Mark Feighery, 25 Feb. 2009; 'Commemorations', http://aprnonline.com/?p=57645 (accessed 27 May 2011). For dissident republican commemorations see, 'Éirígí to commemorate the Egyptian Arch ambush', www.newryrepublican.blogspot.com/2010/10/eirigi–to–commemorate–egyptian–arch.html (accessed 8 Apr. 2011).

11.   John McCoy, Irish Military Archives (hereafter, IMA), Bureau of Military History Witness Statement (hereafter, BMH WS), 492.

Appendix I

Statistics on Sinn Féin and Irish Volunteer Membership

Statistics relating to the membership and composition of Sinn Féin and the Irish Volunteers in Armagh and south Down are based on four samples; two for each organisation.

Sinn Féin Sample One

This sample of 31 prominent Sinn Féin figures from Armagh and south Down was used to generate data on criteria such as age, religion, occupation, father's occupation and quality of housing. In lieu of detailed membership lists for the region, potential candidates for inclusion in the sample were first identified using local press reports concerning Sinn Fein meetings, events, appointments and club proceedings, RIC reports and various other republican sources, such as contemporary correspondence and reports and Bureau of Military History witness statements. Those individuals who could then be accurately traced in the 1911 (or 1901) census returns were subsequently included in the sample. Previous membership of other organisations – such as the Ancient Order of Hibernians, United Irish League, or the Irish Republican Brotherhood – has been identified for a handful of those included in the sample by way of newspaper reports and Bureau of Military History witness statements. Given the means by which the sample has been compiled, it is considered to be reflective of the Sinn Féin elite in Armagh and south Down. It does not purport to be representative of the local party membership as a whole.

Sinn Féin Sample Two

This sub-sample of nine individuals was derived from the original Sinn Féin membership sample of 31. Those included were individuals whose occupation was listed as either 'farmer' or 'farmer's son', or those for whom no independent occupation was listed in the census (e.g. scholars) but who were members of a farming family. The existing census information for these individuals was then supplemented with the rateable land valuation of their farm – or the family farm on which they were sustained – for the year 1911. This information was then used to give an indication of the typical economic background of members of the farming class who became involved in Sinn Féin in the region.

Irish Volunteers Sample One

This sample of 204 Irish Volunteers from the Fourth Northern Divisional area (Armagh, south Down and north Louth) was used to generate data on criteria such as age, religion, occupation, father's occupation and quality of housing. The research presented here predates the Irish Military Archives' recent release – in January 2014 – of the IRA Membership Series of the Military Service Pensions Collection. However, potential candidates for inclusion in the sample were identified using copies of Fourth Northern Division company rolls – included among the Aiken papers – which were compiled for that series in the 1930s in order to assist the verification of pension applications. This was supplemented by information from other republican sources, such as Bureau of Military History statements and contemporary IRA documents. Those individuals who could be accurately traced in the 1911 (or 1901) census returns were then included in the sample. In some instances, the data presented here was based on figures for smaller groupings within the sample; for example, by company, or with a distinction between rank and file members and officers. Where applicable, this is clearly highlighted in the text.

Irish Volunteers Sample Two

This sub-sample was derived from the original Irish Volunteer membership sample, and consists of 33 members of the Camlough, Mullaghbawn and Corrinshego companies whose occupation was listed as 'farmer' or 'farmer's son', or those for whom no independent occupation was listed in the census (e.g. scholars) but who were members of a farming family. The existing census information for these individuals was then supplemented with the rateable land valuation of their farm – or the family farm on which they were sustained – for the year 1911. This was used to provide an indication of the typical economic background of members of the farming class who became involved in the Irish Volunteers in the region. For some of the data presented, a distinction was also made between officers and rank and file members.

Occupational Categories

The occupational categories used in the relevant statistical tables in Appendix II are broadly based on those found in the 1911 census report. The only exception is that those individuals included in the 'Industrial Class' for the purpose of the census have been divided into three further categories; 'Trade', 'Semi-skilled' and 'Unskilled'.

STATISTICS FOR CASUALTIES AND INCIDENTS OF VIOLENCE

Compilation

Casualty figures, and statistics suggesting the incidence of various types of republican violence throughout the years 1919–23, have been compiled from a variety of sources. These include local and national press reports, monthly RIC county inspector reports and other contemporary documentation from the RUC, USC, and the National Army, Bureau of Military History witness statements and contemporary IRA documentation. Statistics for republican casualties have been particularly reliant on information from Bureau of Military History testimonies, Fourth Northern Division company rolls, and a list of casualties for the period included in the McCann Cell Collection at Kilmainham Gaol Museum. This latter source is somewhat problematic as it appears to incorrectly list a number of civilian dead as IRA members, despite having a separate section dedicated to civilian casualties. Consequently, no individual has been classified as an Irish Volunteer/IRA member on the basis of this source alone.

Definition of Casualty

The casualty figures presented here were compiled on the basis of the criteria suggested by Peter Hart, and are indicative of individuals wounded by guns or explosives in incidents of conflict related violence. As Hart has explained, this criterion 'indicates a threshold of violence below which it is very difficult to judge the effect of an incident.'[1]

---

1.   P. Hart, *The IRA and Its Enemies: Violence and Community in Cork, 1916–1923* (Oxford, 1998), p. 319.

POPULATION FIGURES

All figures relating to the demography of Armagh and south Down – in particular the religious composition of the local population – have been obtained from the 1901, 1911 and 1926 census reports for counties Armagh and Down. The figures relating to the religious composition of the townlands of Altnaveigh and Lisdrumliska were compiled from the individual census returns for the two districts. Figures indicating the geographical spread of the signatories of the Ulster Covenant have been compiled using the Public Record Office of Northern Ireland's digitised database.

SELECTED SOURCE LIST

ARCHIVAL SOURCES

IRISH MILITARY ARCHIVES
Bureau of Military History Witness Statements
Free State Army Eastern Command Reports, Civil War Operations Reports, Box No.9

KILMAINHAM GAOL MUSEUM
Fourth Northern Division Casualty List (1919-23), McCann Cell Collection, 20/M5/IP/41/12

NATIONAL ARCHIVES IRELAND
Secretariat Series, North Eastern Boundary Bureau, NEBB/1

PUBLIC RECORD OFFICE OF NORTHERN IRELAND
Annual Land Valuation Revision Lists, VAL/12/B
RIC/RUC Divisional Commissioners Bi-Monthly Reports, HA/5/152

THE NATIONAL ARCHIVES, KEW
RIC county inspector reports, CO 904/107-151

UNIVERSITY COLLEGE DUBLIN ARCHIVES DEPARTMENT
Fourth Northern Division Company Roles, Aiken papers, P104/1295
Fourth Northern Division Reports, Mulcahy papers, P7/A/20
Free State Army Eastern Command Reports, Mulcahy papers, P7/B/60
Free State Army Fifth Northern Division Reports, Mulcahy papers, P7/B/59

NEWSPAPERS

Armagh Guardian
Belfast News-Letter
Dundalk Democrat
Dundalk Examiner
Freeman's Journal
Frontier Sentinel
Irish Independent
Irish News
Irish Times
Newry Telegraph
The Times

OFFICIAL PUBLICATIONS

Census of Ireland, 1901, Volume III, Part I, Province of Ulster, No.2 County of Armagh (Dublin, 1902)
Census of Ireland, 1901, Volume III, Part II, Province of Ulster, No.5 County of Down (Dublin, 1902)
Census of Ireland, 1911, Province of Ulster, County of Armagh (London, 1912)
Census of Ireland, 1911, Province of Ulster, County of Down (London, 1921)
Census of Northern Ireland 1926, County of Armagh (Belfast, 1928)
Census of Northern Ireland 1926, County of Down (Belfast, 1928)

ONLINE RESOURCES

Census of Ireland 1901/1911, National Archives of Ireland, http://www.census.nationalarchives
    .ie/
Ulster Covenant Database, Public Record Office of Northern Ireland, http://applications.proni
    .gov.uk/UlsterCovenant/Search.aspx

Appendix II

TABLES

Table I : *Religious composition of parliamentary constituencies in Armagh, south Down and north Louth, 1911*

Constituency	Catholic	(%)	Protestant (%)		Other	(%)	Total	(%)
North Armagh	13,616	(30.0)	30,699	(67.5)	1,155	(2.5)	45,470	(100)
Mid. Armagh	17,000	(43.0)	21,932	(55.5)	606	(1.5)	39,538	(100)
South Armagh	23,511	(68.0)	10,625	(30.7)	425	(1.3)	34,561	(100)
South Down	24,441	(53.5)	20,168	(44.2)	1,064	(2.3)	45,673	(100)
North Louth	30,930	(90.3)	3,226	(9.4)	86	(0.3)	34,242	(100)
Total	109,498	(54.9)	86,650	(43.4)	3,336	(1.7)	199,484	(100)

Table II: *Occupations of Sinn Féin elite in Armagh and south Down*

Occupational Class	%
Professional	25.8
Commercial	16.1
Agricultural	29.0
Trades	19.4
Semi-Skilled	3.2
Unskilled	-
Unknown	6.5

Table III: *Occupational background of the Irish Volunteers in Armagh and South Down*

Occupational Class	Rank & File (%)	Officers (%)	Total (%)
Professional	1.1	-	1
Commercial	12.2	21.7	13.3
Agricultural	59.4	52.2	58.6
Trades	10.6	8.7	10.3
Semi-Skilled	2.8	-	2.5
Unskilled	12.2	17.4	12.9
Unknown	1.7	-	1.5

Table IV: *Results of Armagh and Down County Council Elections, 1920*

County Council	Sinn Féin	Nationalist	Unionist	Labour	Other
Armagh	3	5	14	-	1
Down	4	1	13	2	-

Table V: *Results of local government contests in predominantly nationalist council districts, Armagh and south Down, 1920*

District Council	Sinn Féin	Nationalist	Unionist	Labour	Other
Armagh Urban	5	5	8	-	-
Crossmaglen Rural	4	4	1	-	-
Keady Urban	1	9	-	-	-
Kilkeel Rural	7	-	3	-	-
Newry Urban	7	5	4	2	-
Newry No.1 Rural	7	5	4	2	-
Newry No.2 Rural	6	1	3	-	-
Warrenpoint Urban	4	3	5	-	1

Table VI: *Casualties in Armagh and south Down, 1919–1921*

Month	Civilian		IRA		State Forces		Total	
	W	K	W	K	W	K	W	K
1919	1	-	-	-	-	-	1	-
1920	5	2	3	4	1	2	9	8
1921*	14	8	7	12	14	7	35	27
Total	20	10	10	16	15	9	45	35

W – Wounded   K – Killed

*Until 11 July 1921

Table VII: *Casualties in the Fourth Northern Division command area, January–June 1922*

Month	Civilian		IRA		State Forces		Total	
	W	K	W	K	W	K	W	K
January	1	-	-	-	-	-	1	-
February	-	-	-	2	-	-	-	2
March	1	3	-	-	4	4	5	7
April	2	1	-	-	1	3	3	4
May	3	2	-	-	9	1	12	3
June	4	12	1	-	2	5	7	17
Total	11	18	1	2	16	13	28	33

W - Wounded   K - Killed

Table VIII (A): *Demographic change in Armagh, 1901–1911*

Denomination	1901	1911	% Change
Protestant	66, 117	63,062	-4.6%
Catholic	56, 652	54,526	-3.8%
Other	2,623	2,703	+2.5%
Total	125,392	120,291	-4.1%

Table VIII (B): *Demographic change in Armagh, 1911–1926*

Denomination	1911	1926	% Change
Protestant	63,062	55,944	-11.3%
Catholic	54,526	49,990	-8.3%
Other	2,703	4,136	+34.6%
Total	120,291	110,070	-8.5%

Table IX: *Monthly averages for casualties inflicted upon the enemy by the Fourth Northern Division, selected periods 1921–1922*

State Forces Jan.–Jul. 1921		State Forces Jan.–Jun. 1922		Free State Army Aug.–Dec. 1922	
W	K	W	K	W	K
2.3	1.4	2.7	2.2	6.8	2.8

W - Wounded   K - Killed

Table X: *Casualties in the Fourth Northern Division's North Louth command area, July 1922–June 1923*

Month	Civilian		IRA		State Forces		Total	
	W	K	W	K	W	K	W	K
July	3	-	3	1	4	1	10	2
August	3	1	4	2	19	5	26	8
September	1	-	-	-	3	3	4	3
October	4	1	-	1	4	1	8	3
November	1	-	3	-	7	3	11	3
December	-	2	-	-	1	1	1	3
January	-	2	-	6	-	-	-	8
February	-	-	-	-	-	-	-	-
March	1	1	1	-	-	1	2	2
April	-	1	-	1	1	1	1	3
May	-	-	-	1	-	-	-	1
June	-	-	-	-	-	-	-	-
Total	13	8	11	12	39	16	63	36

W - Wounded   K - Killed

Sources & Bibliography

—

ARCHIVE MATERIAL

IRELAND

IRISH MILITARY ARCHIVES, DUBLIN
Bureau of Military History, Contemporary Documents
Bureau of Military History, Witness Statements
Civil War Captured Documents Collection
Civil War Operational Reports (Fifth Northern Division & Eastern Command)
Michael Collins Papers
Military Service Pensions Collection
Department of Defence 'A' Files
Truce Liaison and Evacuation Papers

KILMAINHAM GAOL MUSEUM, DUBLIN
McCann Cell Collection

TRINITY COLLEGE DUBLIN
Childers Papers

NATIONAL ARCHIVES IRELAND, DUBLIN
Department of Local Government Files
Department of Finance Files
Department of Justice Equality and Law Reform Files
Department of Taoiseach General Files
North Eastern Boundary Bureau Files

NATIONAL LIBRARY OF IRELAND, DUBLIN
Henry Dixon Papers
Thomas Johnson Papers
Liam Lynch Letters
Colonel Maurice Moore papers
J.J. O'Connell papers
Florence O'Donoghue Papers
Official Military and Civil Papers, 1922

Official Military and Civil Papers, 1923
Sean O'Mahoney Papers
Ernie O'Malley Papers
Sinn Féin Standing Committee Minutes (microfilm)
Michael Collins, 'To the electors of Armagh', 10 May 1921 (Ms 41,525/1)
Eamon de Valera, 'Copy Memo to: Chief/Staff and members of the Executive', 12 Oct. 1922 (Ms
  33,364/2/6)
IRA Dublin No.2 Brigade, GHQ Circulars, February 1923-February 1924 (Ms 17,281)
'William Nelson's Story', 1917-1963 (Ms 41,722)
Rory O'Connor, 'Incidents in connection with I.R.A. that had bearing on outbreak of present
  war', c.1922 (Ms 41,994)
South Armagh By-Election Pamphlets (Ms 25,588)

UNIVERSITY COLLEGE DUBLIN ARCHIVES
Frank Aiken Papers
Ernest Blythe Papers
Eamon de Valera Papers
Desmond and Mabel FitzGerald Papers
Ernie O'Malley Papers
Ernie O'Malley Notebooks
Maurice Twomey Papers

LOUTH COUNTY ARCHIVES, DUNDALK
Dundalk Gaol Register
Louth Oral History Archive

NORTHERN IRELAND

PUBLIC RECORD OFFICE OF NORTHERN IRELAND, BELFAST
Annual Land Valuation Revisions Lists
Best and Gillespie (Solicitors) Papers
J. H. Collins Papers
Martin and Henderson (Solicitors) Papers
Ministry of Home Affairs Files
Ministry of Home Affairs 'S' Series
Minutes of Armagh County Council, 1920-1921
Minutes of Newry No.2 Rural District Council, 1920-1921
Photographs and Documents relating to the formation of the B Specials in Armagh

THE FOLLOWING FILES WERE OBTAINED THROUGH FREEDOM OF INFORMATION
REQUESTS:
Bernard Kelly, Bessbrook (HA/5/2426)
Bi-Monthly Intelligence Summary, 1923–1924 (HA/32/1/212)

J. Woulfe Flanagan Murder, 4 June 1922 (HA/32/1//310)
Kidnapping by IRA of Crown Witnesses, 1921–1923 (HA/32/1/40)
Murder and Attempted Murder, 1922 – 1926 (HA/32/1/297)
Reports on Dangerous Suspected Republican Sympathisers (HA/31/2/326)

CARDINAL Ó FIAICH LIBRARY, ARMAGH
Fr. Louis O'Kane Papers
Cardinal Tomás Ó Fiaich Papers

GREAT BRITAIN

THE NATIONAL ARCHIVES, KEW
Colonial Office Papers
War Office Papers

ONLINE SOURCES AND DATABASES

Census 1901/1911, National Archives, Ireland, http://www.census.nationalarchives.ie/
Dáil Éireann Parliamentary Debates, Houses of the Oireachtas, http://historical-debates.
    oireachtas.ie/
Dictionary of Irish Biography, Royal Irish Academy and Cambridge University Press,
    http://dib.cambridge.org/
Hansard, 1803–2005, Millbank Systems, http://hansard.millbanksystems.com/
'The Irish Election of 1918', ARK Northern Ireland, http://www.ark.ac.uk/elections/ h1918.htm
'Northern Ireland: a Divided Community 1921–1972: Cabinet Papers of the Stormont
    Administration', Gale Cengage Historical Archives, http://www.tlemea.com/proni/
    index.htm
Oxford Dictionary of National Biography, Oxford University Press, http://www.oxforddnb.com/
'The Stormont Papers: 50 years of Northern Ireland Parliamentary Debates', Arts & Humanities
    Data Service: the Centre for Data Digitisation and Analysis, stormontpapers.ahds.ac.uk
Ulster Covenant Database, Public Record Officer of Northern Ireland, http://applications.
    proni.gov.uk/UlsterCovenant/Search.aspx

NEWSPAPERS AND PERIODICALS

Anglo-Celt
An tÓglach
Belfast News-Letter
Armagh Guardian
Belfast Telegraph
Dundalk Democrat
Dundalk Examiner
Freeman's Journal

Frontier Sentinel
Irish Independent
Irish News
Irish Press
Irish Times
Nationality
Newry Telegraph
Northern Whig
Republican War News
Poblacht Na hÉireann War News
Sunday Independent
The Times
Weekly Irish Times

OFFICIAL PUBLICATIONS

Census of Ireland, 1901, Volume III, Part I, Province of Ulster, No.2 County of Armagh (Dublin, 1902)
Census of Ireland, 1901, Volume III, Part II, Province of Ulster, No.5 County of Down (Dublin, 1902)
Census of Ireland, 1911, Province of Ulster, County of Armagh (London, 1912)
Census of Ireland, 1911, Province of Ulster, County of Down (London, 1921)
Census of Northern Ireland 1926, County of Armagh (Belfast, 1928)
Census of Northern Ireland 1926, County of Down (Belfast, 1928)

PUBLISHED PRIMARY SOURCES AND REFERENCE WORKS

Hopkinson, Michael (ed), Mark Sturgis, *The Last Days of Dublin Castle: the Mark Sturgis Diaries* (Dublin, 1999)
O'Malley, Ernie, *No Surrender Here: the Civil War Papers of Ernie O'Malley*, eds Cormac O'Malley and Ann Dolan (Dublin, 2007)
Walker, B.M., *Parliamentary Election Results in Ireland, 1801-1922* (Dublin, 1978)
Walker, B.M., *Parliamentary Election Results in Ireland, 1918-1992* (Dublin, 1992)

PUBLISHED MEMOIRS

Andrews, C.S., *Dublin Made Me* (Dublin, 1979)
_____ *Man of No Property* (Dublin, 1982)
Barry, Tom, *Guerrilla Days in Ireland* (Dublin, 1981)
Breen, Dan, *My Fight for Irish Freedom* (Anvil edn., 1981)
Brennan, Michael, *The War in Clare 1911–1921* (Dublin, 1980)
MacBride, Seán, *That Day's Struggle: a Memoir 1904-1952* (Dublin, 2005)
O'Malley, Ernie, *On Another Man's Wound* (Anvil edn., Dublin, 1978)
_____ *The Singing Flame* (Anvil edn., Dublin, 1979)
Regan, John M., *The Memoirs of John M. Regan: a Catholic Officer in the RIC and RUC, 1909-1948*, ed. Joost Augusteijn (Dublin, 2007)

AUDIO-VISUAL MATERIAL

'Aiken: Gunman and Statesman', Mint Productions, RTÉ, 6 Dec. 2006

INTERVIEWS AND CORRESPONDENCE

Dr Rory O'Hanlon, 13 October 2009
Dr Eoin Magennis, 19 May 2010
Correspondence with Mark Feighery, 24, 25, 27 February 2009

SECONDARY READING

Augusteijn, Joost, *From Public Defiance to Guerrilla Warfare: the Experience of Ordinary Volunteers in the Irish War of Independence* (Dublin, 1996)
_____ *Patrick Pearse: The Making of a Revolutionary* (Basingstoke, 2010)
_____ 'The importance of being Irish: ideas and the Volunteers in Tipperary and Mayo' in Fitzpatrick (ed.), *Revolution? Ireland 1917–1923* (Dublin, 1990), pp25-42
_____ 'Motivation: why did they fight for Ireland? The motivation of volunteers in the revolution' in idem, *The Irish Revolution 1913–1923* (Basingstoke, 2003)
_____ 'The emergence of violent activism among Irish revolutionaries, 1916–1921' in *Irish Historical Studies*, vol. 35, no. 139 (May 2007), pp 327–44
Bardon, Jonathan, *A History of Ulster* (Belfast, 1992)
Béaslaí, Piaras, *Michael Collins and the Making of New Ireland* (Dublin, 1926)
Bell, J. Bowyer, *The Secret Army: a History of the IRA, 1916–70* (London, 1972)
Bew, Paul, *Ideology and the Irish question: Ulster Unionism and Irish Nationalism 1912–1916* (Oxford, 1994)
_____ *Ireland: The Politics of Enmity, 1789–2006* (Oxford, 2009)
_____ 'Sinn Féin, agrarian radicalism and the war of independence, 1919-1921' in D. G. Boyce (ed.), *The Revolution in Ireland, 1879–1923* (Basingstoke, 1988), pp 217–35
Bloxham, Donald, and Robert Gerwarth (eds), *Political Violence in Twentieth Century Europe* (Cambridge, 2011)
Borgonovo, John, *Spies, Informers and the 'Anti-Sinn Féin Society'; the Intelligence War in Cork City* (Dublin, 2007)
_____ *The Dynamics of War and Revolution: Cork City, 1916–1918* (Cork, 2013)
Bourke, Joanna, *An Intimate History of Killing: Face to Face Killing in Twentieth Century Warfare* (London, 1999)
Bowman, John, *De Valera and the Ulster Question, 1917–1973* (Oxford, 1982)
Bowman, John, 'Sinn Féin's perception of the Ulster question: Autumn 1921' in *The Crane Bag*, Vol. 4, No. 2 (1980/1981), pp 50–6
Bowman, Timothy, *Carson's Army: The Ulster Volunteer Force, 1910–1922* (Manchester, 2007)
Bradley, Jim, 'Canon Charles Quin and the Bessborough Commission' in *Seanchas Ardmhacha: Journal of the Armagh Diocesan Historical Society*, vol. 16, no. 1 (1994), pp. 133–94
Brewer, John, *The Royal Irish Constabulary: an Oral History* (Belfast, 1990)

Buckland, Patrick, *The Factory of Grievances: Devolved Government in Northern Ireland 1921–39* (Dublin, 1979)

Campbell, Fergus, *Land and Revolution: Nationalist Politics in the West of Ireland 1891–1921* (Oxford, 2005)

Canavan, Tony, *Frontier Town: an Illustrated History of Newry* (Belfast, 1989)

Coleman, Marie, *County Longford and the Irish Revolution, 1910–1923* (Dublin, 2001)

Collins, Eamon, *Killing Rage* (London, 1997)

Coogan, T. P., *The IRA* (London, 1970)

_____ *Michael Collins: a Biography* (London, 1990)

_____ *De Valera: Long Fellow, Long Shadow* (London, 1993)

Costello, Francis, *The Revolution and its Aftermath 1916–1923: Years of Revolt* (Dublin, 2002)

Cousins, Colin, *Armagh and the Great War* (Dublin, 2011)

Daly, Mary E., *The Buffer State: the Historical Roots of the Department of the Environment* (Dublin, 1997)

Dolan, Ann, *Commemorating the Irish Civil War: History and Memory 1923–2000* (Cambridge, 2003)

_____ 'Killing and Bloody Sunday, November 1920' in *The Historical Journal*, vol. 49, no. 3 (September, 2006), pp 789–810

Donoghue, Florence, *No Other Law* (Dublin, 1954)

Donohue, L.K., 'Regulating Northern Ireland: the Special Powers Acts, 1922-1972' in *The Historical Journal*, Vol. 41, No. 4 (Dec. 1998), pp 1098–120

Donnan, Hastings, 'Fuzzy frontiers: the rural interface in South Armagh', Mapping Frontiers, Plotting Pathways Working Paper No. 26, 2006, from Queen's University Belfast, Centre for International Borders Research website, http://www.qub.ac.uk/research-centres/CentreforInternationalBordersResearch/Publications/WorkingPapers/MappingFrontiersworkingpapers/#d.en.175393 (accessed 20 May 2011)

Duffy, P.J., 'Geographical perspectives on the borderlands' in Gillespie and O'Sullivan (eds), *The Borderlands: Essays on the History of the Ulster-Leinster border* (Belfast, 1989), pp 5–22

English, Richard, *Ernie O'Malley: IRA Intellectual* (Oxford, 1998)

_____ *Armed Struggle: the History of the IRA* (London, 2003)

_____ *Irish Freedom: a History of Nationalism in Ireland* (London, 2007)

Fanning, Ronan, *Fatal Path: British Government and Irish Revolution, 1910–1922* (London, 2013)

Farrell, Michael, *Arming the Protestants: the Formation of the Ulster Special Constabulary and the Royal Ulster Constabulary 1920–1927* (London, 1983)

Farry, Michael, *The Aftermath of Revolution: Sligo 1921-23* (Dublin, 2000)

_____ *The Irish Revolution 1912-23: Sligo* (Dublin, 2012)

Feeney, Tom, *Seán MacEntee: a Political Life* (Dublin, 2008)

Ferriter, Diarmaid, *Transformation of Ireland 1900–2000* (London, 2004)

_____ *Judging Dev* (Dublin, 2007)

Fitzpatrick, David, *Politics and Irish life, 1913–1921: Provincial Experience of War and Revolution* (Dublin, 1977)

_____ *The Two Irelands 1912–1939* (Oxford, 1998)

_____ *Harry Boland's Irish Revolution, 1887–1922* (Cork, 1999)

_____ 'The geography of Irish nationalism, 1910-1921' in *Past and Present*, 78 (1978), pp 113–44

_____ 'Militarism in Ireland, 1900–1922' in Jeffery and Bartlett (eds), *A Military History of Ireland* (Cambridge, 1996)

_____ 'The Orange Order and the border' in *Irish Historical Studies*, Vol. 33, No. 129 (May, 2002), pp 52–67

Follis, B. A., *A State Under Siege: the Establishment of Northern Ireland* (Oxford, 1995)

Gallagher, Michael, 'The pact general election of 1922' in *Irish Historical Studies*, vol. 22, no. 84 (September, 1979), pp 404–21

Garvin, Tom, *The Evolution of Irish Nationalist Politics* (Dublin, 1981)

_____ *Nationalist Revolutionaries in Ireland 1858-1928* (Oxford, 1987)

_____ *1922: the Birth of Irish Democracy* (Dublin, 1996)

Gavin, Joseph, and O'Sullivan, Harold, *Dundalk: a Military History; with Photographs and Illustrations* (Dundalk, 1987)

Gerwarth, Robert, *Hitler's Hangman: The Life of Heydrich* (New Haven, 2011)

Gerwarth, Robert, and John Horne (eds), *War in Peace: Paramilitary Violence in Europe After the Great War* (Oxford, 2012)

Hanley, Brian, *The IRA 1926–1936* (Dublin, 2002)

_____ 'Terror in twentieth-century Ireland' in Fitzpatrick (ed), *Terror in Ireland, 1917–1923* (Dublin, 2012), pp 10–25

Harden, Tony, *Bandit Country: the IRA & South Armagh* (London, 1999)

Harris, Mary, *The Catholic Church and the Foundation of the Northern Irish State* (Cork, 1993)

Harris, Rosemary, *Prejudice and Tolerance in Ulster: A Study of Neighbours and 'Stangers' in a Border Community* (Manchester, 1972)

Hart, Peter, *The IRA and its Enemies: Violence and Community in Cork, 1916–1923* (Oxford, 1998)

_____ *The IRA at War 1916–1923* (Oxford, 2003)

_____ *Mick: the Real Michael Collins* (London, 2005)

_____ 'Youth culture and the Cork IRA' in David Fitzpatrick (ed.) *Revolution? Ireland 1917–1923* (Dublin, 1990), pp 10–24

Hay, Marnie, *Bulmer Hobson and the Nationalist Movement in Twentieth Century Ireland* (Manchester, 2009)

Hepburn, A. C., *Catholic Belfast and Nationalist Ireland in the Era of Joe Devlin, 1871-1934* (Oxford, 2008)

Hezlet, Sir Arthur, *The B Specials: a History of the Ulster Special Constabulary* (London, 1973)

Hopkinson, Michael, *Green Against Green: the Irish Civil War* (Dublin, 1988)

_____ *The Irish War of Independence* (Dublin, 2002)

_____ 'The Craig–Collins pacts of 1922: two attempted reforms of the Northern Irish Government', *Irish Historical Studies*, vol. 26, no. 6 (November, 1990) pp 150–70

Horowitz, D. L., *Ethnic Groups in Conflict* (Berkeley, 1985)

Jeffery, Keith, *The British Army and the Crisis of Empire 1918-1922* (Manchester, 1984)

_____ *Ireland and the Great War* (Cambridge, 2000)

Johnson, D. J., 'The Belfast boycott, 1920–1922' in Clarkson & Goldstrom (eds) *Irish Population, Economy and Society: Essays in Honour of the Late K.H. O'Connell* (Oxford, 1981)

Jorstad, Jonas, 'Nations once again: Ireland's Civil War in European context' in Fitzpatrick, *Revolution? Ireland, 1917-1923* (Dublin, 1990)

Kalyvas, Stathis, *The Logic of Violence in Civil War* (Cambridge, 2006)

Kelly, M. J., *The Fenian Ideal and Irish nationalism 1882-1916* (Woodbridge, 2006)

Kenneally, Ian, *The Paper Wall: Newspapers and Propaganda in Ireland 1919-1921* (Cork, 2008)

Kissane, Bill, *Explaining Irish Democracy* (Dublin, 2002)

_____ *The Politics of the Irish Civil War* (Oxford, 2005)

Kotsonouris, Mary, *Retreat from Revolution: Dáil Courts, 1920-1924* (Dublin, 1994)

_____ 'The courts of Dáil Éireann' in Farrell (ed.) *The Creation of the Dáil* (Dublin, 1994), pp 91–105

Laffan, Michael, *The Partition of Ireland, 1911–1925* (Dublin, 1983)

_____ *The Resurrection of Ireland: the Sinn Féin Party, 1916–1923* (Cambridge, 1999)

_____ '"Labour must wait": Ireland's conservative revolution' in Cornish (ed), *Radicals, Rebels and Establishments* (Belfast, 1985), pp 203–22

Lawlor, Pearse, *The Burnings 1920* (Cork, 2009)

Lawlor, S. M., 'Ireland from truce to treaty: war or peace? July to October 1921' in *Irish Historical Studies*, Vol. 22, No. 85 (Mar. 1980), pp 49–64

Lee, J. J., *Ireland 1912–85: Politics and Society* (Cambridge, 1989)

Leeson, D. M., *The Black and Tans: British Police and Auxiliaries in the War of Independence* (Oxford, 2011)

Leonard, Jane, 'Getting them at last: the IRA and ex-servicemen' in Fitzpatrick (ed.), *Revolution? Ireland 1917–1923* (Dublin, 1999) pp 118–29

_____ '"English dogs" or "poor devils"? The dead of bloody sunday morning' in Fitzpatrick (ed), *Terror in Ireland, 1917–1923* (Dublin, 2012), pp 102–40

Lewis, Matthew, 'The Newry Brigade and the War of Independence in Armagh, south Down and north Louth, 1919-1921', *The Irish Sword: the Journal of the Military History Society of Ireland*, Vol. 27, No. 108 (Summer 2010), pp 225–32

Lynch, Robert, *The Northern IRA and the Early Years of Partition 1920–1922* (Dublin, 2006)

_____ 'Donegal and the joint–IRA offensive' in *Irish Historical Studies*, vol. 35, no. 138 (November 2006), 184–99

_____ 'The people's protectors? the Irish Republican Army and the "Belfast Pogrom", 1920-1922' in *Journal of British Studies*, Vol. 47, No. 2 (2008), pp 375–91

_____ 'Explaining the Altnaveigh massacre' in *Eire/Ireland*, vol. 45, no. 3 & 4 (fall/winter, 2010), pp 184–210

Lyons, F. S. L., *Ireland Since the Famine* (London, 1971)

Macardle, Dorothy, *The Irish Republic* (London, 1937)

MacEoin, Uinseann, *Survivors* (Dublin, 1980)

_____ *The IRA in the Twilight Years 1923-1948* (Dublin, 1997)

Madden, Kyla, *Forkhill Protestants and Forkhill Catholics, 1787-1858* (London, 2005)

Mandle, W. F., *The Gaelic Athletic Association and Irish Nationalist Politics 1884–1924* (London, 1987)

Manning, Maurice, *James Dillon: a Biography* (Dublin, 1999)

Maume, Patrick, *The Long Gestation: Irish Nationalist Life 1891–1918* (Dublin, 1999)

Macardle, Dorothy, *The Irish Republic* (London, 1937)

Macauley, Thurston, *Donn Byrne, Bard of Armagh* (London, 1929)

McCluskey, Fergal, *Fenians and Ribbonmen: The Development of Republican Politics in East Tyrone* (Manchester, 2011)

McConville, Seán, *Irish Political Prisoners, 1848–1922: Theatres of War* (London, 2003)

McDermott, Jim, *Northern Divisions: the Old IRA and the Belfast Pogroms, 1920–1922* (Belfast, 2001)

McGarry, Fearghal, *Eoin O'Duffy: a Self-Made Hero* (Oxford, 2005)

_____ *The Rising: Ireland, Easter 1916* (Oxford, 2010)

McGee, Owen, *The IRB: the Irish Republican Brotherhood, from the Land League to Sinn Fein* (Dublin, 2005)

McMahon, T.G., *Grand Opportunity: the Gaelic Revival and Irish Society, 1893–1910* (New York, 2008)

Mitchell, Arthur, *Revolutionary Government in Ireland: Dáil Éireann 1919–22* (Dublin, 1995)

Moran, Gerard, '"The advance on the North": The difficulties of the home rule movement in south-east Ulster, 1870-1883' in Gillespie and O'Sullivan (eds), *The Borderlands: Essays on the History of the Ulster-Leinster Border* (Belfast, 1989), pp 129–42

Mulcahy, Risteárd, 'The development of the Irish Volunteers; 1916–22: parts 1–3'. *An Cosantóir*, 40 (1980), 35-40, 67–71, 99–102

Murphy, Brian P., *Patrick Pearse and the Lost Republican Ideal* (Dublin, 1991)

_____ 'Nationalism: the framing of the Constitution of the Irish Free State, 1922 – the defining battle for the Irish Republic' in Augusteijn (ed.) *The Irish Revolution 1913–1923* (Basingstoke, 2003), pp 135–50

_____ 'Poisoning the well or publishing the truth? From Peter Hart's The IRA and its enemies to RTÉ's Hidden History film Coolacrease' in *Troubled History: a 10th Anniversary Critique of Peter Hart's The IRA and its Enemies* (Aubane, 2008), pp 29–43

Murphy, Clare, 'The franchise, elections and parliamentary representation for Armagh, 1874–1910' in Hughes and Nolan (eds), *Armagh: History and Society: Interdisciplinary Essays on the History of an Irish County* (Dublin, 2001), pp 917–46

Neeson, Eoin, *The Civil War in Ireland, 1922–1923* (Dublin, 1989)

Nic Dháibhéid, Caoimhe, 'The Irish National Aid and the radicalisation of public opinion in Ireland, 1916–1918', *The Historical Journal*, vol. 55, no. 3 (September 2012), pp 705–29

O'Beirne Ranelagh, John, 'The Irish Republican Brotherhood in the revolutionary period, 1879–1923' in D.G. Boyce (ed.), *The Revolution in Ireland, 1879–1923* (Dublin, 1988), pp 137–56

O'Callaghan, John, *Revolutionary Limerick: the Republican Campaign for Independence in Limerick 1913–1921* (Dublin, 2010)

O'Farrell, Padraic, *Who's Who in the Irish War of Independence and Civil War 1916–1923* (Dublin, 1997)

O'Halpin, Eunan, *Defending Ireland: the Irish state and its Enemies Since 1922* (Oxford, 1999)

_____ 'Counting terror: Bloody Sunday and the dead of the Irish Revolution' in Fitzpatrick (ed), *Terror in Ireland, 1916–1923* (Dublin, 2012), pp 141–158

O'Hegarty, P. S., *The Victory of Sinn Fein* (Classics of Irish History edn., Dublin, 1998)

Parkinson, Alan, *Belfast's Unholy War: the Trouble of the 1920s* (Dublin, 2004)

Patterson, Henry, *Ireland Since 1939* (Oxford, 2002)

_____ *Ireland's Violent Frontier: The Border and Anglo-Irish Relations During the Troubles* (Basingstoke, 2013)

_____ 'Sectarianism Revisited: The Provisional IRA Campaign in a Border Region of Northern Ireland' in *Terrorism and Political Violence*, vol. 22, no. 3 (December 2010), pp 337–56

Phillips, W. A., *The Revolution in Ireland, 1906-1923* (New York, 1923)

Phoenix, Eamon, *Northern Nationalism: Nationalist Politics, Partition and the Catholic Minority in Northern Ireland, 1890–1940* (Belfast, 1994)

_____ 'Michael Collins: the northern question 1916–1922' in Doherty and Keogh (eds) *Michael Collins and the Making of the Irish Free State* (Cork, 1998)

Regan, J. M., *The Irish Counter-Revolution: Treatyite Politics and Settlement in Independent Ireland* (Dublin, 1999)

_____ 'The "Bandon valley massacre" as a historical problem' in *History*, vol. 97, no. 1 (January, 2012), pp 70–98

Rumpf, Ernst, *Nationalism and Socialism in Twentieth Century Ireland* (Liverpool, 1970)

Ryan, Louise, '"Drunken tans": Representations of sex and violence in the Anglo-Irish war (1919-1921)' in *Feminist Review*, No. 66 (Autumn, 2000), pp 73–94

Ryan, Meda, *Tom Barry: IRA Freedom Fighter* (Cork, 2003)

_____ *The Real Chief: Liam Lynch* (Cork, 2005)

Ryder, Chris, *The Fateful Split: Catholics and the Royal Ulster Constabulary* (London, 2004)

Skinner, Liam, *Politicians by Accident* (Dublin, 1946)

Staunton, Enda, *The Nationalists of Northern Ireland 1918–1973* (Dublin, 2001)

Stewart, A. T. Q., *The Narrow Ground: Aspects of Ulster, 1609–1969* (London, 1977)

Tilly, Charles, *The Politics of Collective Violence* (Cambridge, 2003)

Townshend, Charles, *The British Campaign in Ireland 1919–1921* (Oxford, 1975)

_____ *Political Violence in Ireland: Government and Resistance Since 1848* (Oxford, 1983)

_____ *Easter 1916: the Irish Rebellion* (London, 2005)

_____ *The Republic: The Fight for Irish Independence, 1918–1923* (London, 2013)

_____ 'The Irish Republican Army and the development of guerrilla warfare', in *English Historical Review*, 94 (1979), pp 318–45

_____ 'The Irish railway strike of 1920: industrial action and civil resistance in the struggle for independence' in *Irish Historical Studies*, vol. 22, no. 83 (March, 1979), pp 265–82

Valiulis, M. G., *Portrait of a Revolutionary: General Richard Mulcahy and the Founding of the Irish Free State* (Dublin, 1992)

Ward, Margaret, *Unmanageable Revolutionaries: Women and Irish Nationalism* (London, 1983)

Watson, R. P., *Cath Saoirse an Iúir: Newry's Struggle* (Newry, 1986)

Wilson, T. K., *Frontiers of Violence: Conflict and Identity in Ulster and Upper Silesia 1918-1922* (Oxford, 2010)

_____ 'Ghost provinces, mislaid minorities: the experience of Southern Ireland and Prussian Poland compared, 1918-1923' in *Irish Studies in International Affairs*, Vol. 13 (2002), pp 61–86

Wright, Frank, *Northern Ireland: A Comparative Analysis* (Dublin, 1987)

Younger, Carlton, *Ireland's Civil War* (London, 1982)

THESES

Bhreatnach, Aoife, 'Frank Aiken and the formulation of foreign policy: 1951–1954, 1957–1969' (MA thesis, University College Cork, 1999)

Day, Charles Stephen, 'Political violence in the Newry/Armagh area, 1912-1925' (PhD, Queen's University, Belfast, 1998)

Duffy, Dara, 'Frank Aiken TD., (1923–1973) - a pragmatic neutralist' (MA, National University of Ireland, Maynooth, 1994)

Evans, Gary, 'The raising of the first internal Dáil Éireann loan and the British responses to it, 1919–1921' (MLitt, National University of Ireland, Maynooth, 2012)

Gill, Brendan, 'Frank Aiken: from IRA leader to Free State stalwart' (MA, National University of Ireland, Maynooth, 2004)

Grayson, Natasha Claire, 'The quality of nationalism in counties Cavan, Louth and Meath during the Irish Revolution' (PhD, Keele University, 2007)

Hall, Donal, 'Violence and political factionalism and their effects on North Louth, 1874–1943' (PhD, National University of Ireland, Maynooth, 2009)

Hannon, Charles, 'The Irish Volunteers and concepts of military service and defence 1913–1924' (PhD, University College, Dublin, 1989)

Lynch, R. J., 'The Northern IRA and the early years of partition' (PhD, University of Stirling, 2003)

Maguire, Gloria, 'The political and military causes of the division in the Irish nationalist movement' (DPhil, University of Oxford, 1985)

Index

—